Imams and Emirs

Imams and Emirs

State, Religion and Sects in Islam

Fuad I. Khuri

Viva Books

New Delhi | Mumbai | Chennai | Kolkata | Bangalore | Hyderabad | Kochi | Guwahati

First Indian Edition 2010

VIVA BOOKS PRIVATE LIMITED

- 4737/23 Ansari Road, Daryaganj, New Delhi 110 002
  E-mail: vivadelhi@vivagroupindia.net, Tel. 42242200
- 76, Service Industries, Shirvane, Sector 1, Nerul, Navi Mumbai 400 706
  E-mail: vivamumbai@vivagroupindia.net, Tel. 27721273, 27721274
- Jamals Fazal Chambers, 26 Greams Road, Chennai 600 006
  E-mail: vivachennai@vivagroupindia.net, Tel. 28290304, 28294241
- B-103, Jindal Towers, 21/1A/3 Darga Road, Kolkata 700 017
  E-mail: vivakolkata@vivagroupindia.net, Tel. 22836381, 22816713
- 7, Sovereign Park Apartments, 56-58, K. R. Road, Basavanagudi, Bangalore 560 004
  E-mail: vivabangalore@vivagroupindia.net, Tel. 26607409, 26607410
- 101-102 Mughal Marc Aptt., 3-4-637 to 641, Narayanguda, Hyderabad 500 029
  E-mail: vivahyderabad@vivagroupindia.net, Tel. 27564481, 27564482
- First Floor, Beevi Towers, SRM Road, Kaloor, Kochi 682 018, Kerala
  E-mail: vivakochi@vivagroupindia.net, Tel: 0484-2403055, 2403056
- 232, GNB Road, Beside UCO Bank, Silpukhuri, Guwahati 781 003
  E-mail: vivaguwahati@vivagroupindia.net, Tel: 0361-2666386

www.vivagroupindia.com

Published by arrangement with
Westbourne Publishers Limited t/a Saqi
26 Westbourne Grove,
London W2 5RH
UK

ISBN 978-81-309-1317-9

Published by Vinod Vasishtha for Viva Books Private Limited, 4737/23, Ansari Road, Daryaganj, New Delhi - 110 002.

Printed and bound by Mehta Offset Pvt. Ltd., New Delhi.

To Ishaq and Abdul-Qahir

Contents

PART TWO
THE IDEOLOGY OF SECTS

PART THREE
THE ORGANIZATION OF SECTS

Figures, Tables and Maps

A Note on Arabic Words

Proper names of people and places sometimes spelled in English with *e* or *o* will be written with *a, i* or *u*, following their pronunciation in classical Arabic. Thus, Mohammed will be written Muhammad. Exceptions to this rule are those words that have acquired a standardized spelling in English such as emir or emirate.

The ʻayn (ʻ) and the hamza (ʼ) are not transliterated when they occur at the beginning or end of a word. Words are italicized to indicate their foreign origin. Exact transliterations of technical words and concepts are listed alphabetically in the Glossary at the end of the book, following the system published in the *International Journal of Middle East Studies*, vol. 2, no. 4 (1971).

Plurals are written by adding an *s* to the Arabic singular form, e.g. *sayyid, sayyids*. Exempted from this rule are the cases in which the plural form in Arabic is more commonly used than the singular such as *azzaba* instead of *azzabs* or *ajawid* instead of *jawwids*.

The author is responsible for the translation of all Arabic texts. However, many of the Qur'anic verses have been checked with Abdullah Yusuf Ali's translation of the Qur'an published by Dar al-Arabiya, Beirut.

Acknowledgements

It has taken some fifteen years of research and writing to complete this book on Islamic sects. The task would have been impossible without the financial support of many institutions and the encouragement of many colleagues and professors of Islamic studies and Arab cultures. I am very grateful to the Research Committee of the American University of Beirut, the Ford Foundation and the Lloyd Fallers Memorial Lectureship at the University of Chicago for their financial support.

I am also thankful to Professors/Doctors: Ernest Gellner and Bassam Mussallam at Cambridge University, Abner Cohen at the School of African and Oriental Studies, London University, Elie Kedourie at the London School of Economics, Marvin Zonis, Margaret Fallers and the late Morris Janowitz at the University of Chicago, Marun Kisirwani and Sami Makarem at the American University of Beirut, Radwan al-Sayed at the Lebanese University, Beirut, Fritz Steppat at the Free University of Berlin, Roger Owen at Oxford University, Khaldun al-Naqib at the University of Kuwait, Richard Antoun at SUNY (Binghamton), Abdo Baaklini at SUNY (Albany), Edward Azar at Maryland University, Marius Deeb at Georgetown University and Eliya Harik at the University of Indiana (Bloomington). Many of them have read, commented on or sponsored lectures on various topics covered in this work.

I acknowledge with gratitude the many *ulama* (learned men) I interviewed in Lebanon, Syria, Bahrain, Oman and North Yemen. The list is long; it includes, among others, Shaikhs M. Maghnieh, A. Bakkar, H. Zughbi, A. Badr, M. al-Shaikh, Y. al-Marouf, S. al-Madani, A. Jabir, Q. bin Hirz, D. al-Yusufi, A. al-Dawawi, N. al-Dawudi, M. Issa, A. al-Amir, A. Mahdi, M. al-Kharazz, H. al-Ali and many others who gave generously of their time and comfort.

Special thanks must also go to several students who challenged my thoughts and helped me clarify many themes and theories. The seminars I gave at the American University of Beirut were invaluable in restructuring and rethinking my ideas on the subject. I am particularly indebted to Salwa al-Amad, Nabih Beyhoum, Abdul-Rahim Buhusain, Edwin Hanna, Adel Khudr, Françoise Ghurayyib and others who took a personal interest in the work. Many of them have written their Master's thesis on various themes briefly, and sometimes in rather general terms, touched upon in the book.

Finally, many thanks to Sonia Jalbut Khuri, my wife, who tirelessly corrected and recorrected different drafts of this book.

Reading, June 1989

1
Introduction

I have always been fascinated by religion, particularly in Islam, but only decided to approach it systematically in 1978, after I had completed my book on *Tribe and State in Bahrain* (1980). Two things gave rise to this determination: the general sectarian orientation of Bahraini society and the devastating sectarian war in Lebanon. My work on Bahrain had convinced me that 'sectarianism' is a generalized phenomenon in the Middle East, and not peculiarly Lebanese. What is peculiar to Lebanon is the way sectarianism has been dealt with politically as an official policy of government. In Lebanon, it has been a public system; elsewhere in the Middle East, where the ideology of a 'consensus society' prevails, sectarianism is a publicly suppressed private system, a social taboo. Not that it is not a social or political force; it undoubtedly is. But people do not acknowledge it publicly. It is a 'public secret', so to speak.

The present work is a comparative study of Islamic sects with an emphasis on the ideology and organization of religion. 'Ideology' refers to the premises that are held true *sui generis* about the origin and formation of the religious community, and 'organization' to the recruitment, training and performance of the *ulama* specialists in society. Two basic themes dominate the text: one relating to the contradiction between sects and states, and the other between imams (the religious elite) and emirs (the power elite). The contradiction between imams and emirs takes different forms in different religious communities irrespective of whether they are adapted to state structures or to group sovereignties.

The various sects that emerged at different times in Islam were essentially instruments of moral control, operating in peripheral territories lying outside the domain of state authority. In this sense, sect and state stand in opposition to each other; and so do imams and emirs. Whereas sects manipulate moral ties, states use force, coercion and standardized legal references. In fact, one of the main concerns of the book is to deal with precisely the kind of religious ideology and organization that are adapted to state structures, as opposed to those adapted to the sectarian communities. The first is an instance of Sunni Islam; the second of sects in Islam.

In adapting to sovereign communities existing outside centralized authority, Islamic sects have developed peculiar instruments of control based on puritan and rebellious ideologies, diffuse religious organizations, intensified rituals and strict socio-religious codes. Take, for example, the way they deal with adultery, theft and divorce. According to Sunni law, adultery is punishable by stoning or whipping (sometimes to death), theft by hand-cutting and divorce strictly according to the terms of the marriage contract—these are all coercive measures subject to standard procedures. Among sects, by contrast, these transgressions are handled using moral measures. The Ibadis, the Druzes and the Yazidis excommunicate the adulterer and the thief until they repent publicly before a 'court' composed of a pious jury. Whereas the 'jury' in Sunni Islam are versed in Islamic law, among sects they are men of good religious reputation. Adultery among the Druzes is considered a serious crime, like murder or prostitution, and is punished by withholding the 'prayers of mercy' customarily recited at the funerals of the dead. Among the Ibadis, a divorcee is not permitted to remarry, and among the Druzes she is not allowed to see her husband, talk to him or sit in his council. On the other hand, the Sunni and the Shi'a allow the man to remarry his divorced wife after she has been married to somebody else first.

The Sunni insistence on coercive measures and standard procedures is clearly an instance of religious adaptation to state structures. On the other hand, the sects' insistence on the use of moralistic measures such as excommunication, separation, 'mercy-giving' and repentance provide clear instances of adaptation to small-scale sectarian communities. Even the Sunni preference for the exoteric understanding of the Qur'an could be considered an extension of this form of religious adaptation to centralized authority. No state could run its affairs on the basis of the esoteric understanding of the text of law. Unlike the exoteric and the explicit, which can be standardized, the esoteric and the implicit must remain fluid and elusive.

In brief, Sunni Islam, state structures, centralized authority, the exoteric understanding of the Qur'an, the centrality of religion, consensus, the resort to coercive measures in government, the tendency to standardize procedures—all these constitute a 'fabric' fitted together by the logic of power and conquest. By contrast, Islamic sects, peripheral status, the esoteric understanding of the Qur'an, the resort to moral measures and unstandardized procedures constitute a fabric suited to the maintenance of the sovereignty of the sectarian community.

Even the distinction between *islam* (surrender to law) and *iman* (faith) on the grounds that the first is an act of public policy and the second a matter of personal conviction can be interpreted in the same fashion. The Sunni, who use the logic of power and conquest, do not distinguish between *islam* and *iman*; abiding by the dictates of Islam is a measure of faith, and any deviation from one is a rebellion against the other. Religion among the Sunni is not simply a personal matter; it is a public right that cannot be forfeited by individual whims. This contrasts with the view of sects, which draw a sharp distinction between *islam* and *iman*, ranking the latter higher than the former. The Zaidis call themselves *al-mu'minun* (the faithful) and all other Muslims *al-muslimun* (the Muslims); the Ibadis believe that 'there dwells an imam in every soul', thus giving priority to *iman* (faith) over *din* (religion, Islam). The Druzes and the Alawis see *iman* and *islam* as instruments of esoteric knowledge and exoteric understanding respectively, assuming that religion cannot be perfected without knowledge of the esoteric.

The 'peripherality' of Islamic sects is closely linked to their rebellious character. All sects in Islam initially emerged as groups in rebellion against the established Sunni dogma and/or authority and developed later into routinized religious systems. Among some groups, such as the Shi'a, rebelliousness continued as a ritualistic exercise, thus continuously reinforcing the collective consciousness of the sect. It often happened in Arab-Islamic history, however, that sects such as the Buwaihids, the Hamdanis and the Fatimids took power in individual states, but their influence either did not endure or was confined to particular regions in the Arab world. When individual sects came to dominate, they often followed non-assimilative, non-incorporative policies and their territorial expansion was consequently limited. There seems to be an inverse correlation between the status of the state and the rise of sects: as the authority of the centralized state weakens, sects erupt, spread and stabilize. It is not surprising, then, that a large number of Islamic sects emerged in the eighth and ninth centuries when the centralized state authority was weak.[1]

The resort to moral instruments of control among sects has given rise to a comprehensive religious system covering a broad field of social interaction. Among sects, as we shall see, many aspects of social behaviour carry religious significance. Religious specialization and 'presence' proliferate in various directions, thus engulfing the totality of man's day-to-day interpersonal relations. Strictly speaking and from the point of view of social control, *din* (religion)—the public deterrent—in state situations parallels the moral order—the private deterrent—in sectarian conditions.[2]

The fact that sects operate as instruments of control outside the domain of centralized authority by no means reflects upon the quality of faith, either positively or negatively. In this book, religious identity, including beliefs, rituals and symbols, is taken for granted; it is what the faithful believe it to be. We are concerned here mainly with the interplay between religious identity and collective behaviour, the focus being on the way or ways in which religious systems are adapted to state structures or, on the contrary, to the sovereignty of the sectarian community. While state-oriented groups, in this case the Sunni, manipulate the law, *shari'a* (divine law) and coercion to enforce religious (public) order, the sects manipulate moral control. This is a case of law and *shari'a* versus morality, or what the fourteenth-century Muslim Arab scholar Ibn Khaldun calls *wazi* (the internal deterrent).[3]

Sects are seldom studied as religious phenomena. They are often dealt with as if they were mere historical realities, which obviously reflects a Sunni point of view. Ma'ruf's work on the Kharijis (1977), Laoust's on schisms in Islam (1965), al-Zain's on the Shi'a (1979), al-Tawil's on the Alawis (1966), Zakkar's on the Qaramita (1980), Hitti's on the Druzes (1928), Wilkinson's on the Ibadis (1972) and Little's on the Zaidis (1968) are but a few examples that illustrate the point. These works place more emphasis on the historical origin and development of individual sects than on religious ideology and organization, much to the detriment of the sects' self-image.

The 'expressive literature' on sects regrets the fact that sects are dealt with as if they were historical accidents. On the contrary, sects believe they are eternally ordained manifestations of divinity. This 'literature' includes a wide variety of books written by people about themselves and their own sects. Not much of it has yet found its way into academic circles, where Islam has come to be understood mainly as a Sunni and then as a Shi'a phenomenon. Islamic sects such as the Alawis, the Ibadis, the Druzes, the Zaidis and the Yazidis are more intensively studied for their 'historical' performance than for their religious dogma. The books mentioned above are not scholarly in the sense of searching for facts and truths, continuously building upon the findings of predecessors. They are meant to proselytize and to advocate peculiar understandings of religion, a sectarian viewpoint, and precisely here lies their value. Such works are vital for an understanding of religious ideology and organization, sectarian images and self-images, biases and stereotypes—in other words, the irrational elements that count.

In the present comparative study of sects, the emphasis is primarily placed upon present-day religious structures. This has logically led to the exclusion of many sects that emerged briefly in Islamic history but failed to endure. These include the Mamtura, the Mubarakiya, the Muhammadiya, the Qat'iya, the Kisaniya, the Musawiya, the Baqiriya and many others. The bulk of the seventy-two sects that emerged at different times in Arab-Islamic history (al-Baghdadi, 1978) were not able to stabilize into religious systems and will therefore be excluded from the discussion. Only those seven sects that evolved into routinized structures will be discussed: the Alawis, the Druzes, the Ibadis, the Shi'a Twelvers, the Yazidis and the Zaidis, in addition to the Christian Maronites who possess the very ecological, economic and demographic characteristics that distinguish sects from minority groups.

Just as we exclude from the discussion those sects that arose briefly and then disappeared, we shall likewise ignore those classified in this work as religious minorities or religious, patriotic movements. Sects, minority groups and religious movements should not be lumped together into a single category, as many writers on the subject have done.[4] These groups are not alike, either in form or in content. They differ in organization, ideology, general orientation and the way they relate to the state and society.

Sources and Chapters

The data for this book have been collected from two main sources: field-work and the expressive literature.[5] The field-work was carried out systematically in Lebanon between 1977 and 1985; in Bahrain in 1974–75; in North Yemen in summer 1980; and in Oman in spring 1982. In addition, I was able to interview a large number of *ulama* belonging to various religious communities and who happened to be living in Beirut. Specifically, I had the privilege of interviewing Alawi, Ibadi, Zaidi and Yazidi religious officials even though these sects, as total communities, have no significant presence in Lebanon. Beirut before the Lebanese war of the 1970s and 1980s was indeed a meeting-place for all kinds of Arab peoples.

In the first five chapters, a distinction is made between religion and sect on the basis of the centrality of religion as *din* and its adaptation to state structures, as opposed to the peripherality of sects and their attachment to the doctrine of the sovereignty of the community. Chapter 6 distinguishes between sects and religious minorities. Unlike sects, religious minorities live within the city walls subject to centralized (Sunni) authority, and here they seem to have worked out an accommodative formula accepting the ideology of Sunni rule. Whereas sects practise a comprehensive system of production in the territories they control, religious minorities follow a highly specialized mode of activity.

On the basis of this distinction between sects and religious minorities, the Christian Maronites of Lebanon are included in the first, not the second category. Other Christian Churches, plus the Jews, the Sabaeans, the Muslim Isma'ilis and the Baha'is are classified as minority groups. However, it must be borne in mind that this is a dynamic classification subject to economic, demographic and political transformations. Given the proper conditions, sects could turn into minorities and minorities into sects. There are some indications, for example, that the Yazidis of Iraq and the Ibadis of Algeria are slowly being transformed from sectarian to minority status. This issue is discussed at more length in Chapter 6.

Religious movements, like sects, seem to have emerged in peripheral territories lying outside the domain of state authority, but unlike sects, they never developed a rebellious ideology or evolved a dual system of religious organization. In contemporary Arab history, three movements —the Wahhabis of Saudi Arabia, the Mahdis of Sudan and the Sanusis of Libya—have emerged at the periphery, but none developed into a distinctly routinized, stable religious system. These were reformist and fundamentalist movements which, instead of rebelling against the central Islamic state, struggled against foreign colonial rule. The Wahhabis fought against the Ottoman Turks, the Mahdis against British colonialism and the Sanusis against Italian occupation. These religious movements seem to have disappeared as soon as independence was achieved. They became part and parcel of the state structure: either visibly, as in Sudan, where the Mahdi movement turned into a political party; or implicitly, as in Saudi Arabia and Libya, where the Wahhabis and the Sanusis still operate as political forces.[6]

From Chapter 7 onwards, the book discusses the religious structure of each individual sect as compared with the Sunni or Shi'a models, the two mother models from which various formulations have emerged in Islam. The phrase 'religious structure' is used to refer to two related matters: first, the sectarian ideology or world view which includes the origin and formation of the religious community; and, second, the organization of religion which includes the classification, recruitment and training of the *ulama*, and the way they are linked to the society.

Chapters 7 and 8 deal with the disparity between religious and sectarian ideologies, focusing on the Sunni model and the Shi'a model respectively. The theme is that whereas the Sunni focus on the sovereignty of divine law and the centrality of the state, sects focus on the sovereignty of the religious community. Chapter 9 discusses the principle of sovereignty with regard to the Druzes and the Alawis, and Chapters 10 and 11 with regard to the Yazidis and the Maronites. The Ibadi and Zaidi concepts are discussed in Chapter 8.

From Chapter 12 onwards, comparative religious organization in Islam is discussed according to essentially the same style of presentation as in the preceding chapters on ideology. In other words, the Sunni are discussed first (Chapter 12), then the Shi'a (Chapter 13), and these two models are then compared with the other sects. Whereas the Sunni *ulama* assume a subsidiary role to the power elite, the Shi'a *ulama* present themselves as if they were the political elite *par excellence*, performing the tasks normally carried out by the power elite. Unlike the Sunni, sects have developed a dual religious organization adapted differently to different sectarian orientations.

Religious activity and specialization among sects are generalized, diffuse processes. The fact that in Islam Caesar belongs to God does not mean that there is no contradiction between the kingdom of Caesar (emirs) and the kingdom of God (imams). The contradiction in Islam occurs between 'purity' and 'power'—in other words, between the rule of the imam and that of the emir, sultan or pharaoh. How purity and power, as distinct socio-political forces, relate to or oppose each other in various sectarian communities is analysed in Chapters 14, 15 and 16.

The final chapter, entitled 'Brethren or Citizens?', deals with the interplay between religion, nationalism and state organization. This chapter argues that nationalism, as a model of convergence, feeds upon religious symbols, but for these to become nationalistically relevant they have to be transformed from their particular to a wider and more universal meaning—the nation. Religious terms such as *fatih* (conquest), *umma* (community), and *nasr* (victory), the use of the classical language, and so on, have already taken on a more general meaning than their original religious contexts would have allowed. What is treated as an aspect of fundamentalism in the Arab-Islamic world could, conversely, just as well be taken as a measure of national convergence.

Part One

Religion and Sect in Islam

Part One

Religion and Sect in Islam

2
Religion and Sect in Islam

Two points require clarification at the outset. First, the distinction made in this book between religion and sect applies to the Arab-Islamic tradition and cannot—indeed, should not—be generalized to other cultures. Second, although some aspects of this distinction—centrality versus peripherality, for example—may overlap or intervene with other models of stratification, they do not coincide either in form or in content. No society should be dealt with as if it simply constituted a single, monolithic, exclusive system of differentiation embodying the entire ethnographic details of inequality. It is, rather, a question of multiple stratification systems that interpenetrate, overlap or cross-cut at different levels of action or thought.

Religion as *Din* and Sect as *Ta'ifa*

The word *ta'ifa* (sect), meaning a smaller group splitting off from a larger one, recurs more than twenty-one times in the Qur'an. It occurs in the following contexts: 'a sect amongst you', 'a sect amongst them', 'a sect amongst the faithful', 'two sects amongst the faithful', 'a sect amongst the Sons of Israel' and 'a sect amongst the People of the Book'.[1]

Many Muslim scholars and jurists use the term sect interchangeably with team, strain or creed. In his book *al-farq bain al-firaq*, for example, al-Baghdadi uses the word *firqa* (team) to refer to what I would otherwise call a sect. So does al-Shahristani, in his book *al-milal wa al-nihal*, when he uses the word *milla* to mean nation or law (*shari'a*), and the word *nihla* to mean religion or religious order.

None of these terms conveys the meanings implicit in the word *ta'ifa* which, in addition to meaning 'a part splitting from a whole', signifies a sort of religious completeness, the possession of an independent religious personality. For example, the Kharijis constitute a single sect comprising around twenty teams, *firqas* (al-Baghdadi, 1978:54). Or, conversely, a single *milla* may include many sects, as in the *milla* of Israel or the *milla* of Abraham (see the Qur'an 2/130).[2] Moreover, the word *ta'ifa*, as sect, has been continuously used to mean a 'split-off group' possessing a religiously autonomous character. Used in this sense, it is a neutral term, less derogatory than terms such as apostates, schismists, rejectors, polytheists, and so on. Henceforth, the word sect (*ta'ifa*) will be used in this neutral sense.

The term *din* (religion) as used in the Qur'an may mean judgement, faith or divine law. 'Judgement' is the meaning implied in the phrase *yawm al-din* (Day of Judgement) as it occurs in 1/4, 15/35, 37/20 or 51/6: 'And verily judgement must indeed come to pass.' It may also signify faith, loyalty or obedience as it occurs in 2/193, 10/22, 29/65 or 109/6, which reads: 'You have your *din* and I have a *din*.' Here, it means faith. But the most dominant meaning for *din* in the Qur'an is *shari'a* (divine law), which often overlaps with *islam* (surrender or obedience). This is the meaning implied in the phrase *din Allah* (God's religion) occurring in 3/83, 119/2 and other suras, or *din al-haq* (the religion of truth) occurring in 9/33 or *din al-malik* (the religion of the king) as in 12/76.

These seemingly different meanings for religion (judgement, faith and law) are in reality different dimensions of the same linguistic form, *din*. Religion as *din* is an act of 'judgement' (*dainuna*) or sanction according to God's law (*shar'*)[3] and/or surrender (*islam*) to his will. In the Qur'an, 3/19 states: 'The religion [*din*] before God is Islam.'

The verbal root *dana* from which *din* is derived means to judge or to sanction—*kama tadin tudan*, whatever you do you will be sanctioned accordingly (al-Shahristani, 1967:36). When the Prophet Muhammad established himself in Yathrib and began to 'judge' his followers according to the new divine law (Islam), thus founding the first Muslim community, the name of the town was changed from Yathrib to Medina (from *din*)—in other words, the place where 'judgement' is made and sanctions imposed. Once a community surrenders to God's laws it joins Islam and becomes part of the *umma*, the Muslim community, though not necessarily of *dar al-islam*, the abode of Islam, meaning peace. The Islamic *umma* is a form of universal religious brotherhood ('The faithful are brothers,' 49/10), whereas *dar al-islam* is a political adaptation that may include non-Muslims as well. The first is a matter of faith and religion, the second a matter of war and peace. In this sense, *dar al-islam*, which implies a territorial domain, is closer to the concept of state as centralized authority than *umma*, which is simply a form of universal brotherhood.[4]

To combine the concepts of judgement, faith and law in a single linguistic form, *din*, should not be taken to mean that these concepts are all alike. Although some Islamic jurists, especially the Sunni, combine faith and *islam* as acts of religion, the two can still be distinguished on the grounds that *iman* (faith) is a private system and *islam* a public policy. Indeed, the two arenas of belief are separated in the Qur'an, as in 49/14d:

> The desert Arabs say, 'We believe' [have faith]. Say, 'Ye have no faith'; but ye [only] say, 'We have submitted [*islam*] our will to God, for not yet has faith entered their hearts.'

Clearly, the Qur'an places faith in the heart, and *islam* in society as a public policy. The distinction between *islam* and faith recurs in several other verses in the Qur'an, as in 33/35 which distinguishes between the 'faithful' and the 'Muslims', or in 43/69: 'Those who have faith in our verses and were Muslims.'

However, Islamic jurists, especially the Sunni, consider *din* a formulation of public policy where religion, state and faith merge in a single form of action (Uthman, 1979:62, 238). The emphasis on religion as public policy has given rise to two related processes: the supremacy of the *shari'a* in Islam (the Sunni), and the sovereignty of the Islamic community, the sovereignty of religion.

The Supremacy of the *Shari'a*

The supremacy of the *shari'a* among the Sunni manifests itself in two ways: the priority given to jurisprudence in religious training (see Chapter 12), and subsequently the almost dogmatic insistence upon the comprehensiveness of religion. Of course, whoever approaches religion as *shari'a*, a formulation of public policy, will have to give priority to jurisprudence.

The Qur'an can be read and analysed for four related purposes: language and grammar, history, *shari'a*, and esoteric meanings such as those derived from it by the various *batini* sects (sects who are guided by esoteric interpretations) in Islam. The first and second purposes, grammar and history, are not relevant to our inquiry, and will therefore not be dealt with. This does not mean that they are not relevant to the understanding of the Qur'an as *shari'a*; on the contrary, grammar and history are prerequisites for the understanding of the Holy Book, and subsequently for the legal interpretations that emerge from it. In fact, history, which in this context refers especially to the performance of the early Muslim states, is one dimension from which Islamic *shari'a* is derived.

If Islam—Sunni Islam—is a legalistically oriented religion, a formulation of public policy, sent by God to organize human society, it follows that religious specialization must concern itself with matters of marriage and divorce, inheritance and ownership, commercial transactions and contractual dealings, government, banking, investment, credits and debts. The proper execution of these contractual matters according to the dictates of the *shari'a* constitutes the way to salvation.

Herein lies one of the main differences between Islam and Christianity. Whereas Islam places an emphasis on law, Christianity emphasizes sacrament and communion, and therefore the rituals that contain them. Christ's birth, death, and resurrection are sacraments which believers internalize through ritual. Salvation in Christianity lies in the acceptance of the Messiah as manifested in the sacramental rituals of baptism, matrimony, penance, eucharist, unction, priesthood and confirmation. Because of this, Christianity has translated Jesus's life history into a set of rituals performed by specialists with the participation of the laity.

This stands in contradistinction to the Prophet Muhammad, whose life history has been translated into a set of laws and decrees that govern—or should govern—man's behaviour and actions. The marriages concluded by the Prophet, the transactions he made and the treaties or truces he signed are all divine models to be followed by the faithful. They are the way to salvation. While salvation in Islam is sought by following God's laws and decrees, in Christianity it is sought through the acceptance of Christ and the observation of rituals. Correspondingly, religious officials in Christianity are trained in the performance of rituals, and in Islam in the administration of divine law. Indeed, 'love' in Christianity is equivalent to 'justice' in Islam.

The emphasis on sacrament as manifested in the birth, life, death and resurrection of Christ has consciously or unconsciously made Christians elaborate on those rituals that focus on life crises: birth, marriage and death. In Islam, personal rituals are performed with a matter-of-fact attitude. Instead of elaborating on life crises, Muslims seek divine guidance in a wide range of daily transactions including dress, food, drink, mating, the use of cosmetics, and a host of other things. This is what the concept of comprehensiveness of religion in Islam means.

If Islam is a legally oriented religion, which aspects of life does it cover? The answer is: all aspects of life. The comprehensiveness of divine law is a necessary product of the 'perfection' or 'completion' of religion; the Arabic word *kamal* may mean both perfect and complete. Hence the Qur'anic verse 5/4: 'This day I have perfected (*akmaltu*) your religion for you, completed my favour upon you and have chosen for you Islam as your religion.'

One of the main tenets of Sunni Islam is the belief that the *shari'a* for man's society is exclusively and comprehensively contained in the revealed text: 'Government rests in none but God,' insists the Qur'an (6/57). This is what Lewis (1981:9-20) calls the 'universality' of Islam, and Jansen (1979:17) the 'totality' of Islam or, for that matter, what al-Khashshab, professor of Islamic sociology at al-Azhar, meant when he declared, 'The Qur'an is the best book ever written in sociology.'[5] Sharqawi's words are very telling: 'Islam by its nature and essence contains all solutions to social problems and its substance is man.'[6]

The 'comprehensiveness' or 'centrality' of religion is an act of faith, a religious given, a quality of Islam, and as such it must not be confused with human behaviour or the impact of religion on culture. The fact that Muslims hold Islam to be comprehensive does not mean that Islam is comprehensively practised by Muslims. To insist on this syllogism is to slip into what might be called 'the fallacy of normative deduction', mixing behavioural expectation with behaviour. Whether or not Islam is comprehensively practised by Muslims has always been a subject of controversy, an object of reform, and a cause for political dissent and rebellion. This has been so from the early Khariji movement until the rise of Khumaini in Iran, Juhaiman al-Utaiba in Saudi Arabia, Muhammad al-Attar in Syria, and Muhammad al-Islambuli in Cairo, to mention only a few contemporary cases.

Abdullah al-Urwi (spelled Laroui in French), a Moroccan scholar who is considered a leading figure in the modernization of Islam today, bases many of his ideas on the central theme that 'changing Muslims does not simply imply changing Islam.'[7] Nothing offends a Muslim more than to be told that, 'Sooner or later Islam has to change and accommodate itself to modern times.' As one of my interviewees put it, 'The *umma* (community) changes, but religion is eternally fixed.' In this sense, the works of Abdo, Afghani, al-Rida and, more recently, Abdul-Rauf (1979), Chapra (1970), Khalafalla (1981), Sa'b (1979; 1981), Sarker (1980), and others who try to equate Islamic institutions with modern structures and ideologies, must not be dismissed as instances of apology, as some orientalists, notably Gibb (1975:68), have done. These attempts are meant to defend the comprehensiveness of religion, which is itself an act of faith.

A distinction should be made here between two types of comprehensiveness: that of source and that of performance. The first refers to the sources from which religious law is or can be derived, including dogma (i.e. the Qur'an and the *sunna*), history and custom (see Figure 1). Religious legislation can be derived directly from the Qur'an or indirectly from the *sunna* (tradition) on the basis of precedence, i.e. *qiyas* (analogy) or *ijma* (consensus). The *sunna* includes the life histories of the Prophet and his companions who are referred to collectively as *al-salaf al-salih* (the virtuous predecessors). History refers to the performance of government during the reign of the early caliphs. Custom includes those cultural practices held by consensus to be religiously valid.

Figure 1: Sources of Islamic Jurisprudence

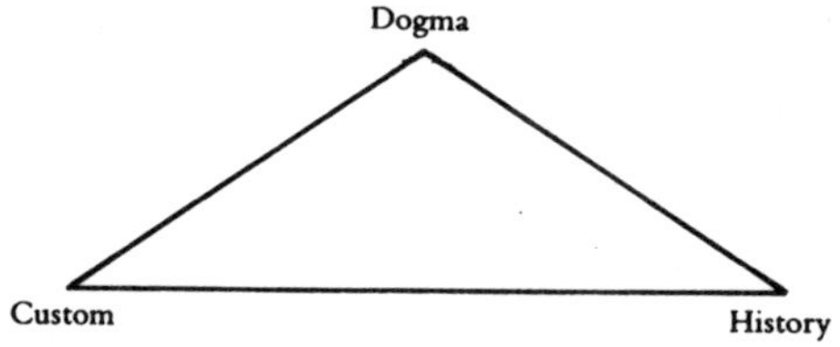

As practised in Islamic jurisprudence, consensus not only refers to the *ulama* agreement concerning the standardized interpretation of the text or to the agreement of 'men of resolution and contract', but also encompasses customary law. When I challenged a member of one of the ruling families in the Gulf, reputed to be a very pious man, by suggesting that the practice of forbidding women from marrying outside the family is not in line with religious teachings, he snapped: 'This is *urf* (custom), and *a'raf* (pl.) constitute an integral part of religious tradition.' The *hadith* related to the Prophet which states, 'My community does not err in consensus,' is taken to mean that consensus (culture and custom) establishes religious validity or, better, divine legality.

Islam is an ideal to be continuously sought after. The comprehensiveness or centrality of religion is an act of faith, a religious given, a quality of Islam, and as such must not be confused with human behaviour or the impact of religion on culture. This is perhaps what Sa'b (1981:34) means when he declares, 'Islam is a continuously interpretive revolution.'

The separation between Islam and Muslims, the ideal and the real, the spiritual and the temporal is not a 'source of tension' in Islam (Kerr, 1966:1); it is rather a form of adaptation to religious teachings. A believer is perfectly in harmony with himself when he states, 'True, I mistreat my wife, but Islam instructs me to be merciful to women.'

The intention here is not to claim that puritans and puritanism, the attempt to reconcile religious demands with community practices, is lacking in Islam. Far from it: the dream of every pious man is precisely to achieve this sort of reconciliation. Some religious communities which sprang from Islamic traditions, such as the *batini* Druzes and the Khariji Ibadis, who are described in the literature as 'puritans', have indeed managed to routinize a religious system that insists on the internalization of religious beliefs.

The Sovereignty of Religion

The incorporation of dogma, culture and history into the body of Islamic jurisprudence can be seen as the logical product of the comprehensiveness of religion as well as of understanding religion as *din*, a matter of public policy. This is an understanding which makes the presence of formal, sovereign Islamic authority imperative for the application of religion—in other words, divine law. The implication here is that the Islamic *umma* is not that which simply implements the *shari'a*, but that which does so under Islamic sovereignty. This explains Islamic jurists' continuous attempts to systematize in some detail the legitimate grounds for the presence of non-Muslims in an Islamic state, while instructing Muslims in non-Islamic states to follow none other than *jihad* (holy war). This also explains why some Muslim Arabs would rather live under Israeli occupation while rejecting the state of Israel than live independently in peace with the Zionist state. Or why the Palestine Liberation Organization (PLO) refrained from making the victory sign only when they were ousted from Tripoli (Lebanon) in 1985 at the hands of their own kind, the Syrian-sponsored Palestinian factions. Or again, why Lebanon has not become an Arab nationalist cause like Palestine even though it has been undergoing a devastating war for more than fifteen years. In these last two instances, Islamic sovereignty is clearly not at stake. Muslims attacking Muslims does not raise the issue of sovereignty.

It is in this vein that Mez' conceives of Muslims within the Islamic state as 'conquerors' rather than 'citizens'—a phenomenon to which he attributes the fragmented structure of Muslim Arab society. One may take issue with Mez' on the grounds that society in Islam is hierarchically conceived in terms of Muslims versus non-Muslims in a formulation where all Muslims are, at least ideologically, conceived of as brothers, not conquerors.

It is precisely this understanding of the *umma* as composed only of brothers that puts non-brothers—in this sense, non-Muslims—in a socially and legally subordinate position. Formal Islam does not conceive of Muslims occupying a minority status even if non-Muslims were to constitute the majority of the population. A society, any society, becomes Islamic if it fulfils two conditions: officially recognizing Islam as the religion of the state, and being governed by a Muslim. This explains why Muslim minorities in non-Islamic states such as those of Europe tend to cluster in 'cultural enclaves' legally and socially separated from the larger society. Those who live in Islamic states take on *taqiya* (dissimulation) as a form of adaptation. This is precisely why sects such as the Shi'a Twelvers, the Isma'ilis, the Alawis, the Druzes and others who have a minority status in Arab society all practise *taqiya*, which formally allows for the concealment of one's religious identity. The Sunni do not practise *taqiya* since they have been the ruling majority in Arab-Islamic society.[8]

These understandings of religion are not uniformly held by all Muslims all over the world. They vary according to the local culture and native traditions, modes of subsistence, social structure, and above all sectarian affinities—in other words, whether or not the religious group in question controls the centralized state authority. Empirically, this means that Sunni Islam, which adapts its ideology and jurisprudence to state structures, centralized authority and ruling regimes, came to enjoy a position of *din*, where other religious communities which adopted rebellious ideologies rejecting state structures came to assume a peripheral, sectarian position.

The consequence of this distinction for the general conduct of the various Islamic communities is clear. Whereas the Sunni, as *din*, have come to concern themselves with the sovereignty of the state and the supremacy of *shari'a*, the sects have concerned themselves with the sovereignty of the religious community. It is true that individual sects have taken hold of independent political entities, such as the Fatimids of Egypt, the Hamdanis of Aleppo (Syria), the Ibadis of Oman and of Algeria and the Zaidis of Yemen, but the polities they have created tend to be peripheral and transitory, and always fail to adopt an assimilative, expansionist policy.[9] There is historical evidence to suggest that as the centralized state authority weakens, sects increase, consolidate and develop. This perhaps explains why many sects in Islam, including the Druzes, the Alawis, the Zaidis and the Ibadis emerged and stabilized as routinized systems between the eighth and ninth centuries when centralized authority was weak.

The association between religion and state sovereignty or *shari'a* supremacy on the one hand, and between sects and community sovereignty on the other, has led to many discrepancies between religion and sect. These discrepancies occur in five different but related fields of action: the level of incorporation of religious and cultural traditions; the centrality of religion and the peripherality of sects; the territorial concentration of sects; the duality of sectarian religious organization; and the adoption by sects of rebellious ideologies rejecting the state, the authority of centralized power.

These fields of action are valid only if taken together. If taken separately, they would fail to distinguish between sects, religious movements and minority groups. Some may argue, for example, that religious movements such as the Wahhabis of Saudi Arabia, the Mahdis of Sudan and the Sanusis of Libya are sects because they emerged and operated in peripheral areas not controlled by state authority. This is true, but it is also true that these movements never developed routinized rebellious ideologies or dual religious organizations. They were basically patriotic fundamentalist movements that formed mainly in opposition to foreign, colonial intervention. As soon as independence was achieved, they were absorbed into the political digestive system of the state.

3

The Incorporative Character of Religion and the Segregative Character of Sects

The main argument of this chapter is that the association between Sunni Islam and state structure has made the Sunni incorporate religious and cultural traditions more than the sects, who stand for the sovereignty of the religious community. This is to be expected since the state, as a political formulation, accommodates a wide variety of ethnic, religious and social groups. The state structure is distinguished by two criteria: the resort to impersonal forms of legislation, including the use of force as an instrument of control; and the heterogeneous or pluralistic character of society. In fact, the one is a necessary product of the other: were it not for the heterogeneous nature of society, there would be no need for formal legislation and coercive instruments of control.

Plurality of ethnic groups implies a multiplicity of moral codes that cannot easily be transferred—as instruments of control—from one group to another. Hence the resort to legislation and the use of force. It is not surprising that the first attempt at legislation, which was Hammurabi's code in Babylon, occurred in around the eighteenth century BC, following the rise of cities, the first settlements in human history that experienced ethnically heterogeneous social structures. Thus one may appreciate Wolf's (1951) contention that Islam in Mecca managed to change the instruments of control from particular criteria derived from kinship and fealty to universal criteria based on religious law.

The Sunni's adaptation of religion to state structure has made them more incorporative of traditions than are the sects. This is well demonstrated in the selection of the caliph or imam, the official recognition of several interpretations of divine law, and many cultural practices including food taboos, style of work, marriage patterns, divorce conditions, naming and numerous other forms of interaction.

The Selection of the Caliph or Imam

Whereas the Shi'a and many other Islamic sects have confined the imamate to the Holy House of Ali and his descendants, the Sunni extended the caliphate to include all the tribal strains of Quraish, and then opened it to any who qualified. According to al-Shafi'i, one of the main Sunni jurists, 'governing is the victor's right'. In fact, the first two caliphs, who are known in Islamic literature as the 'two shaikhs', came from humble family origins. Abu Bakr, the first caliph, belonged to the Bani Tim, and Umar, the second, came from the Bani Adi—both families were of undistinguished origins in Quraish. The most distinguished were the Houses of Hashim and Umayya; Ali, the first Shi'a imam, belonged to the Hashims, and Mu'awiya, the founder of the Umayyad dynasty, to the Umayya. This might explain the chronic conflict between the two Houses.[1]

Although the various sects which branched off from the Shi'a tradition agree to confine the imamate to the holy lineage of Ali, they disagree vehemently over the methods of tracing or terminating it genealogically, and over the ways of designating the proper imam. While the Zaidis trace the imamate from Ali to Zaid bin Zain al-Abidin and terminate it here, the Shi'a trace it through al-Baqir and terminate it with al-Hadi, the Twelfth Imam This is why they are known as the Shi'a Twelvers, henceforth referred to in this work simply as the Shi'a. The Alawis, on the other hand, though tracing it much as the Shi'a do, assign to the imam an entirely different role in religion—a point that will be taken up in more detail later when discussing the Alawis (see Chapters 9 and 15). Other sects such as the Isma'ilis trace the imamate through Isma'il, the son of al-Sadiq; it was from this strain that the Fatimids and the Druzes branched off, as illustrated in Figure 2.

The disagreement between sects on the issue of tracing, terminating or designating the imam is not simply an academic exercise; it is rather a reflection of the general orientation of the sect and the dynamic forces operating within it. In other words, there is a startling correspondence between the personal qualities of the imam (his life, history and political career), on the one hand, and the general social and historical experiences befalling the sect, on the other. There is, for example, a puzzling connection between the life history of Zaid and the almost chronic

Figure 2: Genealogy of Imams among Islamic Sects

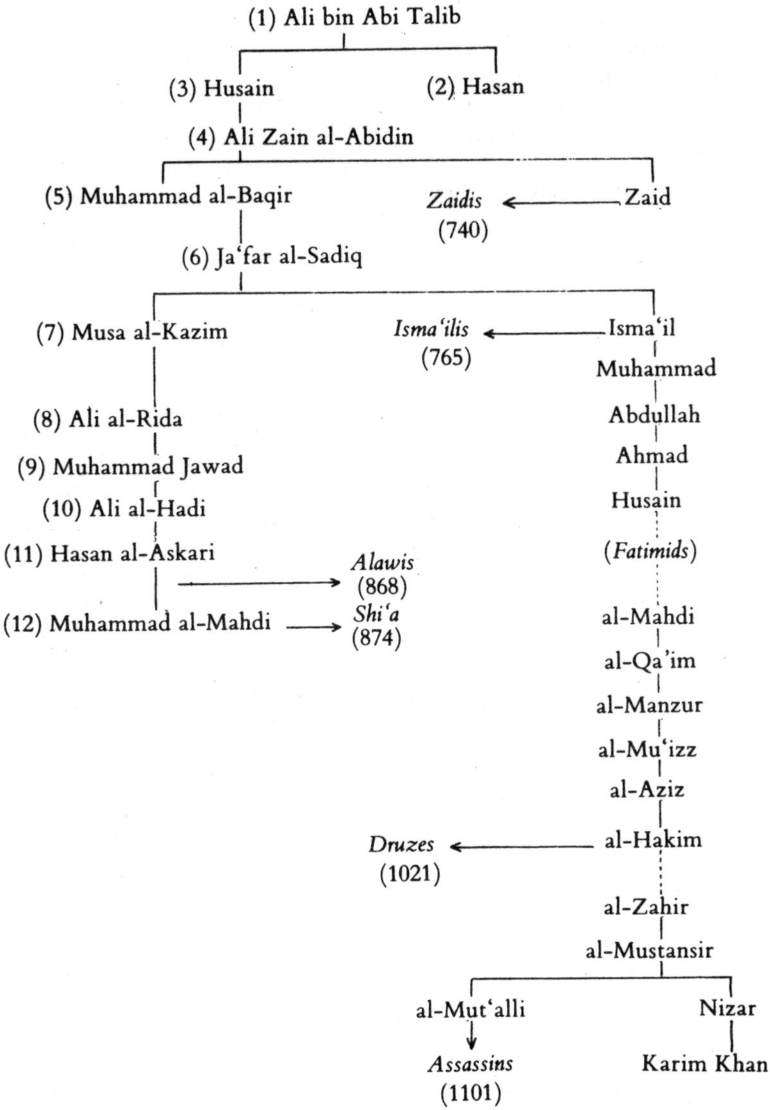

struggle for the imamate among the Zaidi tribal factions in North Yemen. Just as Zaid, the son of a concubine, rebelled against the Umayyads around AD 740 in Kufa and was eventually assassinated at the hands of his own followers, so do the Zaidi claimants to the imamship in Yemen continue to rebel against the ruling imam.[2]

By the same token, the correspondence between the life history of many imams and the status of the Shi'a in the Arab world as an oppressed minority is striking. During the early stages of its formation, towards the first part of the Umayyads' reign, the Shi'a dogma attracted mainly the *mawali* (the oppressed), and it has continued to do so ever since. It appears that the oppressed in society have championed the cause of the underprivileged House of Ali who were repeatedly denied their due right, the government of Islam. This does not mean that all the oppressed have turned to Shi'ism; rather, that those who turned to Shi'ism mostly happen to belong to the oppressed.

Shi'a sources always depict their imams as 'the wretched', 'the tortured', 'the humble poor', 'the worshippers of God' and 'the followers of His religion'. By contrast, the imam's enemies are depicted as 'the usurpers of power', 'the religiously corrupt', 'money mongrels', 'the worshippers of gold'. They speak of Imam Ali as having 'fed on barley' (Kashifulghata, n.d:93), of al-Sadiq counselling the poor and slaves and of al-Rida preferring simple foods and clothes, a man who turned down the caliphate in favour of seeking religious inspiration (Fadlalla, 1973:48). The Shi'a believe that the imams stayed aloof from government in order to safeguard the unity of Islam. Obviously, the personal qualities which the Shi'a attribute to the imams are behavioural preferences of the oppressed and not of the oppressors, the poor and not the rich, the dominated and not the dominant, the weak (or rather, the weakened) and not the strong.

Moreover, these qualities, especially those that pertain to the voluntary denial of government, are organically linked to the ideology of community sovereignty as opposed to state sovereignty. From the point of view of the oppressed and the weakened, one may appreciate the Shi'a insistence on justice being one of the main pillars of Islam (al-Zain, 1979:46), or on the belief that tyranny and injustice govern the world in the absence of the Hidden Imam. Even the messianic concept of the 'expectation of the imam' must be understood as a product of seeking worldly relief from poverty, tyranny and oppression. Just as the ruling Sunni speak of consensus and unity, the oppressed Shi'a speak of justice and expected salvation. The disparity here between Sunni dogma and Shi'ism is a universal phenomenon which distinguishes between the dominant and the dominated, government and opposition all over the world, irrespective of religious affinities or national origins.

The concepts of justice and equality, tyranny and oppression, and *taqiya* and faith can be treated as ideological dimensions, instrumental religious values, which Muslim sects and minorities have used to adapt to, or oppose, Sunni-controlled governments. These concepts help reconcile two opposed positions, rejecting the centralized authority of the Sunni state while upholding the sovereignty of the sect, the religious community. Even the belief in the *batin* (esoteric interpretation) of Qur'anic texts can be taken as a measure of community sovereignty. Like its correlate *taqiya*, the esoteric is an internal deterrent that could only operate in groups bound by community ties rather than in large state orders. State orders require the manipulation of law and force—law as deduced from the *zahir* (exoteric interpretation), the explicit and visible, and not from the esoteric, the implicit and invisible.

Because of their concern with community sovereignty, sects have come to incorporate fewer religious traditions than the Sunni, who managed to adapt religion to state authority. Sects select traditions according to how they fit into the general layout of the community and its historical experiences. Sects are less incorporative but more selective; in fact, one is a logical product of the other.

Variations in Legal Interpretation

The same principle of incorporation and selection can be detected in the official acceptance of the different schools of law in Islam and the way by which precedence is sought or established. Whereas Sunni jurists officiate on matters according to four schools of law—the Shafi'i, the Hanbali, the Maliki and the Hanafi (and some of them may even consult the Ja'fari, which is traditionally followed by the Shi'a)—sects normally adopt one source even if it has to be compiled from various legal traditions. No doubt, the multiplicity of legal reference among the Sunni is again a reflection of their control of the state and the heterogeneous structure of society. It is interesting to note in this regard that as soon as Khumaini came to power in Iran in 1979, his supporters began to call for the 'unity of legal reference', blending the various schools of legal interpretation into one.[3] The attempt, which was unacceptable to the non-Shi'a population of Iran, was quietly hushed.

It should be stressed that the differences between the four Sunni schools of law are no less significant than those between any one of them and the Shi'a Ja'fari law. Gibb (1975:k) is certainly right when he states that al-Mutawakil, the Abbasid caliph, would have officially recognized the Ja'fari law along with the other four schools were it not for the intermittent eruption of Shi'a rebellions here and there in the empire. The recognition of the four schools by the state was obviously a political, not a religious, decision. The Shi'a rejected the decision of the state and opted instead for the Ja'fari law; since then they have come to be known as the *rafada* (rejectors) in Sunni sources.

The more restrictive approach to traditions among sects can likewise be observed in *isnad* (ascription), the process of seeking legal reference by attributing a saying or deed to the Prophet or one of his trusted companions. The Sunni try to incorporate all the Islamic traditions, sometimes preferring some to others, but rejecting none. The Shi'a and other sects, on the other hand, seek legal relevance by tracing references to the Prophet, the imams and a few companions, thus ignoring the sources traced to Abu Bakr and Umar, the first two caliphs, to A'isha, Abu Bakr's daughter and one of the Prophet's wives, or Uthman, the fourth caliph. This the Shi'a do through what they call *ijtihad* (interpretation), an attempt to discriminate between 'reliable' and 'unreliable' sources. The unreliable sources tend to include all those who failed to take Imam Ali's side in his bid for the caliphate.

The process of seeking legal reference is nevertheless similar among the Sunni and the Shi'a, although the people to whom or through whom the ascription is sought vary widely. True, the Sunni often seek reference through Abu Huraira and the Shi'a through Abu al-Abbas, but both of them try to establish the validity of a *hadith* (a saying or a deed attributed to the Prophet) by considering its recurrence, the reliability of its source and whether or not it is in accordance with Qur'anic texts. This is irrespective of whether the act of weighing the evidence is called 'analogy' (Sunni), 'interpretation' (Shi'a) or 'opinion' (Ibadis). The difference between analogy, interpretation and opinion is ideological, not procedural. The Shi'a preference for 'interpretation' is organically linked to an esoteric reading of the Qur'an and the role of the imam in seeking religious perfection. They believe that only through the understanding of the esoteric, as exemplified by the imam, can religious perfection be established. The Sunni, on the other hand, work by analogy, because of their ideological assumption that the Qur'an explicitly contains the perfected religion.

Cultural Practices

The foregoing comments about the scale of incorporation, or for that matter, selection, restriction and segregation, can be generalized to cultural practices as well. The act of segregation among sects is a comprehensive system. Many of these practices, although derived from religious practices, are not directly sanctioned by religion. The incorporation of custom into 'canonized' law could indeed turn any bit of behaviour, however mundane, into a religious act. These practices include naming, eating habits, work patterns and modes of interaction with others. The list is long; I shall try to illustrate the point by citing a few ethnographic examples collected during field trips to Oman, Yemen, Iraq, Bahrain and various parts of Lebanon and Syria.

The Sunni do not discriminate against names as long as these belong to the Islamic tradition. Concerning female first names, they even go beyond the boundaries of their own culture and incorporate foreign elements as well: names such as Sonia, Suzie, Nancy, Natalie and Natasha are commonly used. Unlike the Sunni, the Shi'a and the Alawis avoid the use of the first names of many Muslim leaders who opposed and fought Ali or his descendants. First names such as Bakr, Umar, A'isha, Mu'awiya, Yazid and Marwan are taboo. While forbidding some names, individual sects frequently resort to the use of name sets that fit into their own religious ideology. The Shi'a, for example, who believe in the continuous manifestation of divinity in the House of Ali, use names composed of the names of the imam prefaced by the term '*abd*' meaning 'slave of' such as Abdul-Nabi, Abdul-Husain and Abd-Ali—Nabi, Husain and Ali being the names of the Prophet or imams. The Sunni use '*abd*' only in conjunction with the ninety-nine names of God such as Abdul-Rahman, Abdul-Rahim, Abdul-Naser and Abdul-Ra'uf—Rahman, Rahim, Naser and Ra'uf being synonyms of God.

Druze names are distinguished by their non-committal character in the sense that they are not anchored in any single sectarian tradition, and therefore become peculiar to the Druzes. Druze forenames often signify desirable human moods or qualities such as Salim (safe), Nadim (amusing), Aziz (dear), Laṭif (gentle), Atif (sympathizer), Ra'uf (merciful), Sa'id (happy), and so on.

The avoidance of certain sets of names is counterbalanced by the usage of other sets. The first is an instance of the segregative character of sects, the second a measure of endogamy, the continuous usage of the same set of names down different generations within the same group. The bulk of the Al-Saud in Saudi Arabia are called Abdul-Aziz, Fahd, Faysal, Turki, Sultan, Muhammad, or Khalid; the bulk of the Al-Khalifa in Bahrain, Hamad, Isa, Salman, Rashid, Khalifa or Muhammad; the bulk of the Al-Sabah in Kuwait, Jabir, Mubarak, Ali, Du'aij, Sa'd, and so on. What reinforces the concentration of sets of names in one family is the cultural practice of naming grandsons after grandfathers. Since high-status families keep longer genealogies, name concentration becomes more visible.

The point must not be exaggerated, however, since a large number of names, especially family names, are used by all sects and religions. Biblical names such as Moses, Isa (Jesus), Ibrahim, Ishac, Jacob and Sulaiman are used by all religious communities. So are the names derived from tribal traditions, weather conditions, colours, food, vegetables and flowers, physical disabilities and desirable human qualities.[4]

Certain eating habits follow the same principle of segregation between sects. These habits seem to be derived from local traditions rather than being directly sanctioned by religious dogma. Many a Shi'a in Bahrain, for example, unlike the Sunni, will avoid eating the Hamur fish on the grounds that it 'devours everything'. The Bahraini Shi'a do not eat chicken lungs or lamb spleen and refuse to drink coffee prepared by non-Muslims. Likewise, the Yazidis of northern Iraq are said to avoid eating lettuce, cabbage or cauliflower in case they have been defiled by human refuse. Al-Hasani (1967:107-8) says that the worst insult one can inflict upon a Yazidi is to tell him to eat lettuce. According to him, the Yazidis do not eat lettuce for it carries the name of their Prophet al-Khasiya (lettuce is *khass* in Arabic), or fish because it is the staple of the Prophet Jonathan, or elk because it is of the herd of their Prophet Yazid. The same can be said of the Alawis of northern Syria who, unlike their Sunni neighbours, avoid eating rabbit, camel meat, or the catfish which abound in the region (al-Sharif, 1961:192).

The Druzes and the Ibadis, especially the pious among them, refrain from smoking cigarettes or drinking coffee or tea, and tend to lead a very simple, unpretentious life. The Druzes of Lebanon do not eat a very popular dish called *mulukhiya*, simply because it is popular. They hold that al-Hakim, their divine leader, tabooed it precisely because of people's weakness for it. The Druzes believe in what they call the *tarwid* (exercise) of the soul, which implies the avoidance of what they would otherwise like to do. Those who enjoy a very high status in the religious hierarchy have the reputation of not eating meat, preferring to consume only the foods they themselves produce (H. Abu-Salih, n.d:10).[5]

Even in daily forms of social interaction and participation in work and worship, the sects tend to follow a much more restrictive policy than the Sunni, the people of religion. Except for the pilgrimage to Mecca and visiting the holy places at Medina, which are denied to non-Muslims, the Sunni welcome the participation of others in their worship. By contrast, the Shi'a tend to restrict visits to shrines, participation in rituals, worship and collective prayer to co-religionists. They distinguish between the mosque proper, which is open only to the faithful, and the 'funeral house' or '*husainiya*', which is built for proselytization and open to all. In 1974 the Shi'a of Bahrain vehemently opposed the Sunni government's move to open the Khamis Mosque (a famous historical site) to tourists on the grounds that it was built during Imam Ali's reign, and subsequently became a holy place only to be visited for worship by Muslims. The Shi'a believe that non-Muslims spiritually defile holy places. Shi'a mosques such as the Kadhimiya in Baghdad, or Ali's shrine in Najaf, Husain's in Karbala or al-Rida's in Shiraz, and many others scattered all over the Shi'a world, are open only to the faithful.

However, in a paper he wrote on Ashura (the ritualistic commemoration of the battle of Karbala) as celebrated in a southern Lebanese village, Emrys Peters (n.d) mentions that a Christian peasant took part in the play, acting the role of messenger. This is understandable in a village setting where people are bound by overlapping forms of personal relationships; this form of participation is unlikely to occur in big towns or cities, for instance. Even in a village setting, the role assigned to the non-Shi'a messenger is marginal to the play. I observed in Beirut and Bahrain that non-Shi'a are invited to attend the play as spectators and afterwards partake of *aish al-Husain*, the food prepared for the occasion. In this respect, however, the Shi'a seem to be more incorporative than other sects: the Druzes, for example, who 'closed the door of conversion', lie at the other end of the continuum.

Other forms of interaction, especially marriage and work, are subject to the same patterns of incorporation or segregation. Whereas the Sunni and the Shi'a allow a Muslim man to marry a non-Muslim woman but forbid the contrary, the Druzes and the Ibadis forbid inter-religious marriages altogether. The same applies to work: there is a tendency among the Sunni and the Shi'a, and to a lesser extent the Alawis, to seek job opportunities irrespective of religious constraints. The Druzes and the Ibadis, on the other hand, seem to prefer to work within their own religious communities. The ethnographic details on Lebanon, for example, indicate that Druze share-croppers preferred to work for their own lords, whereas the Sunni, the Shi'a and the Maronite share-croppers worked for other lords. In nineteenth-century Lebanon, many Maronite peasants worked for Druze lords, but the reverse was seldom true. Similarly, Ibadi peasants in Oman worked for Ibadi lords; Sunni peasants worked for whoever was in control. This pattern of work among the Druzes and the Ibadis is undoubtedly linked to their image of themselves as the ones who have 'signed the last covenant with God' (the Druzes) or who are 'the possessors of faith' (the Ibadis).

Given this disparity between the Sunni and the sects it is easy to understand why non-Arab Muslims have always adopted the Sunni dogma, and why the Sunni, who achieved a centralized state authority, seem to dominate in cities and along historic trade routes. The city and the highway have always come under the control of centralized authority.

With the exception of Iran, which turned to Shi'ism in the sixteenth century at the hands of the Safavids, all non-Arab Muslims have gone the Sunni way. Even the Abbasids, who initially usurped power by championing the cause of the House of Ali, turned to Sunni Islam once in power. The active participation of the non-Arab elements in successive Abbasid governments had simply accelerated the process of 'Sunnization'. Until the sixteenth century, Shi'ism was typically an Arab phenomenon. It is possible that Iran adopted Shi'ism following the recurring conflicts with the Ottoman Turks; the conversion undoubtedly helped reinforce the Farsi identity. In Iran today, the Farsis are Shi'a and the non-Farsis (Arabs, Kurds, Baluch and Turkomans) are Sunni.

Because of their incorporative character, the Sunni have become the most numerous of all Muslims, amounting to 80% of the Muslim Arabs and around 83% of all Muslims in the world (Savory, 1981:13). Sunni Islam is so well adapted to the ideology of government and ruling regimes that the leaders of a community would convert to Islam while leaving the rest of the community to follow tribal practices, as happened in Arabia during the rise of Islam; in West Africa and Central Africa until the turn of this century (Trimingham, 1959); and in Syria, Lebanon and northern Iraq until the ascent of the Mamluks towards the fourteenth century. The

Mamluks were urban people and as they began to expand their authority over the countryside, they brought along with them the authority of religion—the Sunni.

4
The Centrality of Religion

The adaptation of religion to state structures, the adoption of Sunni Islam as the dogma of government and the ruling elite, and the incorporative character of the Sunni and their large numbers have all partly combined to turn Sunni Islam into what Shils (1961) calls 'the moral centre', what Fallers (1973) calls 'the cultural mainstream' and what we shall now refer to as 'the centrality of religion'. The phrase 'partly combined' is used because the Sunni, however incorporative, have not yet developed assimilative policies derived from national or cultural traditions. Theirs are still bound by purely religious dogma, brethren versus citizens.

The 'moral centre' is a form of collective sympathy that encompasses a range of ideological and behavioural uniformities and commitments rooted in religion and culture. At this level of analysis, it becomes difficult to distinguish between the cultural and the religious; both merge in a single formulation of action, certain sets of propositions about man, society and the world. These formulations or value orientations continue in the face of social or political fragmentation. This is a case of a 'united culture and fragmented society', as Gellner (1981:14–19) would have put it. The one does not negate the other: while unity takes place at the cultural level, fragmentation occurs at the organizational level.

Shils and Fallers used the concepts of 'moral centre' and 'cultural mainstream' in an attempt to evaluate the prevailing White Protestant (or 'wasp') culture in North America. This is the modal culture which succeeding US governments tried during the first part of this century to translate into an official policy known as the 'melting-pot', designed to assimilate the huge numbers of immigrants. Many social scientists have written about this policy, some arguing for its success, others for its failure.[1] Although it can be seen as having created a cultural mainstream or moral centre, it failed to attract everyone to its contents. Instead of melting immigrants into a cultural, national 'pot', it encouraged the continuity of ethnicities as instruments of organization in cities, workplaces, unions, churches, and even political parties.

Sunni Islam, by comparison, has been incorporative but less assimilative —it has never tried to formulate a melting-pot policy, a deliberate, official attempt to absorb foreign elements into a cultural or national mainstream. On the contrary: perhaps with the exception of Egypt, none of the Arab states has managed to evolve a clear-cut policy of naturalization. One has to be born of Lebanese parents to claim Lebanese citizenship, and to be Bahraini one has to produce documentary evidence that one's parents and grandparents were Bahrainis. Legislation in Arabia, especially in the oil-rich countries, is meant to quarantine rather than assimilate people of foreign stock. There have been Palestinians, Lebanese, Egyptians and Sudanese living and working in the Gulf for over twenty years, but they still have no way of claiming citizenship.

In brief, the term 'centrality of religion' has been deliberately chosen instead of 'moral centre' or 'cultural mainstream' in order to draw attention to three interrelated factors: first, Sunni Islam, however incorporative, is not assimilative; second, there has been no formally and clearly stated policy of assimilation in the Arab-Islamic countries; and third, religious dogma remains the standard by which groups living within the same state are differentiated morally, socially and politically.

State and *Asabiya*: the Sunni and the Sects

The centrality of religion is exemplified in the Sunni control of the state, city and estate. In fact, the control of one has necessarily led to the control of the others. The state, as a centralized authority in the Arab-Islamic tradition, has always been located in the city, and the estate, the feudal order, has always been an extension of city authority. Ibn Khaldun captured the interconnection between state, city and estate and chose to blend them together in a single formulation which he calls *mulk*, a linguistic derivation of *malik* (king) or *mulk* (possession). He distinguishes between the *mulk* and the caliphate on the grounds that the style of rule in a *mulk* setting is based on power and coercion, or what he calls *al-wazi al-sultani* (the sultanic deterrent), whereas in the caliphate situation it is based on the application of religion and divine *shari'a*. In *mulk* situations, *asabiya* (social solidarities) govern the rules of the day including taxes, the treasury, and the distribution of power and wealth; here, the *ulama* assume a subsidiary position, dealing essentially with worship and personal or family law. In the caliphate context, on the other hand, the *ulama*, in consultation with 'men of resolution and contract', take hold of government. Clearly, the position of Ibn Khaldun, himself an *alim*. (learned man), was much like that of Ayatollah Khumaini in Iran.

If we adopt Ibn Khaldun's distinction between the *mulk* and the caliphate, all succeeding Islamic governments, with the exception perhaps of the first four caliphs, were of the *mulk* type, ruling by force and coercion. This was to be expected, given the expansion of Islam into different and varied ethnicities in Asia, Africa and some parts of Europe. The 'moral, internal deterrent' as an instrument of control only works in small-scale, homogeneous communities—families, clans, tribes, neighbourhoods—and not in ethnically complex structures. In complex societies, the 'sultanic deterrent' prevails.

The Sunni dominance of the city and the state made them, *ipso facto*, in control of centralized governments, bureaucracies and civil services. This has been so even where, as in Iraq, for example, they constitute less than the majority of the population. There seems to be a pattern to the Sunni control of governments in ethnically or confessionally complex Arab countries: whereas the Sunni Arabs control the bureaucracy and public services, other ethnicities or solidarities, including sects, control the military or security forces. This is true in Morocco, North Yemen, Oman, Syria, Lebanon and the Gulf states. In Morocco, the Arab Sunni dominate the bureaucracy and public services and the Berbers the military and security forces (Gellner and Micaud, 1973). In North Yemen, the Shawafi Sunni dominate the bureaucracy and the Shi'a Zaidis the military. In Syria, Lebanon and the Gulf states, sectarian and tribal solidarities control the military: the Alawis in Syria, the Maronites (formerly) in Lebanon, the Ibadis in Oman and various tribal strains in the Gulf. In other Arab countries, the Sunni control all aspects of government.

Why this pattern? How did the Sunni come to dominate the bureaucratic structures and other solidarities in the military and security forces? The answer lies in the interplay of three related factors: the Sunni dominance of the city, the internal mechanisms of control among sects and tribes and the emergence of modern states from colonial intervention.

The Sunni control of the state has contributed to their concentration in cities. They are most numerous in 'conquest' cities such as Cairo,

Damascus, Baghdad and Fez; in 'caravan' cities such as Palmyra, Qairouan and Medina; in 'agrarian' cities such as Tripoli in Lebanon, Hama and Homs in Syria, and Mosul in Iraq; and in 'port' cities such as Beirut, Haifa, Jedda, Alexandria, and Casablanca.[2] The Sunni are the urban population *par excellence*. Their concentration in cities has led some orientalists, notably Deffontaines (1948), Fischer (1956) and Planhol (1968), to conclude that the city is the 'citadel of faith in Islam'. Obviously, here they must mean Sunni Islam. Islamic sects spread in rural areas at a much higher frequency than in urban areas. Sectarianism in Islam is a rural phenomenon.

The fact that the bulk of the urban population is Sunni does not mean that all the Sunni are urban. Until recently, the rural population of the Arab world outnumbered the urban population, but since the second half of this century the rate of urbanization, which varies from one country to another, has increased steadily. Statistics for 1984 showed an urban population that ranged from 21% of the total in Sudan to 90% in Kuwait.[3] These ratios—which are likely to continue to increase with rural-to-urban migration, the incorporation of villages into the urban zones and the creation of entirely new urban settlements—all act to some degree in favour of the 'Sunni-ization' process.

Control and dominance breed mutual dependence. The Sunni control of the state rendered the state (the use of force and coercion) the main instrument of control among the Sunni. This contrasts with the sects, where the instruments of control lie in moral measures, social bonds and the prevalence of different forms of inwardly oriented solidarities, which can be summed up in Ibn Khaldun's concept of *asabiya*.

Asabiya, derived from *asab* (meaning nerve), signifies internal cohesion, often brought about by unity of blood or faith. In a state setting, unity is brought about through the use of force; but in an *asabiya* setting, it arises voluntarily through the sharing of moral bonds: blood, descent, marriage, ethnic origin, tribal affinity, faith or through some or all of these mixed together. According to Ibn Khaldun, the *asabiya* structure reaches its zenith when it blends with religion leading to conquest, as happened at the dawn of Islam.

Thus, one may speak of three types of *asabiya*: tribal *asabiya*, meaning solidarity derived from the belief in the unity of descent and genealogical origins; ethnic *asabiya*, meaning unity of ethnic origin (Ibn Khaldun spoke of Arab *asabiya* emerging during the Abbasid dynasty); and sectarian *asabiya*, derived from unity of religious beliefs and practices. An *asabiya* arrangement is always distinguished by two criteria: first, the element of exclusiveness, the group's image of itself as unique; and second, the non-hierarchical structure of its authority. The first criterion will be discussed at length in the chapters on the sovereignty of sects (see Part Two). Suffice it to say at this stage that all sects believe, each in its own way, that they have a special role to play, a special message to deliver, and that they are the last to have signed the divine covenant with God.

The non-hierarchic structure of authority should not be taken to mean that sects lack internal differentiation. It simply means that in sectarian situations, 'vertical' rather than 'horizontal' forms of differentiation dominate people's thinking, where entire collectivities such as Druzes, Shi'a or Maronites, or, for that matter, Arabs, Jews, Berbers and Kurds, are hierarchically ranked. Vertical differentiation is an instance of ethnicity, whereas horizontal differentiation is a measure of class distinction. In the first instance, conflict is bred between sects, religious groups and other forms of ethnic variations; in the second, between social classes. The one may easily slip into the other, however; many a rebellion in Lebanon, including the 1975- war, has begun as an instance of class conflict, but ended as a war between sects (Khuri, 1981d:383–408).

Indeed, the non-hierarchic structure of authority (combined with a strong sense of egalitarian ethics within a sect) helps to draw sharper boundaries between sects. The one induces the other: the stronger the *asabiya* (the internal mechanisms of control), the sharper the boundaries that separate the sects. The reverse is also true: the weaker the *asabiya*, the more fluid the boundaries, and subsequently, the more the group merges with the undistinguished masses of society. According to Ibn Khaldun, a group is in the '*asabiya* stage' when the internal mechanisms of control are strong; when they weaken, the group reaches the *mulk* stage, the zenith of power and the beginning of decline. Whereas austerity, nomadism, a strong sense of equality, and unity of origin maintain the *asabiya* state, the *mulk* is sustained by a luxurious life-style, stratification and the use of force and coercion as instruments of control—in other words, the rise of statehood. Consequently, the rise of statehood weakens the *asabiya* which, in turn, leads to the former's decadence. Hence the cyclical nature of power. To Ibn Khaldun, *dawla* (state, from *dala* which means to rotate power) meant government (or the regime in power), not a territorial structure with a 'juristic personality' that sues and can be sued. It is in this sense that Ibn Khaldun saw the state as passing through five stages: (1) conquest, where *asabiya* (cohesion) is derived from unity of blood and religion; (2) the rise of the 'state', based on military power; (3) the apex, which witnesses the organization of taxes and finance leading to wealth and the display of a luxurious life-style, and marks the beginning of decline; (4) decline, where the state is satisfied with the performance of 'the virtuous predecessors'; and (5) total collapse, which comes simultaneously with the rise of a new *asabiya*.

Leaving aside the cyclical nature of power, Ibn Khaldun's analysis contains an interesting model that could distinguish between Sunni Islam and Islamic sects. The Sunni may be considered as perpetually in a condition of 'state' organization, and the sects as continuously in a state of *asabiya*. Put differently, just as the 'state' (the resort to force and coercion) is an instrument of control among the Sunni, the *asabiya* (resort to moral bonds) is an instrument of control among the sects. (This distinction is elaborated on in Chapter 7.)

Ibn Khaldun saw human society partly as a natural, not a totally divine creation. This is well demonstrated by his giving priority to the ecological variable in modifying patterns of social organization. He saw *asabiya* bonds growing only out of a nomadic tribal setting, and the *mulk* structure rising from a state-city setting. As *asabiya* shifts from the first to the second, it is transformed into a *mulk* form of organization. Ibn Khaldun was a Maliki jurist who presided over many cases of conflict involving the Berber tribes; his model came to reflect a typically North African situation. When he moved to the East and started to write about the Eastern Arabs, he seems to have abandoned the concept of tribal *asabiya* in favour of Arabian *asabiya*, Arabs versus non-Arabs. This is already the ninth century, which witnessed a considerable presence of non-Arab Muslims in Baghdad, the capital of Islam, during the reigns of al-Mu'tasim and his son al-Wathiq.

It appears that whoever studies the North African situation tends inevitably to arrive at Ibn Khaldun's conclusions. Gellner's pendulum theory seems to fit beautifully into Ibn Khaldun's model, in form if not in content. According to Gellner (1968), there exists an implicit alliance between tribal aggregations and city ways, the first providing military might and the second religious scholarship and guidance. Through this unwritten alliance, religion oscillates, like a pendulum, between the principle of stability maintained by the scripturalists who enforce religious law, and the principle of collective sympathy maintained by the ritualists emphasizing spiritual salvation.[4]

Perhaps because Ibn Khaldun was a Sunni imam who rejected sects altogether and dismissed them as undesirable 'novelties', he refrained from dealing with the question of sectarianism, or, for that matter, religious *asabiya*. While *asabiya* forms of organization were to him 'natural' conditions, religion was a divine matter. He might have believed that *asabiya* in religion, unlike that in tribes and ethnicities, is the work of divinity, not a natural matter, and therefore lies outside the realm of human inquiry.

The internal mechanisms of control among sects do not differ in form from those prevalent among tribes and ethnicities. All are forms of *asabiya* (self-contained solidarities) built upon the image of the self as a special creature and upon the non-hierarchic order of authority reinforced by egalitarian ethics. We are dealing here with parallel structures cutting across different collectivities: sects, tribes and ethnicities. Indeed, many variables overlap from one collectivity to another. Many a sect traces descent to a specific set of tribal strains. For example, the bulk of the Ibadis in Oman trace their origin to the various factions of the Hanawi tribe (Wilkinson, 1972); the Zaidis of North Yemen to the tribes of Hashid and Bakil (Little, 1968:12). Likewise, the Druzes of Lebanon trace their origin to the Bani Tim who settled in Wadi al-Taim in south Lebanon, the Bani Ijl who settled in the Shuf area, the Bani Tannukh in the Gharb district and the Bani Lakhm who are the ancestors of the House of Irslan. This is in addition to the Bani Hilal who settled in the Suwaida district of Houran in Syria (Tali, 1961:15-16).

Similarly, the Alawis of Syria see themselves as falling into major tribal factions: the Khaiyatin clans who live around the Kabir River that divides Syria and Lebanon in the north, the Sinjariya clans who trace descent to the Ghasasina and who live near Jabla in Syria, the Bani Ali tribes who settled in the Boudi Mountains, the Mahaliba groups who live at the boundary between Turkey and Syria in north-west Syria, and the Haddadin tribes who settled in the Latakiya district (al-Tawil, 1966:352-73). The Haddadins, who trace their origin to Muhammad al-Haddad, the son of Prince Sinjari, who was the nephew of Hasan al-Makzun, an eminent religious figure in Alawi sources, include the Al-Matawira, the Al-Darawisa and the Azd clan, to which President Asad of Syria belongs.

The Yazidis of northern Iraq, by the same token, are divided and subdivided into tribal factions, each headed by a shaikh called Agha Eil who rules in conjunction with a group of elders called Raspiti—this is a very common form of organization among the Kurdish tribes who live in the area. This is to be expected since the Yazidis are of Kurdish ethnic origin, as evidenced by the language they speak (Jule, 1934:c).[5]

The containment of individual sects within tribal capsules, which reinforces one *asabiya* by another, applies to all Islamic sects with the exception of the Shi'a. The Shi'a, like the other sects, tend to concentrate in peripheral regions, yet, unlike the other sects, the regions they live in are scattered all over the Arab East. They live in north and south Lebanon, in several villages and suburbs around Damascus in Syria, in southern Iraq, Bahrain, Kuwait and Saudi Arabia.[6] Ethnologically, they cannot be easily fitted into any particular type in the Middle East. Some of them are tribally organized, as in the case of those who live in the Hermel-Baalbek area of north Lebanon (such as the Alaw, Dandash and Ja'far tribes), or the sheep-herding tribes of southern Iraq who live along the banks of the Euphrates (such as the Al-Awazim, the Al-Mazalim and the Bani Salih). Some are urbanites as in the Arabian Gulf, many of them being of Persian origin. The bulk of the Shi'a, however, have until recently been peasants living in self-contained villages in southern Lebanon, around Damascus, Mesopotamia, the interior villages of Bahrain and the Eastern Province (al-Hasa) in Saudi Arabia. Since the 1950s, however, many of the peasant Shi'a have migrated and settled in and around the neighbouring primate cities.[7]

The point to be stressed here is that sectarian *asabiya*—reinforced sometimes by tribal origins (unity of blood), and sometimes by ethnic traditions—has enhanced the military capability of individual sects. It is precisely this military capability that enabled the sects to survive and continue for centuries in the face of religious intolerance and persecution. And it is this very capability that allowed them, whenever the opportunity arose, to usurp power and achieve sovereignty, as happened in the second half of the Abbasid era, intermittently during the reign of the Ottomans, and more recently with the advent of European colonialism and the rise of modern states.

Sects and Modern States

The sects' rise to power is inversely related to the Sunni domination of states. Sects come to power when the Sunni state weakens, because of internal strife or colonial intervention, or both together. The prevailing assumption that sects have come to control some modern states purely and simply because of colonial intervention is therefore only half true.

The sects' control of modern states is a product of local tradition as much as it is part of colonial experience.

To appreciate the point, it is necessary to distinguish between what I shall call 'political personality' and what Weber calls 'juristic personality'. Unlike Ibn Khaldun's concept of 'state', which means government or regime, the modern state implies, among other things, juristic capacity: it sues and can be sued. In this sense, the state always stands against religion (any religion), which sues but cannot be sued. This concept of state is relatively recent: states with juristic personalities only began to emerge in Europe between the eighteenth and nineteenth centuries and, like many other European commodities, were transferred overseas through colonization, reaching a climax in the aftermath of the First World War.

The modern state with a juristic personality is a relatively new formulation, but the state with a political personality is an old historical experience. As a system, the Ibadi movement stabilized in the interior of Oman towards the latter part of the eighth century and Oman has had a unique political personality ever since. The same could be said of the Zaidis who established themselves in Yemen towards the end of the ninth century. Mount Lebanon also began to acquire a distinct political personality as of the seventeenth century with the rise of the Ma'nids. The pattern also includes Egypt and Morocco which always had distinct political personalities. In Egypt, this personality became visible with the reign of Muhammad Ali in the early part of the nineteenth century, and in Morocco with the Alawi dynasty who have been in power for no less than four centuries. It also includes Saudi Arabia, which began to acquire a distinct personality in the early part of the eighteenth century with the rise of the Wahhabis, Libya with the rise of the Sanusis, and Sudan with the rise of the Mahdis.

The states of the Arabian Gulf, which correspond to tribal domains, are no exception to the rule. The Al-Khalifa rule in Bahrain, the Al-Sabah in Kuwait, the Al-Buflah in Abu Dhabi, the Al-Buflassa in Dubai, the Al-Qawasim in Ras al-Khaima and Sharja, the Al-Bukhraiban in Ajman, the Al-Buali in Umm al-Qawain and the Al-Sharqi in Fujaira. These tribally controlled states began to acquire political personalities as from the early part of the nineteenth century.

Obviously, there is a dialectic relationship between, on the one hand, the political map of the Arab world as drawn by colonial powers leading to the rise of new modern states, and, on the other, local power dynamics. These political personalities are sometimes rooted in tribal solidarities, as in the Gulf; sometimes in sectarian affinities, as in Oman, North Yemen and Lebanon; sometimes in religious movements, as in Saudi Arabia, Libya and Sudan; and sometimes in historical achievements, as in Egypt and Morocco. Other Arab states that have not had this distinction, such as Iraq, Syria and South Yemen, seem to reject their present status, continuously adopting aggressive, expansionist policies advocating pan-Arab unity.

The Feudal Tradition

The Sunni control of the centre (state and city) has had significant implications for economic organization and the distribution of wealth between religious groups throughout the Arab world. The Sunni came to concentrate in countries with rich, open, fertile plains such as Egypt, Syria and Morocco and simultaneously to dominate in the most fertile lands of other countries where they are less than a majority. In Lebanon they cluster in the rich coastal plains of Akkar, Tripoli and Sidon; and in Oman, in the open Batina region, the coastal plains that stretch from Sharja to Muscat. In southern Iraq, Bahrain and the Eastern Province of Saudi Arabia, the Sunni tend to be the landlords, and the Shi'a the cultivators.

The same pattern can be detected in North Africa, where the Sunni Arabs have been in control of *bilad al-makhzan*, cities and fertile open plains, traditionally under the control of centralized authority, and the Berbers in control of *bilad al-siba*, the less fertile oases and mountainous regions (Abu al-Nasr, 1971:8). The same conclusions can be drawn from case-studies of individual regions. Tou'mah's (1977:44) work on land ownership and political power in Damascus from 1858 to 1958 shows that 24 out of 27 families of feudal traditions in and around Damascus have Sunni affinities. In Iraq, Batatu (1978:ch.4 & 52-61) has shown that out of 52 'landed families', in 1958, 28 were Sunni, 21 Shi'a and 3 belonged to miscellaneous religious minorities—this is in a country where the Shi'a are the majority. The work of Khuri (1980:ch.3) on Bahrain and that of Vidal (1955) on the Eastern Province of Saudi Arabia show that the bulk of palm-groves are owned by Sunni landlords.

The Sunni control of fertile plains must be understood in the light of the fact that Middle Eastern feudalism has historically been an extension of centralized authority. This is very different from Europe, where estate and city were opposed, the first the domain of feudal lords, the second the domain of the king. Feudal estates in the Middle East were allocated by centrally based regimes to sons, brothers, nephews, and sometimes to princes and heads of military expeditions as benefices which were then run as fiefs (Khalidi, 1975; Khuri, 1980). They were not passed on from one generation to another as forms of inheritance according to the rules of primogeniture, as was the practice in Europe. It is thus not surprising that feudalism in the Middle East took the form of absentee landlordism —thus making it necessary for feudal chiefs to stay in the city close to the centre where decisions concerning the allocation of land were made. Some princes helped themselves to estates by using sheer force—those whom al-Mawardi (1979:29) calls the 'usurper princes'.

Another distinction between Muslim and Christian feudal systems lies in the definition of ownership and private property. Whereas Christian ideology allows for private ownership on the basis of the principle 'Render therefore unto Caesar the things which are Caesar's; and unto God the things that are God's' (The Bible, Luke 20:25; Matt. 22:21; Mark 12:17), Muslim ideology follows the dictum 'what is Caesar's belongs to God'. In Islam, man has no right of ownership; only God owns. Man has the right of *ihya* (usufruct), the right of cultivation. Because of this ideological disparity, Christian feudalism followed the principle of inheritance (according to primogeniture), and Islamic feudalism depended on the magnitude of power.

With the introduction of cash crops, mainly cotton, in the nineteenth century and the gradual mechanization of agriculture, the fertile plains—and therefore Sunni dominance—began to undergo a major socio-economic transformation. The process was two-fold: just as tenants shifted from share-cropping to wage labour, the feudal lords were giving way to new 'capitalists', men of commerce and industry, who expanded their investments to include commercial agriculture. Subsistence agriculture began to give way to cash crops. It is no coincidence therefore that Syria, Egypt and Iraq—the countries that contain the open, fertile plains and with a long history of feudalism—adopted socialistic measures earlier than other countries; or that socialism took the form of land reclamation and redistribution. These countries were the first to witness socio-economic transformations, the consequence of which has been the gradual alteration of landed families in Sunni Islam. Two factors were partially responsible for this alteration: the advent of the colonial era, which began to favour, at least in military recruitment, non-Sunni elements; and the rise of secular nationalistic ideologies, which brought to power officers and teachers with no feudal traditions.[8]

It should be noted that this alteration, and sometimes elimination, of the Sunni landed families is counterbalanced by the continuity of feudal houses only in non-Sunni religious communities, that is, the sects. This is well evidenced by the continued survival of sectarian 'warlords' in Lebanon. Two factors explain the continuity of feudal houses among sects: first, the belief that these houses have always protected the religious community; and second, the containment of sects in areas that lie outside the domain of states and cities, the major agents of change.

5
The Peripherality of Sects

The centrality of the Sunni, i.e. religion, is counterbalanced by the peripherality of sects (Map 1). Peripherality combined with a strong sense of territorial exclusiveness work together to magnify the sects' image of themselves as unique and special divine creatures. This image is in turn reinforced by an autonomous politico-religious structure in addition to a comprehensive system of production.

The Territorial Concentration of Sects

Sects are concentrated in exclusive territories located on the periphery of the Sunni-controlled, centralized state authority. The homeland of the Alawis is located in the mountainous region of Latakiya in north-west Syria and then twists northwards, following the mountains to reach Kilikiya in south-east Turkey. This is essentially the mountain range that extends from Antalya on the south-east coast of Turkey to the Kabir River that marks the boundary between Syria and Lebanon (Map 2).

Likewise, the Druzes occupy two highland areas, one on the edge of Damascus and the other where the coastal cities of Lebanon and Palestine are located. There is one concentration in Syria called Jabal al-Druze or al-Arab,[1] and another based in Wadi al-Taim—including Rashaiya and Hasbaiya in Lebanon— and extending north-west to the Shuf and Aley. These two concentrations are joined by a few scattered Druze settlements in the Ghuta of Damascus and in the Golan Heights, and spill over into Druze village communities in al-Azraq in Jordan and in western Galilee, reaching down to Mount Carmel in Israel (Maps 2 and 3). The Ibadis, in turn, cluster in the interior of Oman in a series of neighbouring villages including Nizwa, Bahla, Rustaq, Samayil, Ibra and other small

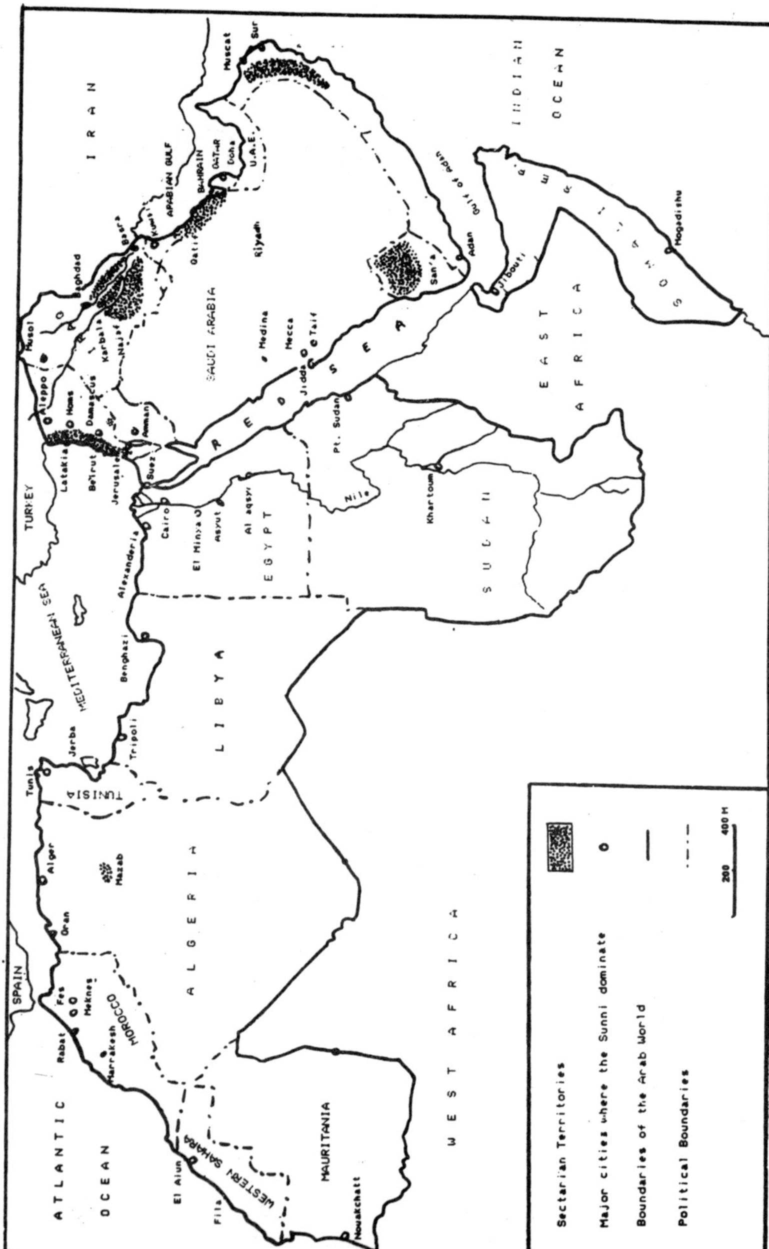

Map 1. Peripheral Distribution of Islamic Sects in the Arab World

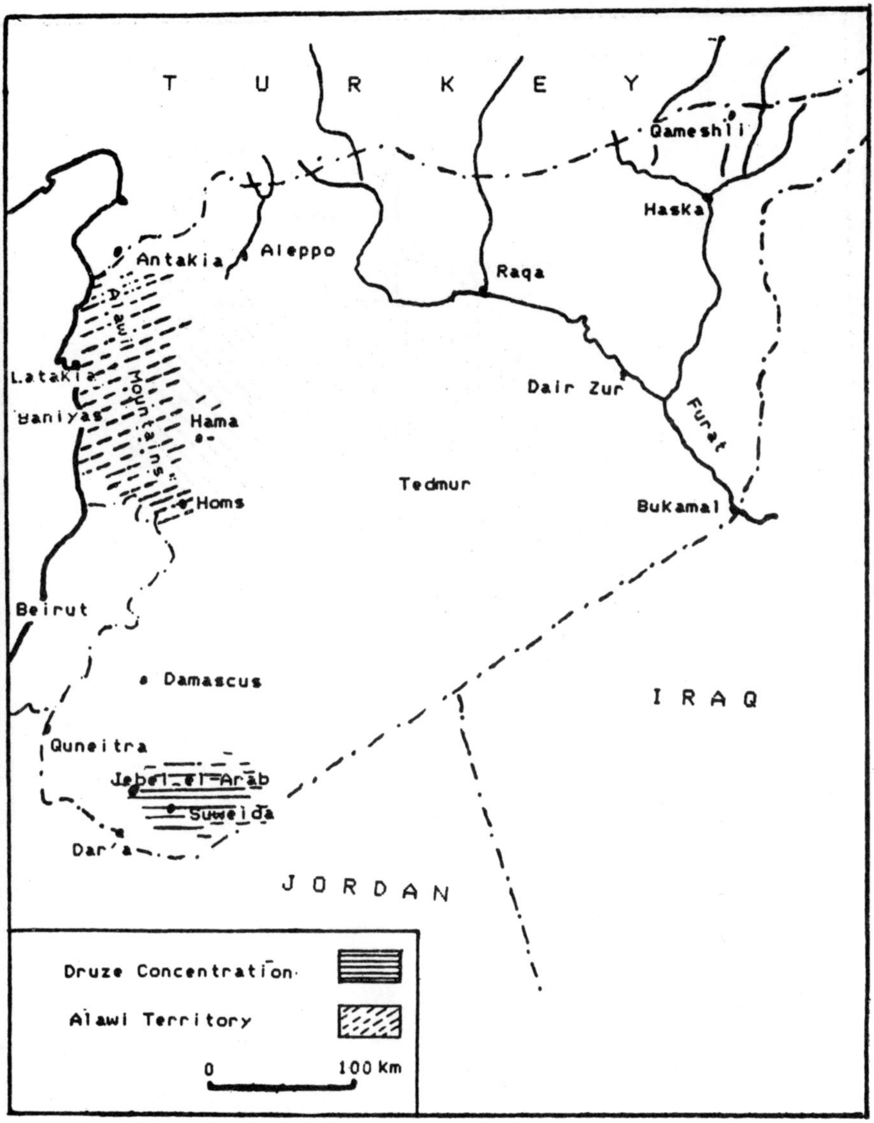

Map 2. Distribution of Sects in Syria

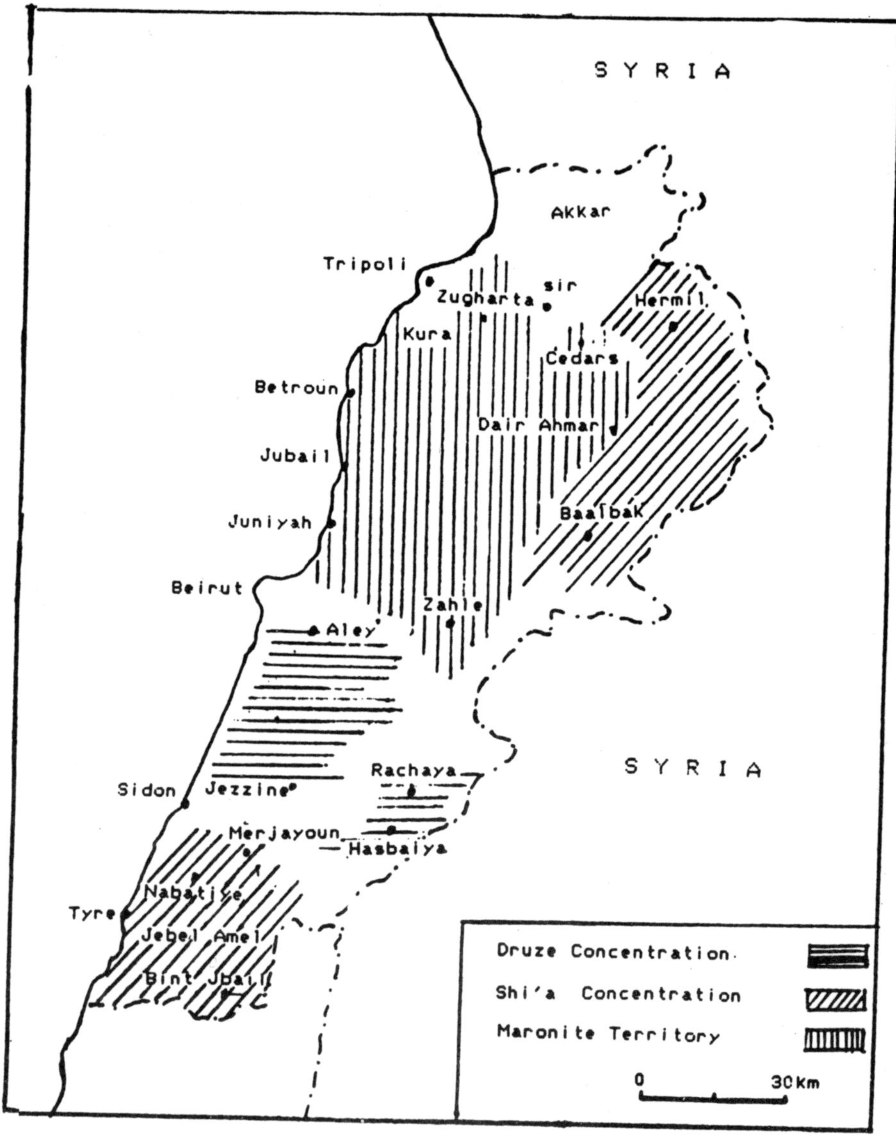

Map 3. Distribution of Sects in Lebanon

settlements scattered over the mountain range that extends from Sohar on the coast to Buraimi in the interior, and stretches southwards to al-Kamil and Sur. Ibadis are also found in small isolated places in North Africa: in the Nafusa Mountains in Libya, in the Mzab Oasis in the southern desert of Algeria and on the island of Jerba in Tunisia (Maps 1 and 4).

Peripherality is characteristic of other sects as well. The Zaidis of Yemen inhabit the northern and eastern sections of North Yemen, in the mountainous area that extends fom San'a in the centre to the east, reaching the Empty Quarter, and to the north reaching Najran, which is inhabited by Sunni Yemeni tribes. The Shawafi Sunni of North Yemen concentrate in the rain-fed maritime hills that extend from the coast roughly to the town of Ibb (Map 4). The Yazidis of Iraq concentrate in Mount Sinjar in northern Iraq, around 160 km to the west of Mosul, on a junction that marks the beginning of the northern Iraqi highlands extending to Kurdistan. Such is also the case of the Christian Maronites, who occupy the central part of Mount Lebanon extending from Zgharta al-Zawiya in the north to Aley in the south-east. This range rises steeply from the coast to the mountain peaks, subdivided by deep gorges and sometimes small, sloping hills. Maronite settlements are found in different parts of the country, where they share territory with other religious communities, both Muslim and Christian (Map 3).

The Shi'a occupy the same pattern. They are concentrated in south Lebanon in Jabal Amil (Tyre and Marj'ayun), and in the north-east part in the Hermel-Baalbek area. In Iraq, they cluster in Mesopotamia, in the alluvial plains that lie between the two cities of Basra and Baghdad (including the provinces of Kut, Karbala, Diwaniya, Shamiya, rural Basra, al-Muntafiq), as well as in the marsh-land along the Shatt al-Arab (Map 5). In Saudi Arabia, they cluster in the Eastern Province and the Qatif Oasis (Map 4), and in Bahrain they tend to inhabit the palm-cultivated sections along the northern coast and the interior villages scattered mainly around the inner desert of the island (Map 6).

Not only do sects occupy peripheral areas, but they also enjoy a kind of territorial exclusiveness that is not available to other religious groups, minorities or movements. The term 'territorial exclusiveness' has been deliberately used here rather than Planhol's (1956:ch.2) 'refuge', in order to underline the sects' image of themselves as independent, autonomous communities. Territorial exclusiveness is expressed in two ways: first, sects concentrate in specific regions that are considered to be 'homeland'

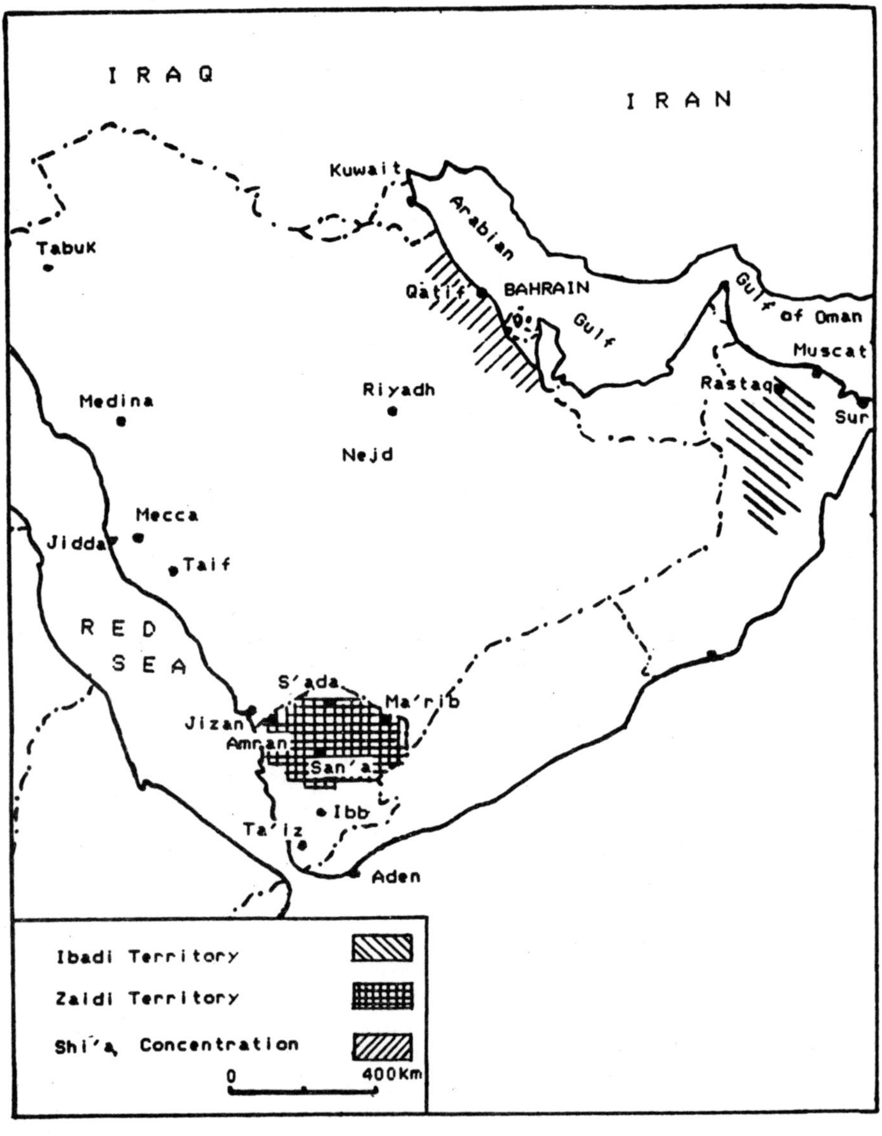

Map 4. Distribution of Sects in Saudi Arabia, Yemen and Oman

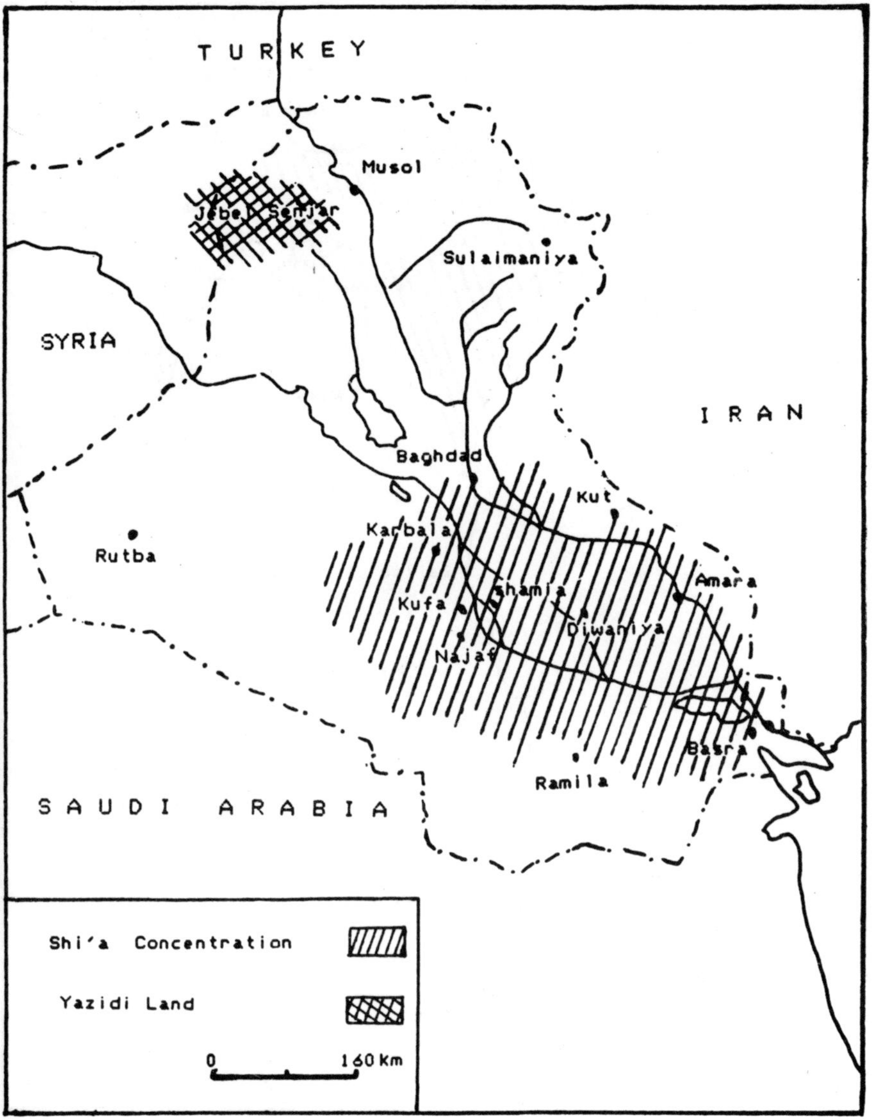

Map 5. Distribution of Sects in Iraq

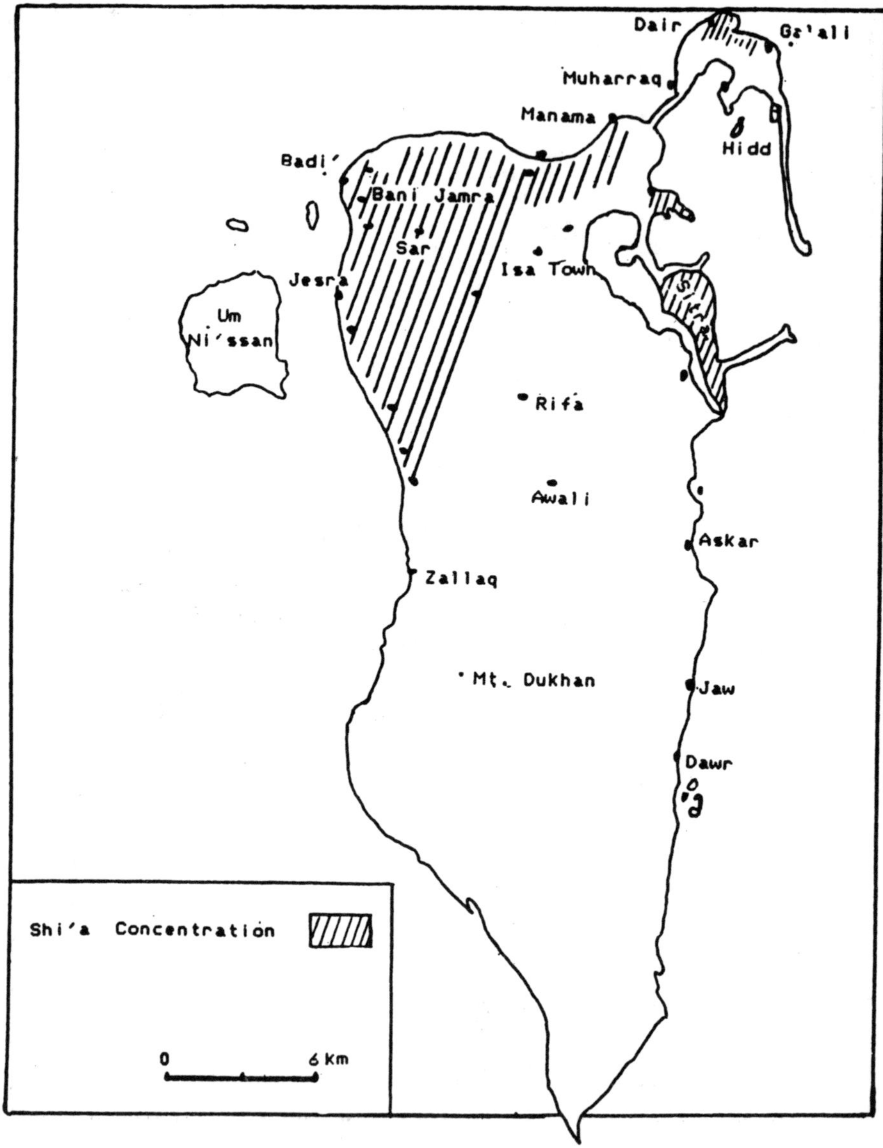

Map 6. Distribution of the Shi'a in Bahrain

or 'sanctuaries'; and, second, there is a comprehensive subsistence economy based on intensive agriculture supplemented by local crafts, which renders the sect structurally and economically a more or less self-sufficient entity.

Table 1 summarizes the rate of concentration of sects in specific regions. It shows that 68% of the Alawis are concentrated in the mountainous range of Latakiya in northern Syria, 82% of the Druzes of Syria live in the Suwaida region and 79% of those in Lebanon in the neighbouring district of Wadi al-Taim, Shuf and Aley. Likewise, 68% of the Ibadis of Oman live in a cluster of villages in the interior. The Shi'a follow a somewhat modified pattern: they are also found in concentrations, but in several different regions of the Arab world. In Lebanon, 68% of the Shi'a live in the north and south of the country; in Saudi Arabia, 91% of them live in the Eastern Province. Other sects fall into the same pattern to varying degrees.

Sects not only concentrate in specific regions; they also form the bulk of the total population (see Table 1 for details). The only exception to this rule are the Druzes of Lebanon, who constitute no more than 45% of the total population in the region where they are concentrated. This statement must be qualified, however, since although they constitute less than a majority, they dominate politically, if not economically. Moreover, the Druze ratio has altered drastically since 1983, following what came to be known as the 'war of the mountain', in which many Christians who had lived among the Druzes for centuries were forced to migrate to other areas. The concentration of other sects ranges between 64% (e.g. the Zaidis) and 98% (e.g. the Shi'a of Mesopotamia).

The data in Table 1 mean more structurally than they do statistically. First, sectarian divisions were noted in past censuses but have been ignored in recent ones: this is true of Syria, Lebanon, Iraq and Bahrain. And second, other countries such as Saudi Arabia and Oman have never taken a count of their sectarian populations. In these countries, sectarian ratios were deduced from case-studies. Statistics on sects are sensitive issues in all Arab countries.[2]

Since these censuses were taken, there has been large-scale rural-to-urban migration from sectarian territories to cities; this is especially true of the Alawis of Syria, the Maronites of Lebanon, the Shi'a of Iraq and the Ibadis of Algeria. Although in-migration undoubtedly altered the ratio, it is not certain that it altered the territorial exclusiveness of sects. During the 1975–89 Lebanese war, for example, the mountainous 'homeland' of the Maronites and the Druzes accommodated considerable migration from cities to villages of origin.

In brief, the territorial exclusiveness of sects is apparent from three related factors. First, sects live in peripheral areas outside the domain of states and centralized authorities. Second, there is a clear concentration

Table 1: Territorial Concentration of Sects

Sect	State	Total population (million)[a] *A*	*B*	% of sect in state	Sectarian regions	% of sect in regions	% of sect concentration
Alawi	Syria	4.025 (1956)	7.845 (1978)	10.66	Latakiya	68.02	75.00
Druze	Syria	4.025	7.845	3.10	Suwaida	81.57	88.18
	Lebanon	1.267 (1950)	2.265 (1970)	6.40	Shuf; Aley; Hasbaiya (Wadi al-Taim)	78.92	44.66
Ibadi	Oman	0.930 (1980)	—	57.60	Interior	67.84	71.21
	Algeria	12.102 (1966)	—	0.42	Mzab	86.32	67.60
Shi'a	Lebanon	1.267 —	2.265 —	18.32	Baalbek-Hermel; Jabal Amil	67.78	68.00
	Iraq	2.857 (1938)	12.000 —	56.43	Mesopotamia	80.48	97.62
	Saudi Arabia	5.000 (1960)	6.726 (1977)	6.36	Eastern Province (Hasa)	91.00	82.74
	Bahrain	— (1941)	0.216 (1975)	54.00	Inland villages	70.16	96.28
	Kuwait	—	0.994 (1975)	26.00			
Maronite	Lebanon	1.267 —	2.265 —	29.11	Mt Lebanon	68.21	75.50
Zaidi	Yemen	4.000 (1971)	5.034 (1978)	51.00	North; East	76.00	64.22
Yazidi	Iraq	8.047 —	12.000 —	0.86	Mt Sinjar	84.20	67.34

Note: [a] Two census data are included: *A* referring to the year when sectarian populations were counted, and *B* referring to the most recent census as indicated in ECWA publication 1980–1, pp. 4–9. See footnote 2 for details, especially where dates or census figures are missing in the table.

of population in these peripheral regions. And third, sects constitute the bulk of the population in these regions. These factors combined allow sects to exercise a measure of religious and political autonomy that is almost impossible for minority groups.

In this sense, sectarian regions are not simply areas of 'refuge'; they are 'sanctuaries' for the sects' holy places. In Mesopotamia, where the bulk of the Shi'a of Iraq live, there lie the holy places of Husain's shrine at Karbala and Ali's at Najaf. The dream of every Shi'a is to be buried close to Ali's shrine: they believe that the closer the distance the more blessed the dead, which has turned the desert strip around Najaf into an expensive real-estate enterprise. The same phenomenon is repeated wherever the Shi'a live; the names of shrines may change but the process is the same. In Bahrain, the Shi'a have erected several shrines, distinguished by black and green flags planted at the top, which they visit for divine blessings.[3]

The Druze shrines that are regularly visited by the community are similarly located in different parts of the Druze territorial base.[4] The Druzes use the word *maqam* (shrine) to refer to the human personage in whom divinity has been manifested. Moreover, in Druze land there are many other religious retreats (*khilwas*) or historical assemblies (*majlises*) which, though possessing no inherently divine value, greatly strengthen the sense of sovereignty of the religious community. The Baiyada retreat in Hasbaiya,[5] which occupies the highest position in religious hierarchy, houses a large number of shaikhs whose job it is to copy by hand the *Rasa'il al-Hikma* (Messages of Wisdom), the Druze holy books, and to bestow them upon the select few who show readiness to receive the word of religion. These shaikhs are reputed to consume only the foods they produce, in case other foods are spiritually unclean.

All the Druze retreats are strategically placed on the hilltops of Mount Lebanon overlooking Druze lands and villages. There are numerous historical religious assemblies, where the Druzes meet to perform collective worship, the most famous being the Ma'nids Assembly in the village of Dair al-Qamar and the Mukhtara Assembly destroyed at the hands of the Shihabi prince in the nineteenth century (Tali, 1961:109).

The Maronites of Lebanon have likewise turned Mount Lebanon into a sanctuary. Shrines of the Virgin Mary and local saints, called *mar* (meaning saint in Syriac), identify a large number of hills and mountain roads. Some of these shrines embody the image of Christ, some the Virgin Mary, and many others the images of local saints including Mar Sharbil, Sarkis, Shallita and Abda. Like the Druze retreats and assemblies,

Maronite monasteries abound on hilltops, 'protecting Maronite lands and villages'.

In meaning and in the way they link to the religious community, nothing parallels the intensity of shrines, monasteries and religious assemblies among the Druzes and Maronites more than the dominant presence of holy tombs among the Alawis. Whoever travels in the Alawi land of Latakiya will notice many oval-shaped tombs marked by white painted domes scattered in different villages, between villages, in valleys and on hilltops. No sooner does the traveller's eye pass one, than another appears. The Alawis speak of these tombs with pride and approach them with reverence. They are the *wilis* (shrines) of eminent religious men to whom the Alawis attribute the power of performing miracles: curing the sick, alleviating injuries, foretelling future events, and so on. Women visit these shrines regularly to make vows, to beg for mercy and to ask for divine blessings.

The Alawis, much like the Maronites, erect shrines whenever and wherever they settle, following the dictum that 'God reveals himself in the weakest of his creatures.' Some recently built shrines include the shrine of Shaikh Ahmad al-Jazri in the village of Balqizia (northern Syria) and that of Shaikh Umran in the Lebanese city of Tripoli. This is in addition to many other shrines built in the Syrian cities of Tartous, Latakiya, Homs, Hama and even Aleppo, where the shrine of Sayyid al-Khousaibi, a prominent religious figure from the ninth century, is to be found (al-Tawil, 1966:466). It is reputed that the tomb of Shaikh al-Jazri acquired the status of *wili* when a bulldozer repeatedly failed to destroy it. Local tradition has it that every time the driver tried to knock it down in order to widen the motorway, the bulldozer broke down. 'It just could not go through the tomb,' my informant insisted. Similarly, Shaikh Umran's tomb was elevated to the status of *wili* because nobody could dig into the ground of his grave. 'When a foolhardy youth tried, a pebble flew into the air and blinded him,' said my informant. Believers take these incidents as clear manifestations of divine power.

In the same vein, the Yazidis of northern Iraq have turned Mount Sinjar, where they live, into a self-contained sanctuary to which they return for worship and the performance of rituals. The lands of the Yazidis contain around eighty-eight shrines, according to al-Hasani (1967:139–42), each specialized in a particular religious activity. Shaikh Adi's shrine in the Shaikhan area is the most revered of them all. Shaikh Adi was the founder of the Yazidi dogma; they attribute to him a range of divinely guided deeds which together place him in the ranks of prophets and divine messengers (Jule, 1934:k). Some writers on the Yazidis believe that Shaikh Adi is none other than Adi bin Musafir, the Sufi leader who travelled and settled in this country around the twelfth century. The Yazidis visit his shrine regularly to offer sacrifices and beg for grace and mercy.

By contrast, the Zaidis of Yemen and (to a lesser extent) the Ibadis of Oman do not display such a high level of shrine-cults. Among the Zaidis the physical display of shrines is not as common, but the principle is the same. Coming out of a Shi'a tradition where divinity expresses itself in a continuous line of imams, they approach the imam as if he possessed the divine power to interfere in the order of nature. They attribute to the imam the power to invite the jinn to support him in battle, or to be a *musarraf*, someone whose body cannot be penetrated by bullets or swords (Serjeant, 1969:296–7).

Shrine-building among the Zaidis is not as common as among the Alawis, Druzes or Christian Maronites, but it is not entirely absent. Zaidi tribal factions each adopt a particular strain of imams, called *hajr*, a term which refers to both the living and the dead—the dead as marked by a series of holy tombs. *Hajrs*, which are frequently visited by believers, are spared in wars between tribes. The most famous of these *hajrs* are the shrines of al-Hadi Ahmad bin Murtada and his sons in Dhafir Hijja, which have remained intact despite the devastating Egyptian air raids on the area in the 1960s.[6]

The Ibadis are the exception to the rule. They do not build shrines, tombs for holy men, spiritual retreats or assemblies, monasteries or edifices. Instead, they have sanctified the whole community. They are the 'Calvinists' of Islam *par excellence*, continuously searching for, building and amending the divine city. Branching off from Sunni Islam, and originally part of the Khariji movement, they believe that 'there dwells an imam in every soul'. In other words, they are a community of imams or potential imams. They confine the caliphate or the imamate to no particular line of descent, neither to the Quraish as the Sunni believe nor to the House of Ali as the Shi'a maintain. They open it to all the faithful on the basis of *sunna* (tradition) and/or *ijma* (consensus)—an imam in every soul. Just as the belief in the continuous manifestation of divinity in human society through imams, holy men and saints has led to the intensive erection of shrines among the Alawis, Druzes, Maronites, Yazidis and to a lesser extent among the Shi'a and the Zaidis, the belief among the Ibadis that divinity has acted once and for all, as narrated in the Qur'an and illustrated in the life-style of the Prophet, has produced the opposite reaction: no shrines or holy tombs.

However, the absence of shrines and local pilgrimages does not mean that the Ibadis have lost the attachment to their lands, the territorial base of the sect. What they have lost through religious dogma they have gained through cultural dictum, the 'myth of origin'. They believe they are the lords of the land, the original inhabitants of the territory, a right that has been passed on from one generation to another since ancient times. In Mzab (Algeria), they call themselves 'the Mzabites', and in Oman 'the Omanians'. And to distinguish themselves from the rest of the population in Oman, they wear a dagger in the centre of the waist, a symbol of manliness and personal freedom. The Baluch in Oman make the dagger and the Ibadis wear it.

All sects are alike in their strong sentimental attachment to their land, the territorial base, the sanctuary, the seat of holy shrines. Visiting shrines among sects has the same religious significance as the pilgrimage to Mecca. So strong is the sects' sentimental attachment to their territory that a considerable amount of personalization takes place in poetry, songs, myths of origin, local histories and naming. 'Ibn al-Jabal' (son of the mountain) is a name by which the Druzes, the Maronites, the Ibadis and the Alawis love to be known or identified. The Shi'a of Bahrain claim to be the original inhabitants of the country and to stress the point they call themselves Bahranis rather than Bahrainis—they use the latter term to refer to the Sunni. The Maronites of Lebanon claim to be of Phoenician origin.

The Comprehensive System of Production

What further strengthens the sense of community sovereignty or territorial exclusiveness among sects is the comprehensive production system they adopt, or rather, used to adopt. This system has recently changed dramatically as a result of mechanized forms of production, rural-to-urban migration and the formation of new states. Until the 1930s or even the 1940s, before the advance of modern technology, sectarian economies were characterized by four interrelated factors: intensive subsistence agriculture, a variety of handicrafts, narrow markets and subsequently small cities.

Practically everybody who wrote in the nineteenth century and the first half of the twentieth century on Mount Lebanon (where the

Maronites and the Druzes live), south Lebanon (where the Shi'a live), the interior of Oman (Ibadi land) or on northern Syria (the land of the Alawis) stressed the intensity of subsistence farming.[7] In the literature, the Ibadis, the Druzes, the Alawis, the Yazidis and the nineteenth-century Maronites are always described as agriculturalists. Intensive agriculture is well demonstrated by heavy terracing, variation of crops and crop rotation, as well as by an elaborate irrigation system. The *falaj* (underground canals) dug in Oman are an example of the complexity of the irrigation systems. Tradition has it that the Lebanese peasants used to carry silt from river-beds to hilltops in order to grow olive trees, grapevines and seasonal vegetables. In my research on palm cultivation in Oman, I found that the distance between palm-trees in Ibadi land in the interior was much smaller than in the Batina region, where Sunni feudalistic orders had prevailed.[8]

Moreover, there is hardly a family living in sectarian territories that does not own a cultivated plot, however small, on which to grow fruit and vegetables. Landless masses simply do not exist here. This is in contrast to the entirely landless villages in the open, fertile plains that came under the authority of the state and subsequently the feudal order. The feudal estates in sectarian territories have always been much smaller than those at the centre. When land reform policies were implemented in the Middle East, the large feudal estates were always to be found in the open plains of Egypt, Syria, Morocco and Iraq, the countries that have traditionally come under the control of centralized authority (Warriner, 1957; 1962). In the Batina region in Oman, where the influence of the state has traditionally been very strong, very large palm-groves are found, each comprising some 2,000 trees. In the interior, where sectarian autonomy has been the rule, such groves contain no more than 800 trees. The same phenomenon can be observed in Bahrain, where the Sunni (the government) own most of the large palm-groves classified as *nakhl*, whereas the Shi'a own much smaller plots, classified as *satr, jubar* or *sirma* (Khuri, 1980).

Confined to narrower and somehow unexpandable territories, sects had to divide the pie more carefully in order to sustain the religious community. There is also a moral angle to this question: conspicuous disparities between groups within the sectarian community—which is greatly influenced by egalitarian ethics—are less tolerable than in a complex, state-controlled society based on power and force. The moral pressure on the 'haves' to redistribute wealth is much stronger in the first instance than in the second. Sectarian societies are 'little communities' subject to strong moral controls.

Oriented towards self-sufficiency within their territorial limits, sects had to follow a comprehensive system of production which, in turn, led to narrow markets. Producing a wide variety of subsistence crops and crafts, sects did not have to seek external markets for exchange or trade. This is very different from the mode of production in those areas that came under Sunni authority, especially the feudal domains, which focused on cash crops such as cotton, grain or fruit for which there was a national or international market demand. Silk production in Mount Lebanon, especially among the Maronites, was an exception to this rule.

Parallel to this mode of crop production among sects was the practice of a wide variety of local crafts. The Maronites and the Druzes of Lebanon, the Ibadis of Oman and the Mzab Oasis, the Shi'a of Lebanon, Bahrain, Saudi Arabia and Mesopotamia—all have traditionally distinguished themselves in specialized crafts such as pottery, jewellery, textiles and mat-making. Whole villages were reputed to specialize in specific crafts. In Lebanon, for example, Rashaiya al-Fakhkhar is known for its pottery, Bint Jubail for shoe-making, Fakiha and Aidamoun for carpets and Shuweir for masonry. In Oman, Sohar and Sur are known for boat construction, Nizwa for silverwork, Samayil for textiles and Bahla for pottery. Needless to say, these crafts flourished in other villages as well, but not in a specialized manner involving the whole village.

Oriented towards self-sufficiency, the comprehensiveness of economic production helped to create narrow markets and subsequently small cities—so small that they are hardly mentioned as cities in the urban literature on the Middle East. The literature notes impressive conquest cities, not small sectarian cities such as Nizwa (Ibadi) in Oman, Karbala (Shi'a) in Iraq, Junieh (Maronite) and Bait al-Din (Druze) in Lebanon, Sa'da (Zaidi) in Yemen or Latakiya (Alawi) in Syria. These towns, however small, are seats of sectarian power and operate as central market-places.

All these factors—the prevalence of *asabiya* forms of social organization, the concentration of sects in specific regions that lie outside state authority, the process of sanctifying sectarian lands, together with the comprehensive production system—clearly distinguish between sects and religious minorities or movements.

6

Sects and Religious Minorities

The distinction between sects and religious minorities is essential to the theme of this book, for it is on this basis that we have limited our inquiry to seven sects. Unlike sects, religious minorities live in cities, subject to the control of state authority. Instead of rejecting Sunni rule, as sects do, minorities adopt and adapt to the ideology of government. A further difference is that religious minorities in cities assume a specialized rather than a comprehensive mode of production.

The Spread of Religious Minorities

Whereas sects concentrate in peripheral regions, religious minorities live within city walls. They are an urban phenomenon, with the scale of urban-dwelling ranging from 62% (the Copts of Egypt[1]) to 100% (the Jews of Syria and Iraq; see Table 2 and Figure 3). Religious minorities concentrate nowhere; they are scattered in different cities. The percentage varies from 0.02% (e.g the Jewish minority of San'a in Yemen) to about 20% (e.g the Copts of al-Minya in Egypt and the Greek Orthodox of Homs in Syria).

However, there is a pattern that governs the spread of religious minorities. The Jews have spread in North African countries, the Greek Orthodox in the Fertile Crescent, the Copts in Egypt and the Syriacs in northern Syria and Iraq. This pattern seems to be organically linked to the variety of ethnic traditions prevalent in the area before the rise of Islam. The Copts claim to be the original inhabitants of the Nile Valley. According to Awad, a Coptic writer, 'the people of Egypt are the Copts irrespective of whether they were Jews, Christians, or Muslims' (Awad, 1932:9). The Greek Orthodox claim to be the original inhabitants of the

Table 2: Distribution of Religious Minorities

Minority	State	% of minority in state[a]	Cities of major concentration	% in urban areas	% in rural areas
Copts	Egypt	6.31	al-Minya, Asyut, Suez, Cairo, Port Said	62.45	37.54
Orthodox					
Greek	Lebanon	9.94	Beirut, Tripoli, Zahle	67.32	32.67
	Syria	4.51	Homs, Latakiya, Hama, Damascus, Aleppo	85.24	14.75
	Jordan	6.40	Amman, Jerusalem, Ajlun	94.38	5.62
Syriac	Lebanon	0.33	Beirut	99.18	0.81
	Syria	1.37	Hasaka, Homs	81.66	18.33
	Iraq	2.93	Baghdad, Mosul	89.18	10.82
Armenian	Lebanon	5.14	Beirut, Tripoli, Zahle	78.22	21.88
	Syria	2.83	Aleppo, Damascus	84.72	15.27
Catholic					
Greek	Lebanon	6.00	Zahle, Baalbek, Sidon	61.16	38.82
	Syria	1.49	Aleppo, Damascus	65.74	34.26
Syriac	Lebanon	0.46	Beirut	99.98	0.01
	Syria	0.51	Aleppo	81.66	18.34
Armenian	Lebanon	1.09	Beirut	97.20	2.80
	Syria	0.51	Aleppo	98.41	1.59
Other Churches (Protestants, Nestorians, Chaldaeans)					
	Lebanon	1.36	Beirut	88.26	11.74
	Syria	0.91	Aleppo, Damascus	98.02	1.91
Islamic minorities					
Isma'ili	Syria	0.99	Salamiya	91.17	8.82
Baha'i	Iraq	<2,000	Baghdad		
Sabaean	Iraq	0.17	Baghdad, Mosul	100.00	
Jews					
	Syria	0.79	Aleppo, Damascus	100.00	
	Iraq	0.03	Baghdad	100.00	
	Lebanon	0.46	Beirut	98.00	2.00
	Egypt	0.003	Cairo, Alexandria	100.00	
	North Yemen	0.02	San'a, Sa'da	88.62	11.37
	Libya	0.28	Tripoli, Benghazi	98.22	1.88
	Tunisia	0.40	Tunis	57.81	42.18
	Algeria	1.23	Algiers, Oran	64.48	35.51
	Morocco	0.50	Casablanca, Rabat, Meknes, Fez	62.56	38.54

Note: a. Total population of countries is the same as in Table 1. The countries that have not been mentioned in Table 1 are Egypt (36.561 million), Jordan (2.348 million), Libya (2.084 million), Morocco (17.300 million) and Tunisia (5.194 million) (*Encyclopedia Britannica*, 1981). For other details see footnote 1.

Figure 3: Distribution of Minorities in Cities

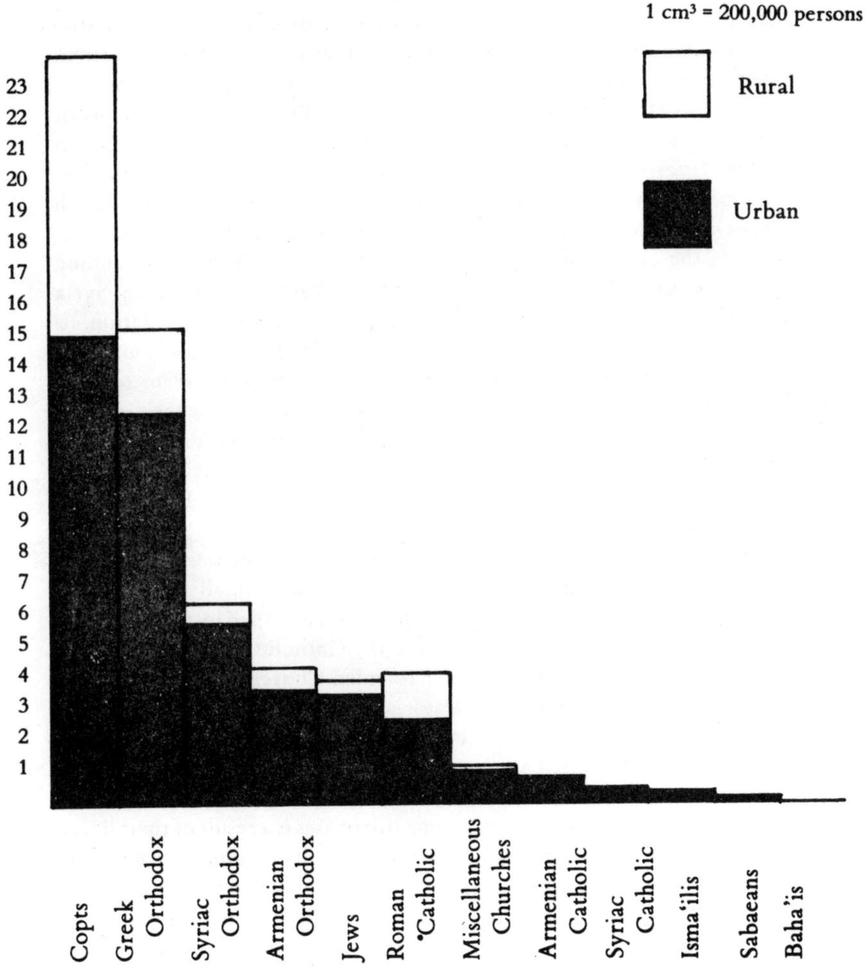

Fertile Crescent, referred to in the Qur'an as *al-rum*, meaning the Eastern Romans. They are called 'Greek' because Byzantium was highly influenced by Greek culture and liturgy. In Byzantium, Orthodoxy was the official dogma of government; the Greek Orthodox lived mainly in cities and the Syriacs in the countryside. The cities spoke Greek and Syriac, and the countryside essentially spoke Syriac. The heretics—the Maronites, the Jacobites and the Nestorians—could be seen as 'nativistic' protests against Greek imperial domination as practised by Byzantium. The three religious movements were ethnically and linguistically Syriac.

The Jews of the Arab world belong to different ethnic strains. Many of the urban professional classes, especially those who settled in North African cities, came in the nineteenth century with European colonialism. Others, known as Sephardic Jews, had come to North Africa at a much earlier date following their persecution in Spain around the third century. Most of the Sephardic Jews had settled inland, predominantly among Berber tribes. The rest of the Jews living in Yemen, Egypt, Iraq, Syria and Lebanon were perhaps the remnants of an old native population.

A large part of the Jewish population of the Arab world moved to Israel following the creation of the state in 1948. They seem to have migrated to Israel in three stages: the first in 1948 following the partition of Palestine and the creation of Israel; the second following the achievement of independence of North African countries in the 1950s and 1960s; the third after the Arab-Israeli war of 1967—see Brace (1964); Clarke and Fisher (1972); Goldberg (1972); and Hoffman (1967).

This geographical dispersion among religious minorities is paralleled by religious and structural fragmentation. Living in small and scattered communities, religious minorities are further subdivided by their national and ethnic origins. The Orthodox and the Catholic Churches are each subdivided into Greek, Syriac and Armenian Churches. Other churches include ancient ones such as the Nestorians and the Chaldaeans, and a host of newly introduced congregations such as the Baptists, Presbyterians, Methodists, Lutherans, Latins and Anglicans. Lebanon alone is said to contain as many as seventeen of these churches.

This religious fragmentation among minorities is a result of their living in cities subject to Sunni-based state control. The Sunni insistence on 'consensus' and, simultaneously, on an 'incorporative' policy has led to two logically connected phenomena: the continued presence of non-Muslims in Islamic states and the fragmented character of non-Muslim communities. The insistence on incorporation made the presence of minorities possible; the insistence on consensus rendered them subsequently insignificant and dispersed. According to Islamic law, religious minorities are classified as *ahl dhumma* (the people in trust), who live under the protection of Islamic authority. According to the anthropologist L. Rosen some Muslim Berber tribes used to fight among themselves each trying to protect their Jews: 'those Jews are ours, we allow none to intimidate them.'[2] To be protected by others, or to seek protection in somebody else's camp, is to assume a secondary position in Arab society. The protector earns prestige and the protected suffer shame.

The Baha'is and the Isma'ilis are the only Muslim groups classified in this work as minorities. While they cannot be strictly classified as *dhummis*—a category that contains mainly Christians, Jews, Sabaeans and Zoroastrians living within the Islamic state—they can no more easily be lumped with sects, for unlike sects, they live in small numbers in cities and are engaged in highly specialized occupations. Most of them are merchants, proprietors or tradesmen.

The Adaptation of Minorities to the Sunni Ideology of Government

There is a clear distinction between sects and religious minorities with regard to the acceptance of the Sunni ideology of government. Whereas sects reject Sunni rule or domination either directly by calling for outright rebellion or indirectly by practising *taqiya*, minority groups accept Sunni rule and adapt to its requirements, however reluctantly. Religious minorities (mostly non-Muslims) apparently tend to be more accommodating to Sunni modes of government than Islamic sects, who share with the Sunni certain religious traditions. Sunni political thought distinguishes between the two categories. It refers to sects as *rafada* (rejectors), *bida* (innovations), *murtadda* (apostates), *bughat* (rebels) or *shu'ubiya* (schismists) and to religious minorities as *ahl dhumma* (the protected people) or *al-musta'min* (the made-secure). The first category is to be continuously fought; the second is to be shown mercy through enforced protection—'enforced' because the *dhummis* have to be protected whether they like it or not.

The terms used to describe sects all indicate a clear deviation from consensus; those describing minorities imply protection, security and 'neighbourliness'. Religious minorities constitute an integral part of the Islamic state; sects do not. In the letters sent by the Prophet Muhammad to Arabian tribes requesting them to submit to Islam, and in the treaties he signed with Christian or Jewish Arabs, the terms 'covenant', 'security', 'neighbourliness' and 'protection' are used interchangeably.[3] At a later date, however, Sunni political jurists began to distinguish between the 'protected' and the 'made-secure' on the grounds that the first category (*dhummi*) is treated as a collective group whose rights are indefinitely guaranteed by the sultan or imam, and the second (*musta'min*) is treated as individuals whose rights can only be temporarily guaranteed by a free Muslim. The 'made-secure' could be affiliated to an external group located in the 'abode of war'. Once the period of grace comes to an end, the made-secure have to decide whether to leave or become *dhummi*.

In the early days of Islam, the *dhummi* category included Christians, Jews, Sabaeans and, at a later date, Zoroastrians[4]—in other words, the non-Muslims living in Islamic states. They were subjected to a wide variety of restrictions imposed on them by different Islamic regimes. Before discussing these restrictions, four points should be stressed. First, Islamic states did not have a standard procedure to deal with non-Muslims. What is today called the 'Covenant of Umar', summarizing all the legal and behavioural restrictions imposed upon non-Muslims, includes a wide variety of precepts collected during the first five centuries AH (seventh to eleventh century AD). Second, different Islamic regimes have used different approaches in dealing with non-Muslims, depending upon the prevalence of particular political circumstances. Third, it would therefore be wrong to assume that all non-Muslims were treated alike, or that they could all be fitted into a definable compartment of legal or behavioural action. Fourth, variations among Islamic regimes led to variations in religious laws drawn from different political experiences. The strictest of all laws were those implemented by Qadi al-Nu'man during the Fatimid period in Egypt; the most lenient or permissive was the Hanafi law as implemented during the time of the Ottoman Empire.

For heuristic purposes, the restrictions governing non-Muslims living in Islamic states will be divided into three categories: civil, religious and behavioural. Although Islamic jurists lump the three categories into one, *shari'a*, they can be distinguished on the basis of the sources from which they were originally drawn. Civil restrictions, for example, are essentially derived from the political performance of the early caliphates, religious restrictions directly from the Qur'an and behavioural restrictions from *urfs* (customs or cultural practices). To deal with them as if they were all religious, as the Islamic jurists do, is merely to affirm the belief in the comprehensiveness of Islam.

Civil restrictions affect the right to conclude formal contracts and transactions about work, ownership, freedom of movement and the appeal to courts, and the right to hold public meetings and occupy posts in government. Many of these restrictions are taken from the decrees and treaties concluded with non-Muslims from the early rise of Islam and the foundation of the first Muslim community in Medina until the end of the fifth century AH (end of the eleventh and beginning of the twelfth century AD).[5]

The first point to be stressed is that Islamic jurists distinguish between non-Muslims as individuals and as groups. The rights granted to them to manage their affairs according to their own religion are bestowed upon them as groups, not as individuals. The moment a non-Muslim moves out of his group he loses the rights and privileges bestowed upon him as a member of a collectivity, in which case he has to choose either to leave the state or to convert to Islam.

Non-Muslims have to pay the notorious *jizya* tax and not the *zakat* paid by Muslims. The difference does not lie in the amount paid, but in the symbolic meaning of the payment. *Zakat* is a voluntary act, done for the sake of earning God's blessings, whereas *jizya* (from *jaza* meaning punishment) is imposed by force and implies a subservient position. This is in accordance with the Qur'an, 9/29:

> Fight those who believe not in God nor in the last day, nor hold that forbidden which hath been forbidden by God and His Apostle, nor acknowledge the religion of truth, even if they are of the People of the Book [Christians and Jews] until they pay the *jizya* with willing submission, and feel themselves subdued.

Because of the subservient position implied by the *jizya*, the Bani Taghlib (Christian Arabs who fought side by side with Muslims at the dawn of Islam) preferred to pay four times as much tax provided it was called *zakat* and not *jizya*.

There is a consensus among Islamic jurists that the *jizya* paid by non-Muslims was intended to cover the costs of their protection.[6] The tax was generally levied from the adult population, except for the old, the insane, the sick, slaves, women, monks and beggars. Some jurists, such as the Hanafis, exempt monks from payment of tax. As long as a non-Muslim *dhummi* pays the *jizya*, he cannot be enslaved by Muslims. Otherwise he will be subjected to the rules and regulations of slavery. Once a *dhummi* converts to Islam, he is automatically exempted from the *jizya*, at which time he relinquishes the right to convert to another religion.

Inequality between Muslims and non-Muslims in Islamic states is not confined to different tax treatment, but extends to customs, the payment of *diya* (blood money), appeals to the courts and holding high office in government. In custom duties, non-Muslims pay double the amount required of Muslims, but for murder compensation, otherwise called 'blood money', they may get a quarter, a half or sometimes the full amount, as the Hanafi law requires. Non-Muslim *dhummis* have the right to appeal to a Muslim court, but have no right to offer testimony or act as witnesses. However, the court's decision with regard to a *dhummi* has to be executed by his own community. Non-Muslim courts operating in an Islamic state have no right to bring a Muslim to trial.

Concerning the holding of public office, Islamic regimes and jurists have observed a wide range of ordinances. Whereas al-Mawardi sees it as right that non-Muslim *dhummis* be given the privilege to hold high public office on condition that these do not imply a position of leadership or meddling in the affairs of Muslims, Ibn Taymiya, in agreement with many other jurists, denies them the right to hold any political or military post, high or low. Ibn Taymiya's interpretation is based on the Qur'an, 5/14: 'But because of their breach of their covenant [meaning non-Muslim *dhummis*], we cursed them and made their hearts grow hard . . .'

It is believed that the Umayyad caliph Umar bin Abdul-Aziz (717–20) was the first to deny the non-Muslim *dhummis* the right to take on political and military responsibilities. Indeed, it is established that Yazid bin Mu'awiya (680–83) recruited *dhummis* in his expedition against Hasan bin Ali at Medina.

The right to property and ownership is almost the same for Muslims and non-Muslims except for two restrictions: the *dhummis* were forbidden to keep Muslim slaves or to partake of the central treasury, the *zakat* revenues. Moreover, all transactions between Muslims and non-Muslims involving wine, pork or debts were strictly forbidden. Among themselves, non-Muslims were left free to engage in such transactions.

Many of the civil restrictions derived from the practice of government in Islam cannot be fitted into a standardized, uniform body of legal action. They vary according to government, state, historical era and/or political circumstances. Indeed, some of these differential practices such as the *jizya* tax, customs, appeals to the courts, blood money, and so on, were wiped out with the introduction of modern states, although they may still be invoked informally to affect interaction between Muslims and non-Muslims. This suggests that the Islamic approach to non-Muslims living in Islamic states is temporal, varies with circumstances and should not be viewed as an eternally fixed dogma. It varies tactically and strategically according to the issues of the day.

On the other hand, the restrictions directly derived from Islamic dogma focus on personal and family law—in other words, inheritance, marriage and the legal status of children. On the question of inheritance, Islamic law is clear: Muslims may inherit from non-Muslims, but non-Muslims may not inherit from Muslims. Likewise, a Muslim male may marry a non-Muslim girl, but a non-Muslim male cannot marry a Muslim girl. This dictum is based on the Qur'an, 2/221:

> Do not marry unbelieving women until they believe. A slave woman who believes is better than an unbelieving woman, even though she allure you. Nor marry your girls to unbelievers until they believe. A man slave who believes is better than an unbeliever, even though he allure you.

Obviously, the social pattern has had a greater impact on the jurists' interpretations of religion than religious dogma has. Although dogma, as stated in the above verse, does not distinguish between Muslim men and Muslim women, the jurists' interpretation has made it the privilege of men. Tradition has it that men of high status may marry girls of lower standing, but not vice versa. A non-Muslim man marrying a Muslim woman would have to convert to Islam first. A non-Muslim girl marrying a Muslim man may retain her religious identity, but the children would have to be Muslim. Even without marriage, a Muslim man may recognize a child as his if it is born of a mistress or a concubine. By contrast, a non-Muslim man cannot recognize a child born to him illicitly from a Muslim girl.

These patterns of 'unstructured reciprocities' or forms of inequality recur in many behavioural restrictions that have no direct reference to the Qur'an. These include horse riding, costumes, wearing turbans, using particular colours, carrying arms, building houses higher than Muslim houses, walking on the right in public streets and many other things of this kind. The various sources on the subject indicate that the *dhummis* were prevented from riding *asil* (thoroughbred) horses, whose riders were given twice as much of the loot in war as ordinary fighters, but were permitted to ride mules. During the reign of the Umayyad caliph Umar bin Abdul-Aziz, *dhummis* were forbidden to wear turbans or military uniforms; the Abbasid caliph al-Mutawakil (846–61) forced them to wear yellow and blue belts. Wearing turbans and sober colours signifies to this day free and high status in society. Custom also has it that *dhummis* were—and in many places still are—prevented, in addition to the above restrictions, from marking their houses with an ownership sign, building new places of worship and holding rituals in public places. They were also forbidden to drink liquor in public, to walk on the right side of the street and, more recently, to teach the Arabic language or Islamic history. They were required to walk either on the left, which is thought to be spiritually unclean, or in the middle of the road, which is often reserved for animals. One of the worst insults you can inflict on an Arab Muslim is to shake hands with the left arm or to use the left hand to take the cup of coffee offered you. Non-Muslims were also expected to give greetings whenever they met or overtook a Muslim.

It must be stressed that these various behavioural restrictions were imposed especially upon non-Muslims living in cities where Muslims dominated. The Christians or Jews who lived in compact rural areas, outside the direct domination of the state, were free from many of these restrictions.

The Correspondence between Religious and Social Stratification

Close examination of these behavioural discriminations reveals the striking correspondence between religious and social stratification. In other words, the contents of religious stratification, which distinguishes between the Muslims and the non-Muslim *dhummis*, corresponds perfectly to the contents of social stratification that distinguishes between the *khassa* (private ones) and the *amma* (commoners), the dominant and the dominated, the upper and the lower classes, the elites and the masses, and sometimes between the old and the young, men and women. The same characteristics overlap and intersect the different models of stratification, irrespective of religious background.

Take, for example, the *jizya* tax and the mode of protection it implies, and subsequently the acts of forbidding non-Muslim *dhummis* from carrying arms and from wearing turbans or military uniforms. In Arab culture, the strong (who dominate) provide protection for the weak (the dominated), which places the protector on a higher social footing than the protected—irrespective of any economic disparity between them. The protector occupies a higher position in society even if he is poorer in economic terms. The stronger person provides protection and the weaker receives it, which is a clear instance of unstructured reciprocity, a measure of inequality. In this sense, the *jizya* tax is a form of 'protection money' exacted from the weak in return for being spared threats and intimidation, otherwise called 'protection'. This is much like *khuwwa* (forced tax) in today's practice, the money which the weak pay the strong in order to guarantee their security. *Khuwwa*, which is derived from the verbal root *khawa*, meaning to be weakened, has nothing to do with *khawa* (to establish brotherly relations). The payment of *khuwwa* is not a brotherly gesture, as some people believe; it is 'the weakened money' which the dominated pay the dominant.

In this sense, *khuwwa* money is the opposite of *bakhshish* (tip), which is money that moves from the strong to the weak and not vice versa. The giver of *bakhshish* earns prestige and the receiver loses it. In *khuwwa* the opposite is true: the receiver earns prestige and the giver loses it. What matters in these forms of exchange is the one who gives or receives from a position of power and strength. Giving *bakhshish* is an act of free will, whereas *khuwwa* is a form of coercion, much like the *jizya* tax.

As an instance of social inequality, the *jizya* and the *khuwwa* payments are subject to the same pattern of reciprocity, or rather, unstructured reciprocity. This is a form of exchange that takes place between individuals or groups of unequal social status. To call the one *jizya* in a religious context and the other *khuwwa* in a social context is not reflective of a different system of exchange so much as being part of a specialized religious code—in the Qur'an the *fasl* (chapter) is called *sura; jumla* (sentence) is *aya* (verse); *musiqa* (music) is *fawasil* (punctuation); and *shi'r* (poetry) is *i'jaz* (miraculous).

If receiving the *jizya* (by the Islamic state) signifies power, and paying it signifies weakness (on the part of the *dhummis*), it is no wonder that the *dhummis* are denied the right to carry arms, be recruited into the army, ride thoroughbred horses or hold positions in government. These practices signify power and authority which the weak obviously do not, indeed should not, possess.

It is on this basis that one may appreciate the position of some Lebanese

Christians, especially the Maronites, who fear that an Islamic takeover in Lebanon would eventually reduce them to a *dhummi* status, effectively turning them into second-class citizens. This explains why the Christian motto in the Lebanese 1975–89 war was 'fear' whereas the Muslims, who were denied the presidency, adopted the charge of 'injustice'. The late president Bashir Jumayil, the founder of the Christian-based Lebanese Forces, used repeatedly to insist, 'We shall not succumb to the position of the Copts of Egypt,' meaning *dhummi* status. In fact, the Maronites were the only Christian community who managed not to join the Millet Council established by the Ottomans in the nineteenth century to monitor the affairs of the non-Muslim *dhummis* living in the empire.

The civil, legal and behavioural restrictions that distinguish Muslims and non-Muslims living in an Islamic state are only part of a wider and more comprehensive social inequality that affects the relationship between strong and weak, dominant and dominated, irrespective of religious affiliation. What is thought to be a religious system is in fact also a social pattern. Field-work by the author in Lebanon, Syria, Bahrain, Oman and North Yemen has revealed that the dominant impose upon the dominated the very stratifications which the Muslims impose upon non-Muslim *dhummis*. The dominant Sunni tribes in Bahrain forbid the dominated Shi'a peasants from carrying arms, riding horses or being recruited into the army or police force. The few who are employed tend to take administrative jobs rather than combat responsibilities (Khuri, 1980). The very behavioural expectations that the dominant Sunni tribes impose upon the dominated Shi'a in Bahrain are also imposed by the dominant Shi'a Zaidis of North Yemen on the Sunni Shawafi (O'Ballance, 1971:23); and by the Ibadis of Oman on the Sunni Baluch; and by the tribal Shi'a of north-east Lebanon on the dominated Sunni peasants. In all these contexts of stratification, the strong allow their sons to marry the daughters of the weak but forbid the contrary; they build higher houses, wear sober colours, and expect the weak to walk on the left and to initiate greetings.

The same argument holds true on other civil, legal and behavioural levels which include appeals to the courts, the payment of blood money and marriage exchange. In these fields of interaction, the dominant in society turn inwards rather than outwards. The institution of what have come to be known in many Gulf countries as 'family courts' is a case in point. In Kuwait, Saudi Arabia, Bahrain and many other Gulf states, the ruling families have special courts, often presided over by the ruler of the country. To appear in the same court would establish a level of equality between the rulers and the ruled, which is unacceptable in a society whose power syndrome is built into a rigidly stratified tribal system. The same principle is observed in Oman, where the Ibadis do not accept the testimonies of others in their courts (Awni, 1964:18).

The tendency of different ethnicities (and sometimes different social classes) to follow different legal references is yet another instance of social stratification. In Bahrain, for example, Sunni tribes follow Maliki law, the Shi'a follow the Ja'fari, the Hawala Sunni the Shafi'i, and the urban Arab Sunni the Hanbali law. Although this differentiation can be partly attributed to ethnic variations, it could likewise be seen as an instance of collective stratification.

Diya (blood money) as a form of exchange follows the same pattern of unstructured reciprocity, or exchange between unequal people. The amount paid as blood money always varies with the social standing of the person or group: the higher the status, the larger the amount. Muslims exact higher rates of compensation than non-Muslims, patron tribes more than client tribes, upper classes more than lower classes. Some ethnographic material indicates that even the acceptance of blood money in compensation for murder is an unacceptable means of reconciliation if the wronged party is to retain its high status.[7] In this case, only revenge cancels the debt.

Marriage exchange between Muslims and non-Muslims, or upper and lower classes, is no exception to the rule. Men of higher standing marry girls of lower standing much more frequently than high-status girls marry boys of lower standing. Some Muslim jurists have even dismissed such asymmetrical marriages as religiously undesirable, in what came to be known as *zawaj al-kafa'a* (qualification marriage), i.e. if the spouses do not enjoy 'equivalent' social standing, divorce may legitimately be granted.

There is strong ethnographic evidence for believing that the incidence of in-marriage, however it is defined, increases with social status.[8] The ruling families of the Gulf consider it a breach of tribal ethics if a girl marries outside the family, much like Muslims forbidding girls to marry non-Muslim men, or Ibadi girls marrying non-Ibadi men. In fact, the few girls who have rebelled against tradition and married outside the ruling families of the Gulf have been, on the whole, isolated, banned and, in rare cases, stoned to death. Marriage across social classes or religious communities is so socially unexpected that Egyptian film producers continuously manipulate it as an appealing element in films and television plots. It is marriage for romance which creates tension in the family and therefore often ends in divorce, separation or bigamy.

Romance aside, men of high standing often marry below them for political purposes, as a move to establish in-law relationships with client tribes. Here, the man's group earns prestige and the girl's group loses it; the latter gain, instead, protection and support. Because of these social implications, and sometimes legal restrictions, marriage between cousins is preferred. It equalizes status and nullifies the effects of marriage on the social value of the group. Giving away girls in marriage to outsiders always carries with it a degrading implication. This is why in some tribal practices in Yemen, girls are given in marriage as a compensation for murder: it is not that the group cannot afford to pay blood money, but the victim's group insists on this form of exchange in order to debase the social stature of their opponents. Many an Arab marries out of spite.

As previously mentioned, building higher houses is yet another measure of stratification that distinguishes Muslims from non-Muslims, the elites from the masses, the *khassa* from the *amma*. The principle is sometimes generalized to include entire areas: the higher the area the higher the status. In Aley (Lebanon), for example, the Druzes dominate and therefore live in the upper section of the town; by contrast, in Bait Miri, a nearby village, the Maronites dominate and therefore occupy the upper section. Physical elevation is so intertwined with social visibility that practically all terms denoting notability in society are metaphorically derived from the upper part of the human body. The notables are known as *wujaha* (from *wajh*, face), *a'yan* (from *ain*, eye), *sadr* (chest), *anuf* (from *anf*, nose), the latter implying dignity in Arabic rather than the English 'nosey' which implies a lack of respect for privacy.

There are, moreover, a multitude of behavioural restrictions imposed upon the non-Muslim *dhummis* which correspond perfectly to distinctions between men and women, the old and the young. Of these, two are of particular significance: first, the use of colours and, second, subsidiary positions in personal interaction. As mentioned previously, non-Muslim *dhummis* were required to distinguish themselves by wearing yellow and blue belts, the bright colours that are normally worn by women, children, slaves and maids. People of noble origin or high status in Arabia wear sober colours, especially black and white, which signify purity, dignity, integrity, seriousness and sometimes masculinity. Bright colours signify meanness, lightness, femininity and humble social origins. Women who want to appear less attractive in public wear black and white shades, the colours of men; but underneath the black or white external gown, they often wear the most fashionable flowery, bright clothes.

In daily interaction, women and children, exactly like the non-Muslim *dhummis*, are expected to initiate greetings, to give way to men and to older people by walking on the left side of the street, and to follow behind men or the old. They sit on the edge of a council, like people of low status: the closer one sits to the chief or prince, the higher his status; the right side is given priority over the left side.

In brief, the stratifications that distinguish Muslims from non-Muslim *dhummis* correspond perfectly with the distinctions between social classes, the sexes and sometimes generations. This is to be expected since these very contents overlap from one model of stratification to another. In Middle Eastern cultures, the single theme around which stratification rotates is power. The poor are described in the Qur'an as 'the weakened'; 'poverty' being an attribute of mankind and wealth an attribute of God. High standing is built upon the ability to use force, to impose oneself on others by coercion. To be dominated is to be weakened, to occupy the lower side of the stratification scale, the place of women, children, client tribes and, for that matter, the masses and the non-Muslim *dhummis*.

This clearly underlines the social fact that non-Muslim *dhummis* living in Islamic states lack power and consequently are stripped of the cultural symbols associated with it: riding horses, carrying arms, joining the army, wearing turbans, walking on the right, building higher houses, wearing sober colours, marrying endogamously, paying *zakat*, collecting *khuwwa*, holding leadership positions in government and offering testimony in court. They lack power, but not economic means. In fact, non-Muslim minorities in Islamic states seem to be economically better off than the Muslim masses. This is mainly because of the economic roles assigned to them, the tasks that particularly serve the elites. Hence the 'specialized' production system among minorities, as opposed to the comprehensive system among sects.

The Specialized Production System among Religious Minorities

The specialized economic roles that religious minorities play in work and production must be seen as an integral part of their living in cities, subject to the authority of the Islamic state. Here, the element of religious ideology becomes manifest: the occupations engaged in by non-Muslim minorities tend to be forbidden by Islam, considered undesirable by Muslims or of menial status. These forbidden occupations (which have strictly been the monopoly of non-Muslims) include wine-making, money-lending and, until recently, banking. Undesirable occupations include professional singers, musicians, dancers and jewellers. It must be stressed at this point that the status of non-Muslim minorities in the Arab world is no different from the status of minorities all over the world. They tend to take up those jobs which the dominant culture sees as religiously unethical or undesirable. Jewish minorities living in Christian-dominated cultures, Christians in Muslim cultures and Muslims in Hindu societies have all tended to be money-lenders, musicians and professional dancers. In Hindu society, only Muslims deal with meat, which Hindus consider to be spiritually unclean.

Other jobs undertaken by non-Muslims (as well as by 'weakened' Muslims) include crafts involving the use of animal organs such as leather-work, dyeing, shoe-making and shoe-repairing; those related to the care of the human body such as hairdressing, nail-cutting, bathing and nursing; and those related to public sanitation, such as street sweeping or refuse collecting. Next in order come the crafts which use natural materials, such as carpentry, weaving and casting. In general, Arabs tend to consider all manual jobs as socially degrading. The word *imtahana*, which means 'taking on a manual job', also means 'causing insult'.

Most of these crafts have been undertaken by non-Muslim *dhummis* or 'weakened' Muslims. The Jews living among the Berber tribes of North Africa, or among the Zaidis of North Yemen, tended to be blacksmiths, weavers, jewellers, masons, stone-cutters, sweepers and refuse collectors (O'Ballance, 1971:21). Except for sweeping and refuse collection, these are precisely the occupations of the Christians of the Fertile Crescent (Lane, 1978), the Shi'a of Bahrain (Khuri, 1980:ch.3) and the Baluch of Oman. Interestingly enough, these crafts were also practised by what came to be known in medieval Islam as *asnaf* (guilds), whose members were often recruited to Sufi orders. In other words, craftsmen were distinguished by being either non-Muslims or 'adulterated' Muslims of questionable moral standards. The same observation holds true for tribal communities in Arabia where blacksmiths, hunters, craftsmen and sometimes prostitutes come from a single strain called the Sliba tribe. The Sliba, derived from *silb* (iron ore), enjoy very low status in society.

The fact that 'weakened' Muslims share some occupational patterns with the non-Muslims does not mean that the two categories are interchangeable. The non-Muslim *dhummis* are 'permanently' committed to second-class citizenship, even though they may be better off economically than the Muslim masses. However, one cannot be sure when the sword of dogma will turn next. By contrast, the 'weakened' Muslims are such for a while, a temporary arrangement depending upon the rise of new opportunities and market resources. The two categories are clearly distinguished in the Qur'an: the 'weakened' Muslims are the *fuqara* (the poor), and the non-Muslim *dhummis* the *masakin* (subdued).[9]

Being condemned to a secondary position in Islamic states, the 'subdued' Christians of the Fertile Crescent and the Copts of Egypt have long been trying to change and reformulate the Islamic approach to government. While outwardly accepting the ideology of Sunni government, they have always tried to restructure it on non-religious grounds. Since the days of the Abbasids, they have been trying to refashion religious beliefs and recast nationalistic attitudes, first by translating Greek thought into Arabic and more recently by laying the foundations of Arab nationalism.[10] All the fathers of Arab nationalism, including Faris al-Khoury, Makram Ubaid, Sati al-Ḥisri, and more recently Michel Aflaq and George Habash, were from Orthodox or Coptic minorities. Whereas minority groups deal with Sunni government from a position of loyalty, trying to refashion the structure of dogma to fit modern times, sects deal with it from a rebellious position, rejecting the dogma of government altogether.

Part Two

The Ideology of Sects

7
The Formation of the Religious Community

Mention has already been made of the fact that the distinction between religion, sects and religious minorities is not entirely confined to ecological, geographical and economic differences, but goes much beyond this to include religious ideology and organization. It should be stressed that our interest here in religious ideology is not comprehensive; it covers only that part of dogma that pertains to the sovereignty of the community and/or religious organization—namely, the recruitment and training of the *ulama* and the way they link to society. Other ideological issues such as the theory of man and his place in the universe, his relationship to God, his salvation, ways of worship, and so on, however significant from the point of view of comparative religion, will not be dealt with systematically here. Although some of these beliefs may be referred to incidentally as they arise in the discussion, the focus is on the comparative study of the religious communities embodying both ideological and organizational criteria, as illustrated in Figure 4.

Figure 4: Structure of the Religious Community

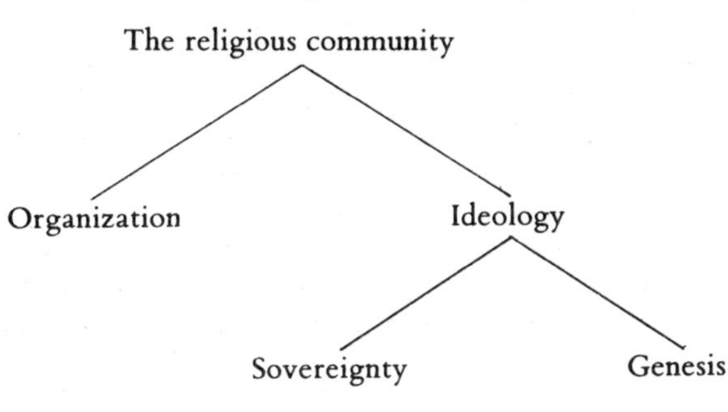

The ideology of a religious community can be seen from two angles: first, origin and formation and, second, the way these contribute to the community's sovereignty as an independent social group. While ideological and organizational issues are dealt with separately, there is a clear interconnection between them. They are discussed separately only to underline the comparative approach of this work.

The Origin and Formation of the Religious Community: the Sunni View

'Ideology' in this work refers to those premises, beliefs and ideas about man and the universe which a person holds to be true *a priori* without needing validation. These are the givens that people manipulate in order to identify themselves as groups and then distinguish between their group and others. The boundaries that separate the self and others, between in-groups and out-groups are not, indeed could not be, clear-cut. There are many overlapping factors—ethnic, economic, linguistic and religious —that combine differently in different settings. Anthropologists such as Dumont (1977:72–80) believe that it is possible to compare whole societies on the basis of the criteria they use to distinguish between their groups and others. Whereas groups and collectivities in Hindu society, for example, are distinguished on the basis of a caste system derived mainly from the ancient vedas, in European societies they are distinguished by a combination of ethnic and class criteria. In Arab societies, the distinction is drawn on the bases of unity of blood or faith, or a combination of the two. Consider, for example, the tribe of Quraish which is distinguished from other Muslim groups or societies both by unity of blood (common descent) and unity of faith (religiously). In this context, tribal stratification corresponds to religious stratification. Consider also the tribal origin of sects discussed in Chapter 4, or again the symbolic meanings of many Qur'anic concepts that combine unity of blood and special divine positions. These concepts include *arham* (from *rahm*, womb, implies kin) as in 8/75 and 26/214 of the Qur'an (author's italics): 'But *kindred* by blood have prior rights against each other in the book of God'; 'And admonish thy *nearest kinsmen*'; and *qurba* (kin) as in 42/23: 'No rewards do I ask of you for this except the love of *those near of kin*'; and many other concepts of this order.

In brief, personal and social identities in Arab culture are uniquely distinguished by family origin or by unity of religious faith, or by both combined. Tribal groups go by the first dictum, the Sunni Muslims by the second, and sects by a combination of the two. The differences between religious communities lie in the kind of prophet or prophets whom they follow, the nature of the call and the time of its occurrence, and the way these link to society. The present work assumes that the state, as a centralized authority, plays a major role in modifying the structure of the religious community, at both the ideological and the organizational level.

Among the Sunni, traditionally the rulers in Arab-Islamic history, the state is the main instrument of organization in religion. The Sunni feel religiously 'lost' once they lose centralized power. Throughout their religious history, they have never been able to develop an alternative to the state as the main formulator of general religious orientation. Hence their insistence that the caliph or sultan should combine purity and power, religious and political authority, and that the state should be governed through the execution of divine law. It follows that the sovereignty of the state is a necessary condition guaranteeing the supremacy of divine law and, for that matter, upholding religion (Islam) as a formulation of public policy. In this sense, the role of public delegation or representation is not to legislate, but to execute the already formulated *shari'a*. Man takes part in choosing the authority to be entrusted with the job of executing laws, but he has no say in making them.[1] The Qur'an is clear on this ideological premise: 'The command [government] rests with none but God' (6/57). If 'command' rests in the hands of God, the pious ruler is not the one who simply abides personally by the dictates of religion, but the one who also sees to it that they are implemented in society. He is not only the one who refrains from drinking alcohol, for example, but also the one who forbids it in society.

To the Sunni, the Muslim community is a human society which has accepted the divine message and works to fulfil its dictates. Islamic jurists refer to this condition as *ummat al-ijaba* (the recipient community)—those who have responded favourably to the divine call—as opposed to *ummat al-da'wa* (the appeal community), which has not yet responded.[2] These two categories divide the whole world comprehensively into Muslims and non-Muslims (or Muslims-in-the-process, who have to be Islamicized).

The Sunni believe that religion has been revealed to man in its complete, perfect form and that man should follow its rules and regulations as contained in the Holy Qur'an. Man's society is an object of revelation and herein lies its uniqueness as compared to other creations of God. The revealed message is 'perfect' and man should therefore continuously strive to abide by its dictates. This assumes that man can abide comprehensively by the dictates of the revealed message only in *dar al-islam* (the abode of Islam) where God's *shari'a* is implemented at the hands of a Muslim imam, and not in *dar al-harb* (the abode of war) governed by non-Muslims. The phrase, 'Islam is *shari'a* and *imam*' (Zaidan, 1963:18) sums up the point. A society, any society, is Islamic so long as it is governed by a Muslim who implements God's *shari'a*, even if the majority are not Muslims.

The Sunni insistence that Islam, as a perfect religion, can be properly implemented only under the banner of Islamic government has had a considerable impact upon leadership and the way authority passes on from one reign to another. The leader in Islam, be he imam, sultan, caliph, king or president, is a 'protector', a 'custodian', a 'guarantor' of faith entrusted with the responsibility of modelling man's society according to God's image. He is a *mukallaf* (trustee) who attends to the execution of divine law.[3]

It is here, in the perfection or completion of religion as public policy, and subsequently in the type of government that implements its dictates, that the major controversies between the Sunni and other Islamic groups actually lie. Under what conditions religion is considered 'perfect' is a controversial issue in Islam. The Sunni belief that religion has been perfected exactly as revealed in the Qur'an, and as modelled by the traditions of the Prophet and his companions, makes them conceive of leadership as a contractual relation between the ruler and the ruled. While the perfect image of man's society is in God's hands, the choice of the leader, essential for the implementation of God's laws, is in man's hands. How to select the leader and validate his authority has been dealt with in numerous treaties on the subject. There is some consensus, however, that the process of selection starts in *shawra* (consultation) and ends in *mubaya'a* (proclamation; homage).

The consultation process takes place among the *ulama* and 'the men of resolution and contract'. Once this is done, the chosen person is publicly proclaimed leader through a show of popular support in which the Muslim community plays the major role. *Mubaya'a*, signifying popular support, is carried out through hand-shaking, which clearly demonstrates the contractual nature of the link between the ruler and the ruled. *Mubaya'a* is derived from the verbal root *ba'a*, which means to sell. Once a sale is concluded, the buyer and the seller shake hands to seal the agreement, much as the Muslims do when they shake hands with a newly proclaimed leader.

Two points are significant here: first, the blending of religious and state institutions in the personality of the ruler; and second, the leader's assumption of power through a dynamic process of political action. The leader is at once a political and a religious figure held accountable in both spheres of action. He is *amir al-mu'minin* (the prince of the faithful), a phrase that clearly alludes to the combination of political and religious authority: 'emir' signifies power and 'the faithful' signifies religious authority. It is legitimate to disobey a leader thus proclaimed only if he deviates from the *shari'a* or *din*. Otherwise, obedience to him is obligatory on behalf of the Muslim community. In this connection, Ibn Khaldun says, 'Let it be known that *mubaya'a* is a promise of obedience.' Umar bin al-Khattab is believed to have said, 'Obey the imam even if he were a slave.'

On this point, Islamic political jurists differ greatly. Al-Baqlani (first published in 1013), for example, believes that the role of the Muslim community must be confined to the correction of the imam should he rule contrary to the *shari'a*; they have no right to dethrone him or withdraw their promised support from him. On the other hand, al-Baghdadi (first published in 1037), who allows for the simultaneous coexistence of several imams, argues that the community has the right to rebel against a tyrant imam. Al-Mawardi (first published in 1058), however, considers the imamate to be a divine right flowing from God, and what God has given no man can take away. Ibn Khaldun, himself an imam, avoids discussing the imamate altogether, but insists that rebellion is legitimate only if directed against an oppressive emir, not an imam. The imam, to him, is an object of consensus, above factional politics, and whoever is in this position does not invite rebellion. According to Gibb (1975), these controversies among jurists were simply *de facto* evaluations of political realities, reflecting the conditions of the Islamic state at the time, and were by no means derived directly from religious dogma.

Gibb's conclusion introduces the second point, namely, that the emir's assumption of power takes place through political competition rather than divine ordinance. True, the Sunni believe that the leader must possess religious knowledge and the capacity to summon the faithful to *jihad* (holy war), but these become relevant only if he, thus qualified, earns the unanimous support of the community, first through consultation and then through public proclamation. These processes, consultation and proclamation, through which consensus is established, are social and political instruments for the exercise of power and authority. If consensus were a sociological reality, it must then vary with group structures, economic conditions and political circumstances. As an act of consensus, the leader's religiosity is then subject to the community's evaluation of it more than it being a personal attribute. It varies from culture to culture and from group to group within the same culture.

The imamate or caliphate, as an object of consensus, cannot therefore be fitted into a monolithic model that operates universally in the same capacity within all groups and at all times. Islamic leadership is a sociological reality, and therefore subject to socio-political variations. The general directives of religion may be the same, but the way they are put into practice varies according to group and cultural tradition.[4]

In this respect, one must distinguish between the universality of the *shari'a* and the relativity of its application; the first is a constant, the second changes with socio-political realities. This is why the radicals in Islamic society, who stand for change, always give priority to consensus in seeking new formulations to suit modern times. Whether defined as the agreement among the *ulama* or among 'men of contract and resolution', or among both, consensus reflects social dynamics. As such, it becomes an acceptable instrument of change, even if change means the modification of people's perception of religious realities.

That consensus is a clue to religious change should not be construed as meaning that it is an instance of deviation from religion. On the contrary, it is the voice of society in religion. The practice of consensus must not be understood in numerical terms; it could be the decision of one person, of a group, or of the whole society. It is precisely this fluidity of definition that makes it an effective instrument of religious change. The Prophet's saying, 'My community shall not err in consensus,' makes consensus at once a means and an end. It is the means through which the 'right' or 'truth' can be sought and established, and simultaneously it is the 'right' itself in the sense that its achievement is an act of religion. Hence the tremendous emphasis in Arab-Islamic culture on consensus, 'unity of action', 'united stand', 'shoulder to shoulder', 'pillar to pillar', even if these ideological commitments are to be accompanied (behaviourally) by considerable organizational fragmentation. Organizational fragmentation appears in various forms: mini-states, tribes, political parties, religious movements, welfare societies, even sports clubs and labour unions.[5]

The ideological emphasis on consensus as an act of religion has had a significant impact on the Muslims' image of society. The Sunni especially have come to regard society as a 'should-be-united' being, irrespective of whether or not it is united in practice. In almost every public speech, whether in the mosques, on the radio or television, or even at professional conferences on the social sciences, the theme of 'unity' and being 'united' comes visibly to the fore. One might almost believe that the Arabs like to stay disunited, precisely in order to make 'unity' a constantly pressing issue. If they once united, there would no longer be a 'gospel' to preach.

The image of society in unity, a society in consensus, has led the Sunni Muslims especially to develop a negative attitude towards any form of collective action that may imply conflict, deviation or even political competition and opposition. The 99.9% of voters who elect presidents in many Arab countries are simply a reflection of the 'should-be-in-consensus' society. The practice of refusing to subject ruling emirs in the tribally controlled Gulf states to popular appraisal (on the grounds that their mode of rule is an expression of consensus) is a corollary of the same principle.

The tendency to suppress the pluralistic character of society, and the insistence that sectarian or ethnic heterogeneity is only a passing episode in the life history of a nation, is an indication of the same mental formulation. In Lebanon, the Sunni have always stood for the monolithic unity of the state, thus rejecting all attempts to resolve the Lebanese conflict through various forms of decentralization.[6] What has been said about Lebanon can easily be applied to Bahrain, Kuwait, Saudi Arabia, Iraq, Morocco and other countries where successive governments have deliberately continued to suppress public debate on sectarian and ethnic issues. No wonder that censuses counting ethnic and sectarian variations have always been suppressed once independence is achieved; such census data have always been taken under foreign, colonial rule.

I recall that in 1976, in the early days of the Lebanese war, a poster was hung in the Sunni-dominated Labban Street reading, 'Oh Muslims! Remember that the Christians rule you! Down with sectarianism.' I thought for a while that this was a self-contradictory statement. But in fact it is in perfect harmony with the image of society in consensus, mixed with the insistence on the sovereignty of Islam. 'Down with sectarianism [*and long live religion*]' was what the poster meant to say. Similarly in 1982, when I was giving a public lecture at the University of New York about the differences between the Sunni and the Shi'a *ulama*, a graduate student responded, in some discomfort, 'What is this thing you call

Sunni and Shi'a? We are all Muslims.' (He was a Sunni of Pakistani extraction.)

The consensus image of society not only affects people's understanding and perceptions of pluralism, but also modifies their response to those ideologies that by their very nature imply conflict. The Arab-Islamic masses have never responded favourably to socialist political parties, except in countries such as Algeria where socialism took the form of a liberation movement. Here, socialism and Islam blended together, however vaguely. Many a socialist nationalist party (such as the Ba'th of Syria and Iraq) has remained, after many years in government, merely the political ideology of the ruling elites, with little impact on the masses. The masses continue to be captured by a variety of religiously oriented models.

By contrast, the appeal of Nasserism to the Arab Muslim masses was striking, mainly because Nasser had always adopted a 'consensus' view of society,[7] which was well expressed in his book *The Philosophy of the Revolution*. Even his brand of socialism, basically restricted to land redistribution, was given the Islamic dimension of social justice.

The mode of recruitment to political parties in the Arab world illustrates the point further. Whereas the Sunni tend to support parties oriented towards pan-Arab, pan-Islamic unity, the non-Sunni champion the cause of parties rooted in conflict models. This is apparent in the long-running hostility between the Syrian and the Iraqi Ba'th Parties. What appears to be a conflict of words (the Iraqi Ba'th give priority to unity over freedom and socialism, and the Syrian Ba'th to freedom and socialism over unity) is in reality a dispute between the Sunni Ba'th who dominate in Iraq and the Alawi Ba'th who dominate in Syria. The same pattern can also be detected in Egypt, Bahrain and Lebanon. Until the 1960s the leftist movements in Egypt, including the communists, were dominated by the Copts (Muhyeddin, 1980:212). In Bahrain, the left tended to be dominated by the Shi'a (Khuri, 1980:ch.10). In Lebanon, the majority of members recruited to leftist parties were mostly Orthodox, Shi'a or Druzes. In fact, the Druzes have founded a socialist party almost entirely for themselves (Khuri, 1975:ch. 7 & 8).

It is perhaps this merger of government with religion in Islam, and the approach to religion as a formulation of public policy, that made consensus not only an instrument of seeking religious truths but the truth itself, and subsequently the image of society as a 'should-be united', monolithic mass. On these premises it is possible to appreciate the Sunni insistence on the 'exoteric' understanding of the Qur'an through *qiyas* (analogy) and precedence, and even the affirmation that the Muslim is not free to deal with his Islam as he wishes. The *din* (religion) of a Muslim is not his own; it is the property of the community, and therefore he alone cannot alter it or seek to change it.

The insistence on the exoteric understanding of the Qur'an is a logical product of treating religion as public policy, as a dimension of state organization. Likewise, the fact that religion is a formulation of public policy makes any deviation from it a crime against the public right, the Muslim community. These three factors—the merger of religion with government, understanding religion as public policy and the consensus image of society—emanate essentially from the process of adapting religion to state structures and centralized authority. After all, is not consensus, or the appeal to consensus, part and parcel of the political language of the ruling elite, wherever and whoever they are? It is the ruling elite who are concerned with the sovereignty of the state which they control and with the law which they enforce.

The Origin and Formation of the Religious Community: the View of Sects

It would be presumptuous to claim that all sects have a unified view that can be captured in a single syllogism—the Introduction to the present book has already argued that sects are distinguished by each having a holistic religious world view. However, there would appear to be some common ground, some general frameworks, into which all sects can be fitted, at least in form if not in content. These frameworks centre on two points: first, the position of the imam as a symbol of the sovereignty of the religious community; and second, the controversy of origin. Irrespective of their differences, all Islamic sects use the word imam, rather than caliph, to refer to the highest position attainable in the community—the position which, like the caliphate, combines religious purity and political power. The choice of the word imam rather than caliph is not accidental. It signifies the sects' resort to moral authority. The imam sets forth the 'perfect' religious model to be followed, interpreted and imitated by the community of the faithful. According to the Shi'a, Druze and Alawi doctrines, the imam is a visible illustration of the 'esoteric' that perfects or completes religion, the only way to salvation. Among the Ibadis and Zaidis, the imam sets the standard for a free and sovereign society. As a model, the imam is to be followed and imitated; much as in masonry, where the word '*imam*' refers to the rope or board according to which blocks are lined up, or when talking of caravans, when it refers to the 'front camel' leading the flock (Ibn Manzur, 1956:42–62).

By contrast, the caliph is a successor (from *khalafa*, meaning to succeed) who rules in accordance with an already formulated governance, the exoteric. He is the executor of ordained law. Unlike the caliph who succeeds to power and authority, the imam is himself power and authority, the 'right path', the 'visible path' as in the Qur'an, 15/79: 'So we exacted retribution from them. They were both an *imam mubin* (a visible path).' Ibn Khaldun's view here is very telling. He calls the leader 'imam' when only one person heads the community, and 'emir' or 'sultan' if there are more than one.

According to Ibn Khaldun, the imam must be a man of deep religious knowledge, physically fit and capable of establishing justice. More important, he must be an object of consensus and therefore cannot be ousted from office. Whereas Ibn Khaldun legitimizes rebellion against the sultan or the emir, he forbids it against the imam. Of course, whoever enjoys a position of consensus does not invite rebellion.

In this sense consensus, a vague concept at any time, becomes almost indistinguishable from *asabiya* (solidarity, the united stand). This explains why Ibn Khaldun sees the imamate as a type of leadership that combines both the *asabiya* form of power (consensus) and the caliphate-like authority, where religious knowledge prevails. This means that sects have a clear preference for the imam structure of government, simply because this summarizes the main tenets of collective action, *asabiya* or consensus, plus religious knowledge. The controversies between sects over the issues of tracing or terminating different lines of imams must therefore be understood as one dimension of sectarian collective identity. Not only does the life history of the imam mirror the socio-political conditions of the sect, but he himself is, in that capacity, an expression of its sovereignty. In brief, whereas the Sunni see sovereignty in the application of Islamic law, the sects see it in the rise of the imam.

The Controversy of Origin

The controversial issue of sovereignty, law versus imam, has given rise to basic disagreements over the origin and formation of sectarian communities. The Sunni, who believe that the perfection of religion lies in the Qur'an as revealed to man through the Prophet, approach everything else (including the genesis of sects) as if it were a historical creation containable in time and place. Many Islamic sects, especially the Shi'a, Druzes and Alawis—who believe that the perfection of religion lies in the Qur'an signifying the exoteric, and in the imam signifying the esoteric—approach the question of genesis ideologically, as if it were a part of the entire system of divine revelation. In other words, the Sunni see the origin of sects in history, as a natural phenomenon; but the sects see their origins as expressions of divine ordinance.

The distinction between history and ideology in this context not only allows for a wider and more comprehensive understanding of sects, but is also more informative about sectarian self-images. No sect traces its origin to the historical (ephemeral) era in which it emerged; all trace their origin to divine roots, to the eternal. The historical material they manipulate is meant merely to validate and supplement the divine origin, the special creation. The point is clarified in the following discussion.

Those who interpret religion historically, whether or not they are historians, trace the origin of the Ibadis to 657. This is the year in which the Kharijis rebelled against Ali bin Abi Talib in protest against his agreeing to settle through arbitration his dispute with Mu'awiya (the founder of the Umayyad dynasty) over the caliphate. The Kharijis were Ali's supporters and wanted him to be caliph. To them, he was the best qualified. The Kharijis considered Ali's loss of the caliphate to the Umayyads as an act of betrayal of his own cause and of their trust: hence the rebellion. Tradition has it that Ali defeated the Kharijis at the famous battle of Nahrawan in 658.

The Ibadis, on the other hand, do not see their origin in accountable historical incidents or events, limited to time and place; rather, they consider themselves an 'ancient' community rooted in Qur'anic revelations. And to validate this claim, they resort to 4/100:

> He who emigrates in the cause of God finds in the earth many a refuge, wide and spacious. And he who parts off (*yakhruj*) from his home [emigrating] to God and His Messenger, and then dies, his reward becomes due surely with God. God is oft-forgiving, most merciful.

To the Ibadis, the words 'part off' signify a spiritual emigration to God, a rebellion against tyranny and by no means an act of deviation from the consensus of the *umma* as many others, especially the Sunni, understand it to be (Mu'ammar, 1964:34–5).

The above comments on the Ibadis can be applied, in varying degrees, to other groups as well. For example, whereas Ibn Hazm traces the origin of the Shi'a Twelvers to the historical era immediately following the death of the Prophet, and Ibn al-Nadim, and many other writers who deal with this subject, trace it to the battle of al-Jamal and Saffin, the Shi'a themselves seek their origin in Qur'anic texts and Prophetic traditions.[8] To prove their point, they quote several verses and traditions that bear witness to what they call *imamat al-nass* (the textual imamate), meaning that Ali's imamate and his successors are ordained by God. They believe that God instructed the Prophet to designate Ali as imam and, from there on, imams always designated their successors down to the twelfth imam, al-Mahdi, who disappeared in Samarra, Iraq (Figure 2). Unlike the Sunni, who consider the imamate or caliphate a product of consensus, a political process, the Shi'a consider it a divine appointment.

The Shi'a trace their claim to the Qur'an, 26/214: 'And admonish thy nearest kinsmen.' They insist that upon this revelation, the Prophet gathered his folk in his house, and after they had eaten, he said to them while pointing to Ali, 'This is my guardian and successor, listen to him and obey his orders.' They refer to many other Qur'anic verses which they say all indicate the authenticity of the 'textual imamate'. These include 33/33:

> And stay quietly in your houses, and make not a dazzling display like that of the former times of ignorance, and establish regular prayer, and give regular charity, and obey God and His Apostle. God only wishes to remove all abomination from you, ye members of the People of the House, and to make you really pure.

The Shi'a believe that the phrase 'the People of the House' in this verse is meant to indicate the Holy House of Ali. They also adduce the fact that there are two more verses, one revealed before the Prophet had declared Ali as his successor and the other immediately after he had done so. The Qur'an, 5/70, revealed before the declaration, affirms:

> Apostle! Proclaim the message which has been revealed to thee from thy Lord. If thou didst not, thou wouldst not have fulfilled His Mission.

Whereas 5/4, which was revealed after the declaration, succinctly states:

> This day I have perfected your religion for you, completed My favour upon you, and have chosen for you Islam as your religion.

The *hadith* (declaration) itself, which occurred on the 18 Dhi al-Hujja, 10 AH, relates:

> Whoever takes me as lord, Ali is his. May God lend support to whoever bids him [Ali] loyalty, fight whoever takes him enemy, dishonour whoever fails him, and turn the truth with him in whichever direction he turns.

The Shi'a take the phrase 'proclaim the message revealed to thee' in 5/70 to signify the designation of Ali as successor, and the phrase 'this day I have perfected your religion . . .' to signify the already-made designation. This is besides many other *hadiths*, all of which indicate the special position Ali occupies in religion. Among them are the following:

> Oh Ali! the faithful love you, the blasphemous hate you.

> Ali sides with the truth, and the truth with Ali.

> Oh father of Hasan! with God's blessing you and your partisans shall enter paradise.

Obviously, the Shi'a prefer to heed their divine origin rather than their historical emergence.

The Druzes and the Alawis likewise see their origin in a universally framed synthesis of religions in which they emerge as the last to sign the covenant with God. This synthetic view is evolutionarily expressed in what is known as *dawr* (the cyclical nature of revelation), which begins with Adam and ends with Muhammad, according to the Alawis, and with al-Hakim, the seventh Fatimid caliph, according to the Druzes. The Druzes believe that al-Hakim's era witnessed the emergence of *tawhid* doctrine, which marks the last divine cycle. Hence, they call themselves the People of Tawhid rather than Druzes. According to the Alawis, the cycles include those of Adam, Noah, Abraham, Moses, Jesus and Muhammad; the Druzes add to these a seventh cycle, Muhammad bin Isma'il, in whom the divine legislative doctrines that define the permitted and the forbidden come to an end. In other words, whereas al-Hakim marks the last call for divine unity, Muhammad bin Isma'il marks the last divine charter.

Clearly, Islamic sects seek their origin in divine designs and eternal structures rather than in historical accidents. In their search for divine origins, they always turn back to the Qur'an.

Because of this controversy over origin, no sect seems to like or agree with the name or names given to them—names that always seem to underline historical origins. They like to be called (as they call themselves) by names that signify their ideological commitments. The Ibadis, for example, simply call themselves 'the Muslims' and bestow no special religious title upon Abdullah bin Ibad, whom the Sunni *ulama*, such as al-Shahrastani and al-Baghdadi, say was the founder of the Ibadi sect. Likewise, the Shi'a would prefer to be known as *imamiyun* (believers in the imamate) rather than Shi'a which simply means 'partisans' (Maghniya, n.d). 'Partisanship' is only one aspect of their much more comprehensive view of the place of Ali in religion. Similarly, the Druzes call themselves 'the People of Tawhid' rather than Druzes after Nashtakin al-Darazi who they believe had betrayed the *da'wa* (religious call) and was subsequently assassinated in 1020 at the hands of a Druze (al-Zu'bi, 1972:17).

The same principle applies to the Alawis, who like to be known as Alawis rather than Nusairis after Abi Shu'aib bin Nusair al-Namiri, the 'door' of Imam Hasan al-Askari, the eleventh imam who lived in the ninth century (al-Tawil, 1966:201). If they accept the name Nusairi, they would rather trace it to *nasra* (support) in reference to the small regiment that came from Medina to support Abi Ubaida in his attempt to occupy northern Syria during the reign of Umar bin al-Khattab (634–44). The Alawi sources have it that after the conquest of the region, this regiment settled in Mount al-Hilu, which came to be known as the Nusairi Mountains (al-Tawil, 1966:97).

The Yazidis follow the same pattern. They believe that they are an old nation directly descended from Adam, whereas other nations are descended from Adam and Eve. However, Sunni sources, such as al-Dimluji (1949:164), trace the origin of the Yazidis to Yazid bin Mu'awiya, the second Umayyad caliph.

The distinction between historical emergence and divine origin seems to suggest that those who follow the exoteric interpretations of the Qur'an, in the sense that it was revealed once and for all, seek historical explanations, whereas those who adopt the esoteric understanding seek a divine origin. The Sunni, and to a lesser extent the Ibadis and the Zaidis, belong to the first category; the Shi'a, the Druzes and the Alawis belong to the second.

Figure 5: Continuity of Divine Manifestation in Human Society

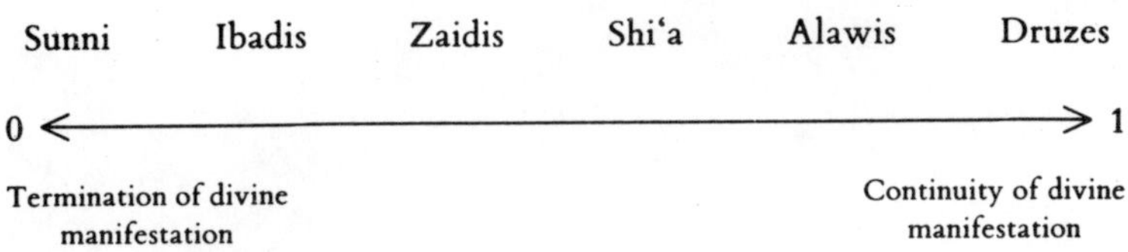

Although sects are alike in upholding the sovereignty of the religious community, they disagree on what actually constitutes the substance of that sovereignty. It is possible to place these differences between sects on a continuum of divine manifestation, with the Sunni at one end and the Druzes on the other, as shown in Figure 5. This concept will be discussed in more detail in the following chapters.

8
The Imam: Martyr or Hero?

This chapter examines the notion of sectarian sovereignty, which causes sects to see themselves as uniquely divine creatures, the people who have concluded the last and the right covenant with God. For heuristic purposes, sovereignty will be dealt with under four headings: (1) the imamate of the hero, which applies to the Zaidis and Ibadis; (2) the imamate of the martyr, which applies to the Shi'a; (3) the society of divine manifestation, characteristic of the Alawis and the Druzes; and (4) the 'survival' society, characteristic of the Yazidis and the Maronites. This discussion on the sovereignty of the religious community continues the preceding discussion on the ideology of religion and of sects; it also serves as a prelude to the forthcoming chapters on religious organization.

The Hero Imamate: the Ibadis and the Zaidis

Irrespective of their differences in religious dogma and/or historical or divine origin (the Ibadis branched off from the Khariji movement and the Zaidis from Shi'a traditions), the two sects are much alike in their approach to religious reality and in the general conduct of their affairs. Much like the Sunni, they believe that religion is revealed to man once and for all, and that man's task is to try to fulfil its requirements and expectations. However, they differ from the Sunni in the structure of government that seeks to implement divine law in society. The Sunni, as of the early days of the second caliph Umar, began to develop a somewhat standardized mode of government with predictable but vague rules of succession. By contrast, the Ibadis and the Zaidis have made government a matter of the personal achievement of the imam as hero. In brief, whereas the Sunni have tried, more or less successfully, to make the caliphate an office, the Ibadis and Zaidis approach the imamate as if it embodied the exploits of an individual. This difference is to be expected, since the Sunni have come to dominate mostly in complex peasant-like societies, whereas the Ibadis and Zaidis have spread among segmentary tribal groups.

The process of becoming an imam is similar among the Ibadis and Zaidis, despite the fact that the former hold the imamate to be open to whoever qualifies for it and the latter restrict it to the House of Zaid bin Ali bin Husain and his descendants. According to O'Ballance (1971:20), however, there are no fewer than 60,000 people from the families of Al-Hashim, Al-Wazir, Al-Mihyuddin and others in Yemen today who all claim descent from Zaid. If this were true, then it is doubtful whether the imamate is restricted to any particular line of descent: 60,000 is a large number. The Ibadis and the Zaidis approach the imamate as a *mas'a* (position to be achieved); it can be neither bestowed nor inherited. In both communities, the syndrome of action and behaviour expected of the imam is much the same, although expressed in different signs and symbols. These expectations can be summed up in two criteria: *ilm* (religious knowledge) and 'sultanic capacity' (the sword), or what is sometimes called 'thought and struggle' or 'purity and power'. 'Religious knowledge' refers to Islamic jurisdiction, traditions and history, as well as a complex religious code, a specialized language mastered only by the few learned men. 'Sultanic capacity', on the other hand, signifies political skills and talent, and the ability to manage and control the community through the use of coercion and/or persuasion, or sometimes through a balanced distribution of loot and benefits. Here, in the personality of the imam as hero, purity blends inseparably with power in a single mode of action.

The Zaidis express these qualifications by insisting that the imam must be a descendant of Zaid, capable of carrying arms and knowledgeable in religious matters. He must be a free-born male with clear mind and strong body, just, firm and pious (Farago, 1938:177; Little, 1968:7). The Ibadis express the same thing by claiming that the imamate is an act of *sunna* (tradition) and *ijma* (consensus). The word 'tradition' here implies religious knowledge whereas 'consensus' implies sultanic capacity. These qualities require the imam to possess the very authority for which he is held accountable. Inasmuch as he is expected to possess religious knowledge and sultanic capacity, he is likewise held accountable by his own followers to perform well in these spheres of action. Because of this accountability, the imamate becomes a highly competitive position; various tribal factions try to seize it, each claiming to champion the cause of the qualified imam. The history of the struggle for the imamate in both North Yemen and Oman, which is replete with internal wars between tribal factions vying for the imamate, illustrates the point.[1]

Marked by the rise of the imamate in 793, the Ibadi movement stabilized in Oman at the hands of four 'messengers' from the Kinda, Bani Smah and Riyami tribal factions. There had been a kind of complementarity of roles in the appointment of the imam: the Yahmud branch of the Azds had provided a list of eligible imams and the Bani Smah had the privilege of selecting the best qualified. Many of these tribal factions lived in the interior of Oman, which explains why the imamate was established for such a long time in villages like Nizwa and Rustaq.

Isolated in the interior villages, the imamate continued to perform its role without major clashes between the various claimants. This era of relative peace continued until the first half of the eighteenth century, when the struggle for the imamate took an entirely different turn, drawing the whole country into a series of devastating internal wars which lasted for about half a century. The new economic resources accruing from the Omani invasion of the East African coast were at the heart of the conflict. The Ibadis split into two warring factions, the Bani Ghafir and Bani Hinna, the first of northern Adnani origin and the second of southern Qahtani or Yemeni origin. Taking advantage of the weakening position of both tribal factions and the subsequent elimination of the key tribal figures, the Al-Busaid family seized the imamate and has continued to control it, in one form or another, until the present day.

Ahmad bin Said from the Al-Busaid family was the first to seize the imamate, in 1749. His rise to power was marked by a drastic transition in the structure of the Omani economy, from a localized peasant mode of production to oceanic, international trade. Following the discovery of the Cape sea route, trade began to shift from the two inland seas—the Red Sea and the Arabian Gulf—to the Indian Ocean. Due to their long experience in oceanic trade and in manipulating the movements of the monsoon winds, the Omanis stood to benefit most from this shift. It is related that a certain Omani pilot called Ahmad bin Majid helped guide the Portuguese across the Indian Ocean from Mombasa on the East African coast to Calcutta on the Indian coast. By this time, oceanic trade had become so active that a new merchant class began gradually to arise in Oman. The merchants were the first to support Imam Ahmad in his attempts to expand trade between the continents. A series of sea ports on the East African coast and on the Indian coast began to rise with an obvious Omani or Yemeni accent. Zanzibar, famous for its cloves, remained clear evidence of the Omani tradition in East Africa until it was annexed by Tanganika in the 1960s; both are now known as Tanzania.

Imam Ahmad died in 1783 and was succeeded by his son Said, but after no more than three years Hamad, Said's son, rebelled against his father and seized power by force. The first thing Hamad did was transfer the seat of government from Rustaq in the interior to Muscat on the coast, thus underlining the shift in the economy from subsistence agriculture to world trade. Hamad had for the first time separated the imamate and the sultanate, keeping his father as imam in Rustaq while appointing himself 'sultan' of Oman in Muscat. This was the first instance of the Ibadis differentiating between the two authorities, the rule of religion and the government of the sultan or emir.

Hamad died in 1792 and was succeeded by his uncle Sultan, who, following in his nephew's footsteps, kept the imamate and the sultanate separate. While he ruled as sultan from Muscat, his brother Said continued to rule as imam in Rustaq. During Sultan's reign, three spheres of influence began to emerge in Oman: the interior, governed by his brother Said, the imam; Sohar or Batina, governed by his second brother Qais; and Muscat, the centre of commerce and trade, under his own authority. Significantly, Sultan bin Ahmad ruled Muscat using the title *sayyid* (descendant of Ali) instead of imam, which was meant to underline his descent, however fictitious, from the 'House of the Prophet'. Ever since then, the Al-Busaid family in Oman have used the title *sayyid*.

On the death of Imam Said bin Ahmad in 1821, the imamate, for the first time since its foundation in 793, remained vacant for about half a century. No successor was elected, selected or appointed. Ibadi political thought, which does not require the continuous presence of the imam, tolerates such an arrangement, which is called the state of *kutman* (concealment).

The separation between the imamate and the sultanate led to a series of wars between various tribal factions, each trying to control the imamate or the sultanate, or both. In a short while, Badr bin Saif, Sultan's nephew, rebelled against him and took over government. Said, Sultan's son, retaliated against Badr, killed him and re-established the right to government of his father's line. Said bin Sultan proved to be a capable ruler, building around him such a strong tribal regime that he could have declared himself both imam and sultan had he so wished. However, he seems to have had much less interest in the imamate than in the more lucrative sultanate that controlled local and international commerce and trade. Indeed, Said used to spend most of his time commuting between Muscat and Zanzibar to oversee his business empire.

In 1846 a certain Hammoud bin Azzan from Sohar, the grandson of Qais bin Ahmad, tried to seize the imamate in an attempt to bring it back to life. He sought the support of some Ibadi tribes from the interior and succeeded in earning their loyalty, much to the dislike of his own son Saif, who rebelled against his father and managed to expel him from Sohar following a short blockade of the castle. The imamate subsequently returned to the state of 'concealment'.

The strongest man in Oman, Said bin Sultan, died in 1856. The empire he had established was divided between his two sons and nephew. His son Thuwaini took over Muscat, Majid took Zanzibar and other ports in East Africa, and his nephew Azzan bin Qais established himself in Rustaq. In 1864 Thuwaini tried to seize Rustaq from Azzan, who was acting in conjunction with the Wahhabis then based in Buraimi. Thuwaini failed, and the Wahhabis continued to use Buraimi as a stepping-stone to Oman. Encouraged by the Wahhabis, Salim bin Thuwaini rebelled against his father and killed him in 1866. Weary of the Wahhabi intervention, the Ibadi tribes of Oman, led by Azzan bin Qais, attacked Salim bin Thuwaini and expelled him from Muscat in 1868. Following the conquest, many tribal chiefs and *ulama* assembled in Rustaq and appointed Azzan as imam. His imamship, however, did not last long. The Ghafari tribes, supported by the Wahhabis, soon rebelled against Azzan and dethroned him in 1870. With the death of Azzan, the struggle for the imamate was quietened; Sayyid Turki bin Said bin Sultan came to power in Muscat and was later succeeded by his son Faysal in 1888.

The imamate continued to be in 'concealment' until 1895, when the Bani Hinna tribes of the interior (mainly because of economic deprivation) took arms against Faysal, destroying a large part of Muscat in the process. Through the distribution of gifts and loot, Faysal managed to earn their trust for some eighteen years. However, in 1913 they rose against him again, this time led by a locally renowned Ibadi shaikh, Said bin Khamis al-Kharrousi. Al-Kharrousi accused Faysal of corruption and blasphemy, and of committing religiously prohibited acts including the importation of wine and tobacco, mixing with and concluding commercial deals with non-believers (Christians) and being unable to speak Arabic correctly and therefore unable to understand the Qur'an. It is true that Faysal was not fluent in Arabic; he spoke Swahili, the *lingua franca* of East Africa. The rebels took hold of the interior villages of Oman and declared al-Kharrousi the imam of the faithful, seated in Nizwa. Were it not for the intervention of the British fleet, they would have taken the coastal port cities as well. The disparity in wealth between Muscat, the centre of commerce and international trade, and the interior, engaged mainly in subsistence production, was the main cause of these repeated insurrections against the sultan.

The war between Muscat and the tribes of the interior lasted for some seven years; it ceased temporarily following al-Kharrousi's assassination at the hands of a Wahhabi tribesman. Al-Kharrousi was succeeded by Imam Said bin Khalfan al-Khalili, who successfully negotiated a workable treaty with Taymur bin Faysal, the sultan of Muscat. While the sultan agreed not to impose tariffs on goods entering Muscat from the interior, nor to restrict the movements of Omanis coming into the flourishing coastal cities, the imam in turn pledged not to attack or loot the villages or towns that lay under the sultan's authority.

The treaty, which was signed in al-Sib near Muscat, was the first of its kind in the history of Ibadism, whereby the imamate entered into a formal treaty with the sultanate and thus recognized the separation between the authority of religion and the dictates of power. It was clearly understood, however, that Imam Said al-Khalili was acting on behalf of the tribal chiefs, which meant that the treaty was, in reality, between the chiefs and the sultan.

When Sultan Taymur died in 1932 and was succeeded by his son Said, Imam Said al-Khalili was still alive but the tribal coalition, composed mainly of different segments of the southern Bani Hinna groups, came under the strong leadership of Isa bin Saleh. The political skills of bin Saleh overshadowed the imam's ability to manoeuvre for autonomy. As soon as bin Saleh died, the imam began to impose his own rule on the villages and towns of the interior. He demonstrated his autonomy by forbidding oil excavators from entering the area he controlled on the pretext that they, being Christians, might defile the purity of the Ibadi land. Of course, this was a gesture indicating rejection of the sultan's government rather than obedience to the dictates of religion. Following the death of Imam Said al-Khalili in 1954, Ghalib bin Ali was appointed imam in Nizwa, a move that came to reflect the power of his brother

Talib, the tribal chief who had recently been appointed to the governorship of Rustaq.

Much to the dislike of the sultan, Talib continued to oppose oil excavations in the areas subject to his rule, always bargaining for the lion's share in the endeavour. Supported by the Saudis, he simultaneously began to lead a separatist movement in the interior, demanding total independence from Muscat. Unnerved by these moves, the sultan decided to attack Nizwa, the rebels' stronghold, occupied it in 1955 and took Imam Ghalib hostage. His brother Talib fled to Saudi Arabia and sought asylum there, later to be joined by Imam Ghalib. Encouraged by Saudi Arabia and Nasser's Egypt, in 1957 the two brothers waged a new attack on Oman, occupying a series of villages in the interior from which they hoped to descend upon Muscat. In 1959, with the help of the British, Sultan Said bin Taymur retaliated, crushed the rebellion and re-established Muscat's authority over the interior villages.

Using sometimes Egypt and sometimes Saudi Arabia as a base, Imam Ghalib has continued to oppose the sultan ever since, if not physically, then by radio, calling for rebellion against the 'blasphemous regime' of the sultan; but in vain. The imamate, as the Ibadis would say, is again in concealment. The unprecedently long absence of the imam now poses many questions. Will the imamate ever come back to life again? If it does, will it be able to capture and cope with the dictates of modern government? Will it disappear for good? If it does, will the Ibadis simply follow the Sunni model? Or will the imamate and the sultanate coexist as separate authorities as they did during Imam Said al-Khalili's days?

The struggle for the imamate, and that between the imam and the sultan, demonstrates two points: first, the concept of sovereignty of the religious community is closely linked to the position of the imamate; and second, the imamate is an object of competition between the various political factions in Ibadi society. This is clearly reflected in what the Ibadis call the four situations of the imamate, namely, those of *zuhur* (rising), *difa* (defence), *shira* (spread) and *kutman* (concealment) (Mu'ammar, 1964:93–4). In the 'rising' situation, when the imam is visibly in power, the Ibadi community is in full control of its own affairs, independent and free of all foreign intervention. This is a state where the laws of God and the rules of religion are put into effect. It is an expression of sovereignty, precisely in accordance with the Qur'an 63/8:

They say, 'if we return to Medina, surely the more honourable will expel therefrom the meaner', but honour belongs to God and His Apostle, and to the believers; but the hypocrites know not.

The second situation, 'defence', takes place when the community falls under the influence of foreign, non-Ibadi rule, at which time they, led by the imam, rise up against foreign aggression (Mu'ammar, 1964:94). If the imam fails to mobilize the community in total uprising against foreign influence or occupation, then any small number of believers, not exceeding forty, could, without an imam, wage wars against foreign aggression—this is the state of 'spread'. The last stage occurs when all the aforementioned attempts to free the community fail, and the community consequently surrenders to foreign rule; at this point, the imamate is said to be in 'concealment'. (The Ibadi concept of 'concealment' or the 'concealed' imamate is entirely different from the Shi'a concepts of *taqiya* and the 'hidden' or 'absent' imam, as will be demonstrated later in this chapter).

Just as the rise of the imamate signifies the sovereignty of the religious community, its concealment signifies foreign domination. Clearly, the imamate is an expression of the political status of the Ibadi community, and in this sense it comes to symbolize the collective religious consciousness of the group. The close linkage between the imamate and the community's sovereignty continuously requires of the imam that he act as a 'hero', a 'liberator', more than simply an *alim* (a man of religious knowledge). In other words, the imamate is a personal achievement, not a divine appointment; the imam is a 'builder' of cities and states rather than a succeeding manifestation of divine justice, as the Shi'a hold him to be.

The Zaidis present a comparable situation, especially if we consider the imamate from the point of view of performance and its link to the issue of sovereignty of the religious community. This comparability is demonstrated by the struggle for the imamate in Yemen since its inception in 901 at the hands of al-Hadi Yahya. According to Zaidi sources, al-Hadi Yahya, the grandson of al-Qasim al-Rassi (called this after al-Rass Mountain near Medina), migrated to Yemen between 893 and 894 and settled among a branch of the Sharafa tribe. In fact, they invited him to come and live in their midst, always guiding them through the 'righteous path', obeying God's word and enforcing his laws. He soon chose to return to his homeland the Hijaz, however, for the tribal chiefs who had originally invited him failed to appreciate his staunch adherence to divine law and the dictates of religion. They preferred to go by tribal law rather than the law of religion.

As soon as he returned home, a branch of the Khawlan tribes who lived in and around San'a appealed to him, once again, to return to Yemen to help resolve a dispute between the warring tribal factions. Relying upon the rules of God as demonstrated by the political skills of the early Muslims, he established peace among the Khawlans and then moved to Najran and likewise put an end to their internal rivalries (specifically between the Bani Wadi'a, Shakir and Yam, on the one hand, and the Bani Bil and Harith, on the other). He was reputed to have been able then to establish peace between these Muslim tribes and the neighbouring Christian tribes of Najran.

The Zaidis believe that the work of Imam al-Hadi in bringing about unity and peace between the warring tribal factions was following in the footsteps of his grandfather, the Prophet Muhammad, and then set an example for future imams. Since its foundation in Yemen towards the end of the ninth century, the imamate has always been an instrument of reconciliation between warring tribal factions, afterwards leading them in conquest to uphold the word of religion. The pattern rotates in a vicious circle: the imam sets up the religious order by virtue of tribal support, but as soon as he does this the very tribes who first rushed to his cause turn against him. This is predictable since they initially came for loot and not out of piety. The conflict weakens both sides, at which time another tribal coalition, perhaps led by another claimant of the imamate, steps in and tries to impose its dominance. Hence, the vicious circle of conflict. The alliance between a set of tribal factions with a specific strain of imams may continue from one generation to another. The 'house' of imams who do so are known collectively as *hajr*; thus *hajr* Sa'da or *hajr* al-Hut means the strain of imams attached to the Sa'da or al-Hut tribes.[2]

The continuous internal struggle for the imamate in Yemen did not necessarily weaken the country's capacity to resist foreign intervention. After the coming to power of the Al-Hamiduddin in 1597 under the leadership of Imam Mansur al-Qasim, the Yemenis fought a series of wars against the Ottomans, the Egyptians and the tribal chiefs of the south. None of the aggressors was able to conquer the Zaidi country and subject it to its rule.

Not all the Zaidi imams were heroes of war, however. Much like the Ibadis, some were war heroes, some were managers of divine justice and some combined both skills—a combination deeply admired by the faithful. As a matter of fact, the Zaidis distinguish between two types of imam; one they call *sabiq* (predecessor) imams and the other they call *muhtasib* (accountable) imams. The first wage wars, levy taxes, defend the community by the sword and therefore hold Friday prayers; the second administer religious law and refrain from holding Friday prayers. (In Shi'a religious practice, the holding of Friday prayers means that the congregation believe that it is possible to establish 'justice' in the absence of the 'hidden' imam; not holding it means the contrary.)

The separation between *sabiq* and *muhtasib* imams provides the Zaidis with the opportunity to reconcile their belief that there should be only one imam at a time with the reality of having simultaneously a multitude of claimants to the immate. Although the Zaidis believe in the 'singularity' of the imam, and the Ibadis in the multiplicity of imams, they are alike in terms of action. The two communities have had two or more contemporaneous imams governing the faithful simultaneously in different places. Early in the tenth century, the Ibadis had separate imamates, one in North Africa and one in Oman; likewise, the Zaidis had one in Yemen at the same time as another in the Caspian Sea region. This means that the Zaidis' insistence upon the singularity of the imamate is simply a reflection of their belief in the sovereignty of the religious community. The singularity of the imamate stands for the ever-expected but rarely accomplished unity of the tribally fragmented religious community.

The correspondence between the rise of the imamate and the issue of sovereignty does not mean that the first comprehensively embodies the second. The imamate is only one dimension or component of sovereignty. The organization of the *ulama*, their recruitment and training, the unique and comprehensive dogma of the sect, the more or less different sources of law—all these operate to reinforce the image of a sect as a sovereign community. This is, of course, in addition to geographical isolation, ecological conditions and the comprehensiveness of economic production, which greatly enhance the community's sovereignty.

From the point of view of Islamic law, the Ibadis developed a distinct legal code around 643 at the hands of a certain Jabir bin Zaid al-Yahmudi al-Omani, which agrees on several points with the Sunni laws. Unlike the Sunni, however, the Ibadis tend to be more egalitarian, and stricter in their adherence or more literal in their interpretation of text. For example, they, like the Sunni, speak of merit, but unlike the Sunni, who give priority to the Quraish, the Prophet's House, they do not restrict the caliphate to any house or strain. If the imam errs and refuses to repent, the Ibadis legitimize a rebellion against him; the Sunni differ on this point. Moreover, the Ibadis do not adopt perpetuity inheritance like the Sunni, nor do they deny women the right to full inheritance.

The Ibadis also differ from the Sunni in other beliefs: they maintain that God cannot be seen in the after-life and that man cannot be permanently committed to hell. In patterns of worship, they are closer to the Sunni Maliki order than other orders in the Islamic world.

The Zaidis, on the other hand, differ from the Sunni in two ways: first, by following the style of Zaid bin Ali in their performance of religious duties; and second, by restricting the imamate to his descendants. Apart from these two points, they follow the four Sunni schools of law, and many of them hold Friday prayers side by side with Sunni worshippers. They are so close to the Sunni that Lambton (1981:219) chose to refer to them as the 'political Shi'a'.

However, the fact that the Sunni and the Zaidis share many items of belief and/or worship is not enough to make them alike in sociological terms. The question is how these ingredients of faith and practice combine with each other and with other social, ecological and structural criteria to make the group a unique socio-religious reality. These ingredients include endogamous marriage, patterns of loyalty, shrine visits, distinct historical accounts and interpretations, literature and a highly specialized religious language. Just as these fields of interaction reinforce the identity of a sect as a unique, sovereign divine creature, they likewise define the boundaries between one sect and another. In other words, the boundaries that set one group apart from another are defined religiously as well as socially and economically; it is a manifold process.

The Martyr Imamate: the Shi'a

One of the main criteria by which the Shi'a are distinguished from other Islamic groups is the belief that the community of believers falls under continuous divine surveillance or guidance, and that this happens through a continuous, unbroken line of imams. This belief is embodied in what they call 'the textual imamate', which is to say that the imam is designated by God in the texts of the Holy Qur'an. From there on, existing imams designate their successors in an unbroken line until the last and twelfth imam, the Hidden One, the Expected, the Owner and Possessor of Time, in other words, the Timeless. Because the faithful will always need divine surveillance in order to 'perfect' religion, the imamate strictly speaking cannot, and should not, terminate or be broken. It continues and prevails in different forms.

The Shi'a believe that the place of the imamate in religion is almost equivalent to the Qur'an and the *sunna* (Traditions). This they express in the concept of the 'two weights': the 'heavy weight' which refers to the Qur'an and the *sunna* and the 'light weight' referring to the Holy House of Ali and his descendants (al-Zain, 1979:44). In other words, the practice of religion depends upon the Qur'an and the *sunna* which illustrate the 'exoteric' and upon the unbroken line of imams who individually and collectively demonstrate the 'esoteric'. By demonstrating the implicit meanings of religion, the imam becomes infallible, a *muqallad* (imitable model), the epitome of piety, a manifestation of divine perfection.

If the imam signifies the esoteric in religion, and religion is perfected by the pursuit of both the exoteric and the esoteric, it follows that the practice of religion can only be complete through the Qur'an and the imam. In the absence of the imam, who went into 'concealment' in the ninth century (Figure 2), religion cannot be perfected and therefore divine justice cannot be established. Only with the coming of the imam will justice be established. In his absence, tyranny and oppression will prevail and the world will be governed by 'sultanic' and 'pharaonic' styles based on power and coercion rather than the application of divine law or justice.

These ideological commitments have generated two related political attitudes throughout Shi'a history: first, the continuous tendency to oppose sultanic governments even if they are controlled by Shi'a people, thus reinforcing the rebellious character of Shi'a religious ideology; and second, the oscillation of Shi'a political behaviour between two extremes, the *taqiya* and the *ta'bi'a* (mobilization) positions. The *taqiya* position is one of indifference towards the political regime of the day whereby the Shi'a, especially the *ulama*, take no active part in politics, confine themselves to the administration of religious law and leave the privilege of decisions entirely in the hands of men of power, the sultans, the emirs and the shahinshahs. Hence, the word *taqiya* means piety as well as the concealment of one's right to politics in favour of the practice of religion.

The *ta'bi'a* position is an act of mobilization whereby the community of the faithful, led by the *ulama*, try to seize power and take hold of government directly—as an attempt, of course, to establish the rule of God. It must be stressed here that in both positions, *taqiya* and *ta'bi'a*, the

Shi'a are guided by the style of behaviour modelled on their imams. Just as Hasan, the second imam after Ali (who ceded the caliphate to the Umayyads in order to save Islam from devastating internal strife), stands for the practice of *taqiya*, so Husain, the third imam, who rebelled against the Umayyads in order to restore the right of the Holy House of Ali to government, stands for the practice of *ta'bi'a*. Husain, the Martyr, rebelled against the Umayyads at the famous battle of Karbala in southern Iraq, where he and a large number of his family and close relatives were ruthlessly slain. In their actions, Hasan and Husain have set a permanent, divine precedence, a model followed by Shi'a throughout the world, depending upon the political circumstances of the day.

In pursuit of Hasan's model, the *taqiya* people try to adjust their roles to the various political regimes. The *ta'bi'a* people, on the other hand, call for outright rebellion against 'sultanic' regimes in an effort to control government and impose the rule of God or Islamic law. The first group refrains symbolically from holding Friday prayers on the grounds that justice cannot be established in the absence of the imam. While awaiting his coming justice, they deal with the sultanic authorities at the hands of the emirs. The second group, by contrast, holds Friday prayers under the pretence that although it is impossible to establish justice in the absence of the imam, they, the *ulama*, are more fit to rule than the sultans—hence the prayers.

Correspondingly, the Shi'a in many countries of the world are split into two complementary factions, one calling for *taqiya*, accommodating various power regimes, and the other calling for *ta'bi'a* with the aim of assuming power under the authority of the *ulama*. Ayatollah Khumaini of Iran is a good illustration of the second type, Ayatollah Muntaziri of the first. In Lebanon, Shaikh Qabalan, the head of the Ja'fari courts, would stand for *taqiya*, whereas Shaikh Fadlalla, the spiritual leader of Hizbollah, the Party of God, stands for *ta'bi'a*. In Bahrain, the Shi'a are likewise divided into two factions, the Akhbar who hold Friday prayers and call for outright rebellion against government, and the Usul who refrain from doing so, calling for adaptation. In Bahrain in 1975 there were three shaikhs after whom the Akhbar used to hold Friday prayers; these shaikhs were said to possess the qualities of 'upholding righteousness and uprooting viciousness'.

In fact, one of the main themes of Khumaini's book, *Wilayat Faqih/The Islamic Republic*, was precisely to affirm the right of the *ulama* to government. The book discusses many traditions relating to the Prophet and the imams, all of which indicate this right. For example:

> The imams, peace be upon them all, imposed upon the *ulama* very important duties, expecting them to live up to and maintain the dictates of religion . . . There should be no resort to *taqiya* in every case, however small or big. The resort to *taqiya* is legitimate only if it is intended to safeguard the self and others from the dangers resulting from the application of subsidiary religious rules. But if Islam, all Islam, is in danger, there is no room for *taqiya* or silence.

Khumaini adds:

> If the circumstances of *taqiya* require some of us to place themselves in the service of the sultan, we should in this case refrain from doing so even if our lives are at stake. The practice of *taqiya* must be addressed only to the conquest of Islam and the victory of the Muslims.

Under the title 'Expel the Sultans' *Ulama*', he writes:

> Those are not *ulama*. Some of them have been turbaned by foreign intelligence to call God to the service of the sultans and to bestow His mercy and compassion upon them [the sultans]. Those we must expose; they are the enemies of Islam (Khumaini, 1979:142–3).

Thus, through the mobilization of the *ulama* and the faithful, Khumaini was able to challenge and destroy the Shah's government in Iran, one of the strongest in the Third World.

Once in power, Khumaini was expected to take control of government in Iran and refashion it according to an Islamic model, 'the Islamic republic'. Many students of Islam were curious to know how the 'Islamic' republic would differ from other republics. Instead, Khumaini, once in power, styled himself 'the counsellor of the revolution', leaving the management of the affairs of government to his immediate aides and relatives. Besides, the devastating Iraq-Iran war left Khumaini and his *ulama* supporters practically no time to try to build up the democratic institutions of the Islamic republic. What institutions are democratically Islamic is not clear.

What concerns us in this debate is clearly the Shi'a's ideological commitment to the formation of a religious community. To say that human society is under continuous, direct divine surveillance, first through the infallible imams and then through the *ulama* who are the heirs of prophets, is to believe that society must be in perpetual mobilization, always awaiting the perfection of religion, which actually cannot be perfected in the absence of the imam. The difference from the Sunni in this understanding is the belief in the continuity of divine surveillance, which subsequently requires continuous attention to God on the part of man. If this is so, then the imamate could not possibly come to an end; it merely disappears. Ending or terminating the imamate is a 'historical' affirmation; its continuity *in absentia* is an ideological reflection. The imam is 'the timeless', 'the possessor of time', i.e. beyond time and history.

From this angle, the position of *taqiya* and that of *ta'bi'a* are just two extremes along the same continuum. And this is precisely what Ayatollah Khumaini meant by the statement mentioned above: 'The practice of *taqiya* must be addressed only to the conquest of Islam and the victory of the Muslims.' In this sense *taqiya* is another form of religious struggle, often referred to in Shi'a writings as 'the bigger *jihad*'. It is a religious struggle against the self when the circumstances of religion require the Shi'a to be in a state of subdued opposition.

In brief, *taqiya* and *ta'bi'a* are two positions through which the faithful continue to attend to or respond to God's continuous surveillance of man. At any given period, the Shi'a oscillate between this and that position depending on the political circumstances of the time. *Taqiya* and *ta'bi'a* are both rebellious positions which reject the dictates of mundane authority and demand eternal justice, the justice of the imam's rule. Whoever is in this position, the position of perpetual rebelliousness, comes therefore to be symbolized as a 'martyr' and not as a 'hero'. Just as the heroic imam comes to signify the establishment of the social order where God's law is executed, as is the case among the Zaidis and the Ibadis, the martyr imam comes to signify the community in perpetual rebellion in search of divine justice, as is the case among the Shi'a. Consider the following excerpts from Shaikh Mahdi Shamsuddin's speech during the Ashura commemorations in Lebanon in 1983:

> Islam is a continuous rebellion, a continuous movement, a continuous rejuvenation process in man. It is a perfected achievement at the theoretical level and a continuous movement at the historical level. It is

a perfected achievement at the theoretical level as evidenced by God's words: 'today I have perfected your religion', etc. It is likewise a continuous movement as evidenced by His words: 'you were the best community . . .'

Because Islam is, at the level of history, a continuous movement and a continuous rebellion, it always provides martyrs. At its dawn, Islam provided martyrs who led it to conquest against the powers of the age of ignorance; and after its perfection it continued providing martyrs in order to keep and sustain the conquest against the forces of the apostates and religious deviants . . .

In every rebellion, there arises a martyr . . . martyrs to achieve victory and martyrs to sustain victory. And in every rebellion there arises a counter-force that aims to destroy the rebellion, destroy its aims and its values. The counter-force hopes to assassinate the rebellion and assassinate the future for which it stands. From here, the greatness of martyrdom that stands against the counter-rebels. It is the martyrdom of the victorious who did not fall captive to the privilege of conquest; they instead continued on the thorny route, even after their victory, in order to attain a greater grace, the grace of martyrdom.

And so were Imam Husain and his companions. Husain was the victorious. He could always, had he wished, have enjoyed the privilege of Islamic conquests. But he saw the counter-force growing under the cover of Islam, trying to transform it into a rigid, petrified institution, a Caesar-like or Chosroes-like kingly structure. Being aware that Islam is a continuous rebellion, and that as such Islam is exposed to assassination, retreat and petrification, exposed to become an instrument of coercion and violence . . . from this awareness, Husain chose the path of martyrdom, the choice that helped preserve Islam and the conquests of Islam.

The Islam that Husain had sacrificed himself for is not a theory hanging up there in a vacuum; it is Islam on earth. It is the Muslims and the Muslim community. It is their fears, their hopes, their lives, their dignity and the future of their coming generations.

Husain and his companions were not martyrs only when they were killed; they were martyrs also while alive. Martyrdom is not achieved only in death; it can be achieved in life as well. Rallying behind a just cause affecting the whole society rather than a person or family, a cause linked to God and His teachings, and to carry this cause across with piety and determination . . . this is what gives life and death the meaning of martyrdom. To live for the service and salvation of people . . . to unite the fate of the martyr with the destiny of man, is what bestows upon a person the grace of martyrdom . . .

This is the reality of the rally of martyrs at Karbala. The universality of Karbala, the humanness of Karbala, are what have made it survive in the minds, feelings and conscience of people until this very day.[3]

Many ideas and expressions contained in Shaikh Shamsuddin's speech clearly indicate the fact that 'perpetual rebelliousness' and subsequently 'martyrdom' are integral parts of Shi'a ideology, the formation of the religious community. Consider the following: 'Islam is a continuous rebellion', 'a continuous movement', 'a continuous rejuvenation process', and as such, it 'always provides martyrs'. Martyrdom thus becomes the 'greatest act of grace'. On the contrary, the lack of rebelliousness opposes Islam; it implies rigidity, petrification, standardization, 'Caesar-like' and 'Chosroes-like' rules, governments based on 'sultanic' rather than religious authority. Here, in these non-rebellious, non-Islamic structures, the continuous divine surveillance of man's society would have to terminate. It can only be activated by acts of martyrdom that aim to re-establish the 'link to God', the continuity of 'God's caring', which makes martyrdom a logical outcome of rebelliousness and therefore of Islam. It is in this sense that 'martyrdom' occurs in life and death alike.

This understanding of human society—a society always on the alert, on the move, continuously mobilized to respond to God's care—obviously does not agree with the conception of 'state' rule based on and derived from standardized, stable routine structures or procedures. The continuous manifestation of God's care requires man to be continuously active in seeking God's words and directions. Herein lies the idea of perpetual rebellion and subsequently the continuous provision of martyrs.

Through these ideological commitments there emerges the issue of sovereignty of the religious community. The Shi'a community is always ready and willing to receive the word of God, always awaiting his directions, his justice, through the coming or return of the imam, the coming that perfects (completes) religion. Without taking these ideological premises into consideration, it is difficult to understand Shi'a religious organization.

It is true that many of these ideological premises were not reflected in the course of Shi'a history, as evidenced by the fact that the Shi'a have established, and continue to establish, states characterized by stable structures. But it is also true that these states were shaped by these premises. Unlike the Sunni, the Shi'a states have always been distinguished by the following five features: (1) the *ulama* taking up the opposition even where government is controlled by the Shi'a; (2) the oscillation of political commitments between the position of *taqiya* and *ta'bi'a*, both of which reject worldly authority; (3) the intensity of ritual life, which makes the impact of religion felt in the day-to-day activities of man; (4) the wide variation and proliferation of religious specialists, permeating the entire structure of the religious community; and (5) the element of 'rebelliousness' implied in the various forms of collective worship and ritual, which almost entirely derives from Husain's martyrdom at the battle of Karbala.

It must be stressed here that the element of rebellion is religiously bound, emanating from religious teachings in Islam, and has nothing to do with revolutionary ideologies of the time. It is important to make this distinction because the two positions may at times meet, at least at the level of current political mottoes and slogans such as 'social justice', 'equality', 'the rights of the oppressed', and so on. The fact that the two rebellious positions meet does not make them synonymous; they meet but do not mutate. Their accord or alliance holds only tactically, temporarily, as it did in Iran on the verge of Khumaini's rebellion, or in Bahrain during the general parliamentary election of 1973. As soon as either group comes to power, they necessarily split into opposing camps, since their basic ideologies are far apart. From the point of view of religious dogma, rebelliousness is a constant, a never-ending activity awaiting the establishment of divine justice, whereas from the point of view of secular ideologies, rebelliousness is historically instrumental, a method of seizing power for the sake of establishing justice, human justice, if I may say so. In the first instance, rebelliousness is constantly anti-structure, in the second, it is the prelude to another structure.

This point will be taken up again in Chapter 13 on Shi'a religious organization. Before then, the discussion turns to the concept of the sovereignty of the religious community among other sects.

9

The Society of Divine Manifestation: the Druzes and the Alawis

In Chapter 7, all Islamic sects were placed on a continuum of divine manifestation, with the Sunni at one end and the Druzes at the other (Figure 5). All religions and sects are 'the Chosen People'; the differences between them lie in the nature of the relationship that binds them to God.

The Sunni believe that God's will is perfected in the Qur'an as revealed to the Prophet, who is the last to come, and that this will can be accomplished by the execution of divine law at the hands of a centralized authority or caliphate. The Ibadis and the Zaidis essentially agree with the Sunni, but try to execute God's will with the imam, who leads the community and establishes the 'city of God'. The Shi'a, on the other hand, believe in the continuity of divine surveillance in human society through an unbroken, unending line of imams who could also act *in absentia*. However, the Twelfth Imam, 'the Timeless', disappeared, which left the community in a permanent search for divine justice. In the absence of the imam, the Shi'a believe they are in a 'perpetual rebellion or movement' seeking his return, without which no 'justice' can be done on earth.

Unlike the Shi'a, the Druzes and the Alawis believe that divinity has never, and could never have been, terminated; it flows on indefinitely in human society through a continuous manifestation of divine will. According to them, divinity permeates society diffusely, as demonstrated in what the Druzes call *maqam* and the Alawis *wili*—the enshrined personage through which divinity has chosen to manifest itself. The belief in the divine permeation of man's society implies that souls are eternally created and reincarnated generation after generation. Souls do not die, and therefore are neither resurrected nor reborn. They neither go to heaven nor to hell, nor do they face the last judgement. It is on this earth that man is 'judged' and here lie both paradise and the inferno.[1]

One of the main tenets of Alawi and Druze beliefs is that divinity, or rather divine knowledge, can be realized by man, or make itself available to man, depending upon man's readiness for it. From here, it is possible to appreciate two central themes in Alawi and Druze religious thinking: first, the synthetic outlook on religion, and second, gradation or ranking of religious knowledge. These themes constitute the essential commitments upon which sovereignty of the religious community is based.

The Synthetic View of Religion

The Alawis and the Druzes believe that all heavenly religions (meaning the Semitic ones, for they exclude Hinduism, Confucianism, Buddhism and others from their framework) have been revealed to man in evolutionary cyclic stages depending upon man's readiness to appreciate and accept them.[2] They express this belief in the concept of *dawr* (evolutionary stage or cycle) which the Alawis restrict to six and the Druzes to seven. According to the Alawis, these include the cycles of Adam, Noah, Abraham, Moses, Jesus and Muhammad; the Druzes add a seventh stage, which is the cycle of Muhammad bin Isma'il with whom, according to them, the legal decrees were terminated. In his banned book *The Druze Way*, al-Najjar (1965:94) says:

> the seven cycles correspond to the seven heavens, the seven manifestations of divinity (*maqam*), the seven imams, the seven reasons for the spiritual world, the seven regulators of the world, the seven days, the seven esoteric pillars and the seven rules of *tawhid*.

Tawhid to the Druzes is not simply the belief in the unity of God; it is 'the knowledge of the unity of being in God'.

In this symbolic classification of cycles, heavens, imams, reasons, pillars, and so on, into sets of sevens lies the other implication of the synthetic view of religion—namely, that it embodies other beliefs (religions) as well as the entire cosmic order. In other words, the Alawi and the Druze orders do not concern themselves only with man's society, but also with the whole universe. The practice of religion therefore entails an understanding of the revealed texts (the Bible and the Qur'an) and also of the cosmic pattern, and the interconnection between them:

the extent to which religious patterns correspond to cosmic realities, and vice versa.

However, the Ạlawi and Druze concern with other religions must not be exaggerated. It is basically restricted to the concept of the cyclic manifestation of divine revelation, its timing, and these sects' participation in others' rituals. It is related that the Alawis, for example, observe many Christian rituals including the New Year, Easter and St Barbara's Day, as well as the Persian New Year called Nayruz (al-Alawi, 1972:174; Uthman, 1980:118–20). The Druzes, in their turn, take part in the Muslim celebration of Ramadan without fasting, and observe the Adha (sacrificial) feast. The scale and meaning of this participation have sometimes been greatly overstated, especially by certain orientalists who saw in them an extension of Christianity. For example, whereas R. Dussaud and H. Lammens (who both wrote on the Alawis) trace the word 'Nusairis', the name by which the Alawis are collectively known, to *nasara* meaning Christians, the Alawi sources trace it to *nasra* meaning military expedition or support (al-Tawil, 1966:97). In the Qur'an, the Christians are referred to as *nasara* meaning the followers of the Nazarene—i.e. Jesus who lived in Nazareth (in Arabic al-Nasira) as a child. This is much in keeping with Arab traditions whereby all names have a *nisba*, the place to which a person is related. Jesus in Arabic is also referred to as al-Nasiri meaning the person who relates to al-Nasira; hence his followers are *nasara*. Other Alawi practices such as visits to local Christian saints, the use of candles and scent in worship and permitting wine-drinking while forbidding drunkenness are thought to be of Christian origin. Lammens (1899) treats the idea of *hulul* (spiritual occupation) among the Alawis as if it were the same as the concept of *tajassud* (embodiment of Christ), which it is not. It must always be remembered that many of the early orientalists came to the Middle East to look for the origin of Christianity and tried hard to find, perhaps invented, what they were looking for.[3]

Among the Druzes, the same principle of synthesis can be observed, though in a different manner. Their sources abound in names, ideas and religious traditions that appeared before the rise of Islam, especially those recurring in the Bible and in Greek philosophy, particularly Neoplatonism. After the rise of Islam, the Druzes relied heavily on the writings of the Mu'tazila writers such as Ikhwan al-Safa, and well-known masters of Sufism such as Rabi'a al-Adawiya and Ibn al-Farid.

It must be stressed, however, that the Alawị and Druze recognition of other religions, through a complex process of religious synthesis, does not correspond to or reflect those religions' views of themselves. The kind of Christianity or Judaism they talk about is different from the Christian beliefs in Christianity or Jewish beliefs in Judaism. The Alawi and Druze synthesis is almost entirely dependent upon esoteric interpretations of Qur'anic texts. They tend to refer to the Bible only in support of their own religious discourse, which suggests that their synthetic views of religion are indeed a formulation of a new and unique dogma. In this sense, all religions are synthetic in one way or another; they are all new combinations of old ingredients. The Alawi and Druze insistence on being syntheses of previous religious dogmas, which they summarize in the theory of the 'cycles of revelation', is indeed an act of faith, a given. Both the Alawi insistence that their holy book, *Kitab al-Majmu* (The Book of Synthesis), contains everything one needs to know about other religions and the Druze claim that their book, *Rasa'il al-Hikma* (The Messages of Wisdom), guides man to the holistic knowledge of existence, which they call *tawhid*, must be taken as acts of faith.[4] In his book, *The Druze Faith*, Sami Makarem writes, 'The Druze dogma has it that God is the only existence; He is the whole' (Makarem, 1974:41).

The other side of the synthetic view of religion, concerned with the entire cosmic order, is an attempt to seek correspondences between the esoteric understanding of some Qur'anic texts and natural, cosmic or celestial conditions. According to Muhammad al-Tawil (1966:203), a well-known Alawi writer, 'The message of the Prophet Muhammad is an act of mercy which encompasses the Muslims, the People of the Book, the entire humankind, all the creatures who have souls, as well as the entire universe.' In this attempt to seek corresponding analogies between 'religion' and the universe lies one of the main differences between the Druzes and the Alawis. Whereas the Druzes seek correspondence, or rather, 'unity of the cosmic order' on the basis of symbolic classification, the Alawis do so through a free system of substitution between man, the moon, the stars and other cosmic creatures or features. Indeed, some Alawi shaikhs with top positions in the religious hierarchy have a deep knowledge of astrological techniques, which they call *jafr* (al-Tawil, 1966:199).

Although a discussion of these issues is outside the scope of the present work, it is worth stressing that the Druzes and the Alawis consider such knowledge to be 'high religious culture' which only the select few can, or indeed should, know. It is private knowledge that can be acquired only privately and must be kept as such. In brief, it is inferable but incommunicable knowledge. The following is an illustration of how 'cosmic unity' is understood through a system of symbolic classification as cited in *Kitab al-Naqd al-Khafi* (The Book of the Hidden Critique), which is attributed to Hamza bin Ali, one of the most important interpreters and founders of the Druze dogma. He says:

> There is no God but God [*la ilah illa al-lah*]: two words, four chapters, seven paragraphs, and twelve letters. The two words signify 'mind' and 'soul', the chapters signify the four 'interpreters', the paragraphs signify the seven 'speakers' [*nutaqa*], who are Adam, Noah, Abraham, Moses, Jesus, Muhammad and Muhammad bin Isma'il, as well as the seven heavens, skies, earths, mountains, and so on.

How the Qur'anic text, 'There is no God but God', came to symbolize the mind, the soul, the interpreters of religion, the prophets, the skies, the mountains, the heavens, and so on, is private knowledge and obviously cannot be communicated publicly to the outside world. Cosmic unity is established through the classification of creatures and features into sets of sevens whose meaning is necessarily implicit.

The Alawis, on the other hand, try to establish the 'unity of the cosmos' through a system of free substitution or transformation, again based on esoteric meanings of Qur'anic texts. They divide the verses into two types: those with *muhakkamat* (explicit meanings) and those with *mutashabihat* (implicit meanings). Al-Tawil (1966:197) says that 'every verse whose meaning is not obviously real or metaphorically clear carries an implicit meaning'. Not all verses that have implicit meanings are interpreted in a controversial way. Some, such as 20/5: 'The Most Gracious [God] is firmly established on the throne', or 48/10: 'Verily those who plight their fealty to thee do no less than plight their fealty to God: the hand of God is over their hands', are interpreted in the same way by all Islamic groups. God does not sit on thrones: it is the 'throne' of authority. He has no hands: it is the hand of power.

There are other controversial verses, however, which the Sunni see as having explicit meanings and the Alawis implicit meanings. Most, if not all, of these verses centre around the position of the Holy House of Ali in religion. Take, for example, 67/5: 'And we have adorned the lowest heaven with Lamps, and we have made such [Lamps] missiles to drive away the evil ones . . .' or 67/3: 'He who created the seven heavens one above the other . . .' These are subject to controversial interpretations.

The Alawis do not interpret such referents as 'lamps', heavens' or 'missiles' metaphorically, as the Sunni do, but rather as implicit indicators to the House of Ali where the one is organically transformed to become the other. In his book on the Alawis, Shaikh Ali Ibrahim al-Alawi (1972:227–31) says that 'there are no less than 300 words or phrases that refer to Imam Ali in the Qur'an'. These include the phrase 'a Witness from Himself' as cited in 11/17, or 'the Great News' in 78/2. Indeed, a good deal of religious discourse among the Alawis centres on implicit interpretations of such Qur'anic verses, so much so that the word *ilm* (religious studies) is used basically to refer to studies that specialize in the House of Ali, 'the People of the House'.[5]

The Stratified View of Religion: the Alawis

The synthetic and the stratified views of religion are closely interlinked: one derives from the other. The belief that religions have been revealed to man in stages, depending upon man's readiness to appreciate and accept the divine message, implies that some are readier to receive the divine message than others. Hence the stratified view of religion. The Alawis believe that the final manifestation of divinity took place through Imam Ali, and the Druzes through the Fatimid caliph al-Hakim. They were the first to respond to the last divine call. Although the Druzes and the Alawis agree in understanding the concept of revelation by stages, they disagree as to the contents of these stages, especially the last stage, the focal point.

The concept of stages, which is originally an Isma'ili concept (al-Aiyash, n.d), implies that revelation takes place through divine manifestation, which in turn appears to man in a dual form: first, through the *rasul* (messenger or speaker), and, second, through the *asas* (base or foundation) in whom divinity is manifested. For every messenger there is a 'base': Habil was the base of the messenger Adam, Sam of Noah, Isma'il of Abraham, Harun of Moses, Sham'un al-Safa of Jesus, and Ali of Muhammad. This means that Ali and his House are the last in whom 'the will of God' or, as al-Tawil (1966:183) puts it, 'the source of the will of God', has been manifested.

It is in this special position occupied in religion by Ali and his House, and in the special role they play in Islam, that the uniqueness of the Alawi dogma lies. The Alawis believe that this special position has been allocated to Ali and the People of the House in accordance with 33/33:

> And God only wishes to remove all abomination from you, ye the People of the House [members of the family] and to make you spiritually pure.

Thus, the People of the House, including Fatima, the Prophet's daughter, and Salman al-Farsi,[6] are the source of manifestation of God's will and in this sense 'they are infallible in their words, deeds and intention' (al-Tawil, 1966:182).

The literature on the Alawis is divided on this issue. Some, especially the non-Alawis writing on the sect, such as Druzah, Shak'a and H. Uthman (1980), place the Alawis among the Isma'ili branches, whereas Alawi writers such as al-Alawi (1972), Salih, al-Sharif (1961) and al-Tawil (1966) always seek Shi'a affiliation. The journal *al-Nahda*, published in the late 1930s during the rise of the Alawi state in northern Syria, contained many articles written by Alawi scholars supporting the second view. Under the title 'The Awakening of the Alawis', Abdul-Rahman Khair says:

> They are Nusairis as they were called before, and Alawis as they were called during the French Mandate, but they are true Arabs, Muslims who believe in the infallibility of imams.[7]

In fact, al-Tawil uses the terms Alawi, Shi'i (a Shi'a individual) and Nusairi interchangeably. It is not easy to assign the Alawis to any particular tradition since they seem to depend upon Shi'a sources for legal action, on Isma'ili sources for organization, and on both for some of their beliefs.

What matters is the way these diverse elements combine in a harmonious, communicable religious ideology, irrespective of the varied origins of its constituent parts. The Alawis are unique among Islamic sects in entrusting Ali and the People of the House with a religious role almost equivalent to the role of the holy books. This is evidenced by the insistence that religious studies be confined to the People of the House, who set forth the style of Islamic conduct, rules and obligations. The Alawis agree with the Shi'a that religion has been perfected through the delegation of the imamate to Ali and his descendants after him, but they disagree with them on the scale of perfection. Al-Tawil (1966:75) says, 'At the time that religion was declared perfect, a fraction of it was deliberately concealed until the present day for its privacy.' He adds,

'The concealment of that fraction of religion itself amounts to part of its perfection.'

In this connection, al-Tawil goes on to relate the following anecdote:

> When the Prophet was called upon to meet the face of his God, he gathered his family and supporters around him and said, 'Bring me a pen and some ink, I want to write for you a text after which you will never be [religiously] lost.' Those whose hearts were full of hatred towards Ali thought he was going to further endorse Ali's right to the caliphate and therefore intervened to prevent him from completing his will—the will that would have otherwise truly perfected religion (al-Tawil, 1966:76).

The Shi'a in general, and the Alawis in particular, think that religion can only be perfected by the completion of the 'will' which God has ordained. This is so because the will itself is part and parcel of the entire divine message, Islam.

The Alawis, however, believe that the will was concealed from the common Muslim masses, but not from the People of the House, Ali and his descendants, which means that religion can only be perfected by focusing on the studies of the People of the House. They make a clear distinction between the prophet and the imam: the first is a 'speaker' who delivers the message as dictated by God through the Archangel Gabriel; but the second is a 'base' who is a direct 'source of divine will' as such, without 'inspiration or intermediation—his words, deeds and intentions correspond exactly to God's will' (al-Tawil, 1966:183). If so, it follows that the imam is infallible and his understanding of the Qur'an is in total agreement with God's will. According to the Alawis, this role of the imam is what is meant by 36/12:

> Verily we shall give life to the dead, and we record that which they send before, and that which they leave behind, and of all things we have taken account in a visible imam.

The will that perfects religion was imparted to each of the People of the House individually, every one of whom passed it on to his infallible progeny until the Twelfth Imam. Afterwards, the main constitution of the will was entrusted to 'the very select' among the believers in the Alawi way, who themselves constitute 'the very select among the

Muslims' (al-Tawil, 1966:77). In other words, of all the Muslims, the Alawis are called upon to know, or be 'entrusted' with, the knowledge of what is concealed of religion; this knowing itself perfects religion. Just as Ali and his House were 'selected' to know the 'perfected message', so the Alawis are 'selected' to specialize in the studies of the People of the House—a discipline that perfects religion.

It can be deduced from the preceding discussion that the sovereignty of the Alawi community is based on two formulations. First, a gradation of religious knowledge begins with the manifest and the explicit, and ends with the latent, the implicit and the concealed which perfects religion. Second, it is the Alawis who are called upon to know the 'perfected message', in this case religion or Islam, through the studies of the People of the House.

The issue is much more complex than it sounds. The belief in the concealment of the (perfected) religion is an act of faith, a religious given, which must be continuously sought; it is a perpetual religious demand or practice. The term 'concealment' here also means sacrament, divine privacy or secret, or even divine existence as exemplified in the People of the House, the imams. This presents a puzzle, however, since the line of imams was terminated with Muhammad al-Mahdi, the Twelfth Imam, which means that the sources of divine will have disappeared. But the Alawis believe that the disappearance of the imam could not possibly prevent the faithful from seeking to know what is concealed, otherwise religion would remain indefinitely imperfect, leaving the world in perpetual chaos. Knowledge of the concealed continues through the *bab* (door), who instructs people in what is to be known, followed and believed.

The Alawis believe that every imam has a 'door' according to the *hadith* related to the Prophet: 'I am the city of religious knowledge and Ali is its door', or another *hadith* which stresses: 'Whoever seeks religious knowledge, he has to rely upon the door.'[8] Seeking to know the concealed part of religion is therefore allowed through the continuity of the 'doors' of knowledge in human society. It is believed that Muhammad bin Nusair was the 'door' of the Eleventh Imam, Hasan al-Askari, and continued in this capacity during the reign of the Hidden Twelfth Imam, Muhammad al-Mahdi, the Timeless.

The 'door', who assures the faithful of the continuity of the search for religious knowledge, is not a source of divine will, as is the imam, but is an *alim* (learned person) who comes next to the Prophet in religious hierarchy. The 'doors', often referred to in the literature as 'the heirs of prophets', perform the same role as the imams without having a divine quality. Here, the position of the 'door' is equivalent to the position of the top religious shaikhs, and in this capacity the role continues from one generation to another. Sometimes they operate in the open and sometimes they are hidden, depending upon the prevailing political circumstances. Following the death of Muhammad bin Nusair, many 'doors' or *sayyids* came to lead the Alawi community, the most famous of whom include Sayyid Abdullah bin Muhammad al-Junbulani who established a special order known among the Alawis as the Junbulaniya, or Sayyid Husain bin Hamdan al-Khusaibi who wrote the famous book *al-Hidaya al-Kubra* (The Great Guidance). The Ala'wi sources say that al-Khusaibi was born in 873, the very day Imam al-Askari died, and died in 957 in Aleppo. His shrine is frequently visited by the faithful today.

After al-Khusaibi, the Alawi community was fragmented into various movements and orders, each faction following its own 'door' or *sayyid*. In the meantime, the Ishaqiya order had arisen, but it was destroyed around the eleventh century by Hasan al-Makzun al-Sinjari. In this era, Sayyid Srur bin Qasim al-Tabarani also appeared in Latakiya, leading the Junbulaniya faction. His revered shrine is today located in the Sha'rani Mosque on the Latakiya coast. To these historic figures the Alawis add a long list of newly established leaders including Ibrahim al-Adham, al-Hajj M'alla, Shaikh Yusuf Hayy, Shaikh Ghanim Yassin, Shaikh Mustapha Mirhij, Shaikh Ahmad al-Shaikh and many others who have had a far-reaching influence in the field of religious interpretation.

In summary, four points must be stressed. First, the rise of 'doors', *sayyids* or 'men of knowledge' is a continuous process in Alawi society—the last to emerge were Shaikh Ahmad al-Jazri in Balqizia village in Syria and Shaikh Umran in Tripoli (Lebanon) in the 1940s and 1950s. Wherever the Alawis settle, there arises an enshrined shaikh, following the dictum, 'God manifests himself in the weakest of his creatures.'

Second, the rise of these *ulama* or shaikhs is a clear witness to the continuity of divine manifestation in human society. This is commonly referred to among the Alawis as *zuhur* (the manifest [divine] reality, the personification of divinity). *Zuhur* may come up after death through the performance of miracles such as healing the sick, fulfilling the wishes of the faithful or injuring those who meddle with holy shrines. It may also show in 'persons' who unite the Alawis and establish their supremacy, which is what Sulaiman al-Murshid did in the late 1930s and early 1940s.

Many Alawis, known today as the Murshidiya, thought he was the 'divine manifestation' *par excellence* and dealt with him on this assumption.

Third, only through the continuity of divine manifestation is the knowledge of the 'concealed', which perfects religion, assured. Otherwise, religion remains imperfect, in which case chaos prevails in the cosmos.

Fourth, the Alawis strive to know the 'concealed' part of religion, the sacramental, in order to perfect religion, not to be 'secretive' about it, as many outsiders believe. The Alawis hold that their search for divine reality is a private practice which they alone are called upon to engage in: hence their self-image of being the 'select' Muslims. Many of these beliefs have a significant bearing upon Alawi religious organization, as will be shown later.

The Stratified View of Religion: the Druzes

As mentioned earlier, the sects which broke away from the Isma'ili tradition, including the Druzes, are alike in their synthetic view of religion and the gradation of religious knowledge, which they express in the concept of cyclic revelations. As also mentioned, these similarities do not go beyond general frameworks, the formal skeletons of religious activity. The contents, which make up the autonomous structure of the religious personality, are different, each sect believing it is the last to be called upon to accept the divine message and conclude the last covenant with God. While acknowledging the 'occurrence' of previous 'divine messages', every sect places itself at the top of the scale of revelation. In this latter part of the system lies the image of sovereignty of the religious community.

The Druze dogma or ideology is not easy to deal with, for two reasons: first, the multiplicity of sources from which their ideology has been drawn; and second, their belief that *tawhid* (high religious knowledge) is only privately acquired and therefore cannot be communicated to the outside world. In his book, *The Druze Faith*, Makarem (1974:100), under the heading 'The Necessity of Keeping Divine Knowledge Secret', writes:

> Once filled with the feeling of his oneness with God, a famous mystic, al-Hallaj, is said to have exclaimed, 'I am Truth.' Being unprepared for this knowledge, those who heard him speak in such a way accused him of blasphemy. Al-Hallaj was beheaded. Seeing this, other mystics

> reproached him for having divulged a secret which his listeners and those who executed him were not prepared to understand. He betrayed the secret of his God by proclaiming to all and sundry the supreme mystery which ought to be reserved for the elect.
>
> He also caused his executioners to commit the sin of murder and to do injustice to truth itself. Had al-Hallaj not divulged this truth he would have spared both his head and the sin of those who killed him.

Makarem adds:

> Scripture must be protected from those who do not deserve it.

On the evidence of the available sources,[9] the Druze religious ideology seems to fall into two main formulas: the concept of cycles and the structure of meanings. Except for some mild modifications, the concept of cycles is essentially Isma'ili in origin. Much like the Alawis, the Isma'ilis believe that Semitic religions have been revealed to man in stages depending upon his readiness to understand and accept them, the last stage being the seventh, that of Muhammad bin Isma'il. They also see revelation taking place through a duality composed of the speaker or proclaimer and the base or foundation. The first represents the explicit and the visible, the second the implicit and invisible. In assigning these roles to prophets and imams they follow more or less the pattern mentioned earlier. There is some disagreement among the sources, however. Whereas Makarem, for example, cites Ali as the 'base' of Muhammad, al-Najjar places Salman al-Farsi in this position.[10]

According to the Druzes, these cycles are hierarchically arranged in evolutionary stages, in the sense that each one follows from the other. The attainment of one stage necessarily requires the passing of the preceding stage, which means that those who are at the top (the last *tawhid* stage) have passed through all the other stages (Makarem, 1974:71). The Druzes claim that they have attained the last stage, and therefore they are an ancient people, 'the People of Tawhid'.

The belief that revelation came about in stages, and that those who have attained the highest position on the scale have passed through all the stages, necessarily and logically leads to a belief in reincarnation and the limited number of souls. Through reincarnation souls pass through all the stages of revelation, and to do so they have to be the same souls—in other words, limited in number. According to al-Dhubyani (1967:90) 'the recurrence of souls again and again has made the children of today more knowledgeable than yesterday's children'. Al-Najjar (1965:57) adds, 'The recurrence of the same personality-soul in different bodies results in the accumulation of spiritual experience.' In support of these views, the Druzes frequently resort to the Qur'an and sometimes to the Bible. According to al-Dhubyani (1967:43), for example, reincarnation is implied in the Qur'an, 2/28:

> How can ye deny God! You were dead and He gave you life, then He will cause you to die, and will again bring you to life, and again to Him will ye return.

And a limited number of souls is what is meant by 19/94:

> He [God] hath taken count of them all, and hath exactly numbered them all.

Or as it recurs in the Bible (Matt.10:30; Luke 12:7):

> The very hairs of your head are all numbered.

In brief, the Druzes believe that human society is composed of souls which are reincarnated, and in the course of their recurrence souls evolve from one stage of divine knowledge to another. In every stage, man experiences divine reality depending upon his *kathafa* (corporeality) and the extent of his purity. 'God reveals himself to man according to man's capacity.'[11] Divinity cannot be perceived by the human mind as such; it is beyond nature, beyond time and place. Divinity exposes itself (*takshif*, from *kashf*) to man according to his readiness. If this is so, different religions represent different stages in the evolution of man's knowledge of divinity, much like 'mirrors' reflecting the advancement of man's knowledge of 'divine light'. Man's knowledge of divinity evolves through stages beginning with the seven legal doctrines, from Adam to Muhammad bin Isma'il, and ending with the doctrine of *tawhid*, the last stage of divine knowledge. Some Druzes, such as al-Najjar (1965:94) for example, go even further and specify the number of years covered by each stage.

However, the coming of one stage (a new religion) does not eliminate that which precedes it: the latest being the closest to the realization of divine knowledge. The last to appear was the *tawhid* stage 'realized' in the evening of 1 Muharram, 408 AH (1017 AD). The Druzes believe that the lapse of time separating the stage of Muhammad bin Isma'il (when the legal doctrines were completed) from realization of *tawhid* knowledge was a period of preparation.

What concerns us in this work is the last stage of *tawhid* knowledge, wherein lies the issue of sovereignty of the religious community among the Druzes. According to Makarem (1974:82), the knowledge of divinity has:

> passed through three stages: direct revelation or divine instruction (*tanzil*), allegorical interpretation (*ta'wil*), and *tawhid*. Direct revelation or instruction concerns itself with the exoteric, the explicit and visible and is carried out through speakers and messengers. It focuses on the legal aspects of religion, divine law, the public policy. Interpretation, on the other hand, focuses on the esoteric, the implicit and invisible and is carried out through bases and the imams. It concentrates on faith and the inner convictions. The last stage, *tawhid*, leads to the true knowledge of divinity through direct 'exposition' or 'manifestation' (*tajalli*); this, however, occurs to only the few select, those who were ready for it [i.e. the Druzes, the 'People of Tawhid Knowledge'].

Thus, Makarem (1974:77) says:

> After more than four hundred years since the advent of Islam, and a little more than one millennium since the birth of Christ, the knowledge of God's unity was finally revealed.

He adds (1974:77):

> Now a man no longer was obliged to observe the rituals of Islam (the legal doctrine), taught al-Hakim, because Islam now reached the utmost reality, i.e. *tawhid*. For instance, praying five times a day developed into prayer as a constant state of being. The Divine Message also was freed from the figurative treatment behind thick curtains of material and superficial forms.

Clearly, the concepts of 'revelation', 'interpretation' and *tawhid*, as mentioned in these contexts, imply progressive stages in the search for the knowledge of divinity. *Tawhid* knowledge is a form of 'mental awareness' of divine reality, and as such it goes far beyond legal codes, forms of worship or rituals. Makarem (1974:90–1) says:

> After the true believers were being nourished by the literal meaning of the divine message and then by its implied meaning through allegorically interpreting the religious law, the time has come to divulge *tawhid* as such, i.e. the true knowledge of God's unity.

Makarem goes on to explain the manifest, the latent and the *tawhid* meanings of each of the five pillars of Islam—testimony, prayer, *zakat* (alms), fasting, pilgrimage and the holy war—while comparing them with the seven pillars of the Druze faith.[12]

Space does not allow a detailed exposition of these treaties. As an illustration, let us turn to what Makarem (1974:101–2) says about fasting:

> From the exoteric point of view, fasting entails abstaining from eating, drinking or coitus. As for the inner meaning (esoteric), it came to be abstaining from divulging the inner meaning of the divine message to people who cannot understand it, that is to the people who only adhere to the apparent meaning of the Qur'an.
>
> But the real (*tawhid*) meaning of fasting aims at man's realizing himself in the unity of God.

In his explanation, Makarem (1974:101–2) relies upon the writings of Hamza bin Ali, who taught that 'fasting is the avoidance of those beliefs that deny existence, which subsequently lead to the commitment of fallacies and sins'. Likewise, it is related that al-Muqtana Baha al-Din, one of the five main interpreters of the Druze religion, said, 'The belief in unexistence denies existence, which leads to blasphemy.'

According to al-Khatib, the Druzes are an ancient people who have evolved through reincarnation until they have reached the final stage of knowledge of divinity—*tawhid*. In the Druze literature, *tawhid* is referred to as 'the last exposition' [of divinity] which took place on Thursday, 1 Muharram, 408 AH (1017 AD). This is the first time in the history of religion that the 'last [divine] call' has been exposed to those who were ready for it. In 409 AH (1018 AD), the door of the divine call was closed for the first time, and opened again after about one year, this time on a Friday, 1 Muharram. It was then closed down for good on 27 Shawwal,

411 AH (1020 AD), the time that al-Hakim disappeared. Those who were (spiritually) ready to receive the 'call' responded favourably to it—they are 'the People of Tawhid Knowledge', the Druzes. Others who were not ready for the call ignored it. And since the door of 'accepting the call' was closed for good, they have lost the privilege for ever.

Although the Druzes as a whole are distinguished from other religious communities by having accepted the last call for which they were spiritually ready, they seek divine knowledge, each according to his own capacity or 'corporeality'. The Druzes are a highly stratified community, as will be seen in the discussion of Druze religious organization (see Chapter 15).

10
The Survival Society: the Yazidis

The title 'survival society' is intended to highlight the fact that the Yazidis (and the Maronites, see Chapter 11) belong to religious traditions preceding Islam. The word 'survival' implies continuity, endurance and steadfastness. The Maronites are Christians who split from the Byzantine Orthodox Church towards the latter part of the fourth century, two and a half centuries before the rise of Islam in Arabia. The Yazidis, on the other hand, emerged after the rise of Islam, but their religious dogma combines various elements drawn from ancient Semitic and Persian religious beliefs. According to Menzel, the Yazidis have taken the concept of the duality of good and bad from the ancient Manichaeans; some food taboos from Judaism; baptism, the Last Supper and the use of wine in rituals from the Christian Nestorians; and fasting, circumcision, pilgrimage and Adha festivities from Islam. Likewise, they have taken from some Islamic Sufi orders the tendency to consider religion a private practice and visiting the shrines of holy men regularly. From the Sabaeans they have taken the concept of reincarnation, and from the Babylonians certain funeral rights, divination techniques and ritual dances.[1]

The Yazidis, however, do not acknowledge the religious elements they share with others or have taken from existing religious traditions. They consider themselves sovereign and unique in their theory of creation, their view of the cosmic order and their religious practices and taboos. In this respect they differ from the Maronites, who consider themselves part of a wider and more universal religious order, the Catholic Church. The image of sectarian sovereignty among the Maronites is not drawn from a unique religious dogma so much as from assigning to themselves and

Lebanon, the land they live in, a unique religious and historical role. The Yazidis will be described in this chapter and the Maronites in the next.

The Society of Angels: the Yazidis

The Yazidis believe that they are a very ancient people whom God alone created through Adam, whereas the rest of the human world was created from Adam and Eve. They trace this special creation genealogically through Sheeth, Anush and Noah during the First Flood, and through Miran in the Second. Unlike other peoples who are descended from Ham bin Noah during the First Flood, the Yazidis believe they are descended from Miran bin Sam bin Noah in the Second Flood. The myth of special creation among the Yazidis is part of the more universal view of the cosmos detailed in their two holy books, *Kitab al-Jilwa* (The Book of Manifestation) and *Mishaf Rash* (which means The Black Book in Persian). The first treats divinity and the arrangement of the universe including creatures and souls, while the second deals with the genealogical strains of mankind.[2] The Yazidis further believe that God spoke to Adam and the angels in Kurdish, which suggests that they were meant to be the receivers of these divine messages.

In brief, the Yazidis hold that God created the world in seven stages, exemplified by seven angels who were created successively in seven days, and then he authorized each angel to rule, in harmony with other angels, over a particular group of creatures. On the first day, Sunday, he created the angel Azaz'il, and not the satan Azra'il as some Sunni sources such as Azzawi and Taymur (1347 AH:4) have it. Azaz'il is embodied in the angel Peacock (*tawuss*) whom God appointed to be the head of the angels, responsible for the conduct of the world, good or bad. On the second day, Monday, he created the angel Yuda'il, then Israfil, Mika'il, Jibra'il, Shimna'il, and lastly on Saturday, Nura'il. These angels came from divinity itself, and they were made to rule over the world successively, each for a thousand years. It is worth noting here that the peacock was used in many ancient Sumerian religions to signify the sun, which in turn stood for continuity and survival. In their rituals the Yazidis still use many statuettes representing the peacock, the highest authority among the world of angels.

The angels do not exist in isolation; they reincarnate and blend in human bodies from generation to generation, thus forming an inseparable unity between personality and soul. The soul of every angel is blended with the personality of the Yazidi chiefs who combine religious and mundane authority. In this manner, the soul of the angel Peacock had blended with Shaikh Adi bin Musafir, one of the renowned Sufi leaders of the seventh century, and the soul of the angel Yuda'il with Shaikh Hasan, Israfil's with Shaikh Shamsuddin, Mika'il's with Shaikh Abu-Bakr, Jibra'il's with Shaikh Sirajuddin, Shimna'il's with Shaikh Nasruddin and Nura'il's with Fakhruddin.

The cosmos of the Yazidis is made up of angels who succeed one another in the government of the universe; as such, the Yazidis seem to be, if anything, 'angel worshippers', rather than 'devil worshippers', as many sources have dubbed them.[3] It is possible that the confusion over what kind of worshippers they are has arisen from the dual role played by the angel Peacock. Being the head of the angels, he may leave paradise and return to it any time he wants, sometimes taking the form of a snake or scorpion, or any other creature (Jule, 1934:78). On earth he assumes responsibility for the good and the bad that happens. The Yazidis believe neither in a paradise where the righteous live for ever, nor in a hell where the sinful are burned. Theirs is a world which continuously oscillates between good and evil, both under the command of the angel Peacock. The angel Peacock, therefore, while fostering the good, could likewise cause evil. According to Yazidi myths, the angel Peacock repented so deeply for the evil he had caused in the world that he wept for seven thousand years until he filled seven jars, and his tears were used to put out the flames of hell for ever.

The Yazidis see themselves as part of a universe where the souls of angels and men blend together, one taking on the form of the other in a unique combination, eliminating none. This integration appears in the names of the seven chiefs who represent the seven dominions that make up the Yazidi land. The seven dominions correspond to the seven angels who rule the seven regions of the world, as well as to the seven shaikhs who were transformed into angels through reincarnation. The most notable among these shaikhs are Shaikhs Dawud, Shamsuddin, Yazid bin Mu'awiya, Adi bin Musafir, Hasan al-Basri and al-Hallaj.[4]

Shaikh Adi bin Musafir, whose soul mingled with the angel Peacock, occupies the highest position in the hierarchy and assumes a central role in Yazidi rituals. Because of this, it is strange that the sect are called Yazidis after Yazid bin Mu'awiya, the founder of the Umayyad dynasty. Yazid has no special place in their religious thinking, and in fact they do not call themselves Yazidis. They call themselves al-Dawasin or al-Dawashin, and the Yazid they recognize seems to have been a Sufi practitioner, not a dynastic figure. While recognizing the term Yazidis, they, like many other sects in Islam, trace their origin to the Qur'an, 19/76: 'And God doth enhance [*yazid*] the guidance of those who seek guidance.' They were perhaps called Yazidis simply because they first appeared as a distinct group following Adi bin Musafir during the reign of Yazid bin Mu'awiya.

Through reincarnation and transmigration, Adi became the angel Peacock, whom God entrusted with command of the universe. The Yazidis believe that God created the world and left its management to the angels headed by the angel Peacock. To this day, most of the Yazidis' rituals focus on the angel Peacock, as exemplified in Adi bin Musafir and his descendants. Today, all the *ulama* among the Yazidis claim descent either directly from Adi bin Musafir or indirectly from Hasan al-Basri, whose essence blended with Adi's through the transfer of souls. These include the families of Shaikhs Hasan and Fakhruddin who live in the villages of Ba'ashqiya and Bahzani in the Sinjar area of Iraq; the Fakhruddin family has a monopoly of '*baba-shaikh*', the highest position in the religious hierarchy (al-Dimluji, 1949:42). They also include the family of Sharafuddin, who provide the line of 'imams', those who act as first-hand assistants to *baba-shaikh*, as well as many other families such as the Sajjadin, Amadin, Nasruddin, Shamsa, Abi Bakr and Mand who hold high religious titles and positions in the land.

The fact that the descendants of Adi bin Musafir control the highest religious positions has not prevented other families from having a religious role. Indeed, Yazidi society is made up of various family strains, each controlling a religious function of a kind. It is a rigidly stratified society. At the top of the hierarchy stands a group known as the *birat* (literally, the old men), who are responsible for the spiritual guidance of the community. This is followed by the *fuqara* (the poor), who seek solitude in order to sustain the values of the society. Next in order come the *qawwalin* who chant religious hymns, the *kowjak* who collect the *zakat* tax and supervise religious performance, and finally the common Yazidi worshippers.

What makes the Yazidi community unique, however, is the belief that through reincarnation and the transfer of souls, the angels become exemplified in particular family strains on earth, and thus penetrate deep into Yazidi society, blend with people and act with and upon them. Yazidi society is seen as continuously under angelic, divine surveillance, which may explain the intensity and richness of their ritualistic life, as will be shown later (Chapter 14). In brief, they are an extension of God's 'special creation'—a fact that is continuously assured by the free communication between man and deity.

11
Lebanon, the Unique Identity: the Maronites

The concept of sovereignty among Islamic sects is essentially based on religious dogma. Each sect believes that it has a special arrangement with God; and as such, it contains 'the people' chosen to execute God's will or message on earth. The Sunni hold that they execute the contents of the divine message through the establishment of a centralized state authority, the Ibadis and the Zaidis through the intermittent rise of the state of religion at the hands of the imam (the hero), the Shi'a through perpetual movement and rebellion awaiting the coming of the Hidden Imam (the martyr), the Druzes and the Alawis through the continuity of divine manifestation or exposition and the Yazidis through special creation and the transfer of souls between man and angels. By contrast, the Maronites do not draw their notion of sovereignty from a unique dogma so much as from the distinct politico-religious role they play in Lebanon, the divine country. The Maronites and Lebanon combine, so to speak, through a complex process of ritualization, to become a single religious phenomenon.

The Maronites are part of the Catholic Church headed by the Pope based at the Vatican. This has been so since 1215, when they began a special relationship with Rome—a relationship that did not deprive them of a measure of autonomy in their internal affairs.

Although the Maronites' image of sovereignty is not derived from a complete and consistent religious dogma, it is nevertheless fashioned from religiously based criteria. Since the thirteenth century, the Maronites have developed a unique religious and national personality based on three interrelated factors. First, they consider themselves (and are now considered by others, especially the Vatican) to be a symbol of

Christian resistance and steadfastness in the Near East, the birthplace of Christianity, the Holy Land. Second, there is a 'mental merger' between this form of continuity and Lebanon, the 'unique identity'. And third, they enjoy a certain autonomy in administrating some of their religious affairs independently of the Vatican.

Of the large number of Christian Churches in the Islamic world, only the Maronites have adopted an ideology of resistance. The difference between 'continuity' and 'resistance' here is very clear. Many a Christian Church in the Arab world today considers itself a continuation of an ancient, pre-Islamic civilization. The Nestorians, for example, believe they are the descendants of the Assyrians; the Copts, the descendants of the Pharaohs of Egypt; the Maronites, the descendants of the Phoenicians. Many of these Churches hold that they were able to survive the Islamic tempest by the strength of faith and/or Islamic tolerance. But none believes, as the Maronites do, that they survived because of their resistance to religious oppression. Their view of themselves in history, beginning with Mar Marun, the founder of the Maronite Church in the first part of the fifth century, and ending with the achievement of Lebanese independence in 1943, reflects this ideology of resistance. They express it by referring to Lebanon as the 'bronze fortress' or the 'shielded castle' (al-Sawda, 1979:153).

From this historical perspective, there emerge two identities: the Maronite identity and the Lebanese identity. The two soon merge into one, however: 'the Sons of Marun', the group, are transformed into 'the House of Marun', the land (Daw, 1978:13). Just as the Maronite identity concentrates on a history of struggle for survival, the Lebanese identity concentrates on an ancient civilization 'invading the world'.[1] The history of the struggle for survival covers a long period of time stretching from the fifth century until the present day. It includes the formation of the Maronite community in the Asi River basin in Syria and their concurrent spread in Homs, Hama and Aleppo (and even as far as the town of Tikrit in Iraq) and then their gradual mass migration and settlement on Mount Lebanon from the end of the seventh century (Vaumas, 1955:516). It must be stressed that mass migration among Arabs, including the Palestinians today, is always seen as a form of resistance to external aggression or oppression, the idea being that the hardships of migration are compensated for by the achievement of group sovereignty.

The internalization of resistance as an instrument of survival in the history of the Maronites has led them to focus on particular eras during which they were able to achieve the ideal they stood for. The history of their struggle is enriched by a series of affective events that succeed one another in time. The group's image of history matters much more here than the bare facts of historiography. The Maronites see their origin among the Marada, who began to settle in Lebanon around 671, as well as in the rise of the Ma'ni and Shihabi Emirates, followed ultimately by Lebanese independence. Maronite sources such as Dibs (1905: 41–7) and Duwaihi (1890:186) argue that the Marada were themselves the Maronites who had often and successfully challenged the Islamic conquest and managed to keep their Christian identity. Other sources relate the origin of the Marada to a 'heretical' group who split from Orthodoxy following their disagreement with the Byzantine emperor Justinian II, al-Akhram.[2] None of the Maronite historians, whom Harik (1982:99–112) calls 'the founders of the Maronite ideology', ever questions the Marada origin of the Maronites.[3] The term Marada, meaning 'the rebels', is an attractive origin for a community that made resistance an instrument of survival and continuity. Even today, during the Lebanese war of 1975–89, the Maronite fighters of the north chose to call themselves 'the Marada'—a label which, while paying tribute to the past, aims to establish or maintain a sovereign future.

After the Maronites had passed through the Marada episode towards the end of the seventh century, they began a new era of struggle, the mass migration from the Asi basin in Syria to Mount Lebanon in search of religious freedom. The hero of this era of migration and settlement was Yuhanna Marun, who was consecrated bishop of Byblos in 677 and then became Patriarch of the Maronite Church in 702 (Hayek, 1964:24). Once their migration to Lebanon was complete (between the eighth and ninth centuries), they quietly settled down in the mountains until the coming of the Crusades in the eleventh century; at which time the Maronites began to be incorporated into the Catholic Church.

This process of incorporation has had a significant bearing on the Maronites' self-image. Since then they have regarded themselves, and are regarded especially by the Vatican, as the symbol of continuity of Catholicism in the Orient. This is the time when Pope Leo X (1513–21) coined the phrase 'flowers among thorns' to designate the Maronites and their environment. The new relationship with Rome was so effective in helping the Maronites reorganize their Church and monastic orders that it has been truly called 'the era of reformation'.[4] The monastic orders came to assume a leading role in education and agricultural modernization in, for example, land reclamation, silk production, printing houses, and free schools especially for the poor.

The era of reformation was a formative period during which the identity of the Maronites as an enlightened community became apparent. The foundation of the Maronite School at the Vatican, and subsequently the spread of formal education among the Maronites in Lebanon, produced an intelligentsia whose writings have considerably enriched Arabic language and literature. It is not surprising that Lebanon came to be known at this time as 'the land of light'. The Maronites' role in education was paralleled by their role in economic innovation. The introduction of silk-making linked Lebanon with international markets, and the cash flowing therefrom made it possible to establish the semi-autonomous regimes which Lebanon had within the Ottoman Empire, namely, the Ma'nis (1591–1697), the Shihabis (1697–1842), the two Qa'im-maqamiyat (1843–60) (an administrative unit) and the Mutasarrifiya (1860–1915). The first two emirates were achieved through a Druze-Maronite reconciliation in which the Druzes had a leading role in politics and the Maronites in administration and commerce.

The continuous interaction between the Maronites and the wider Catholic world created a unique position for the former within the Ottoman Empire. The Maronites were the only Christian Church who refused to join the 'millet system' established by the Ottomans to control and monitor the empire's non-Muslim subjects. They were outstandingly successful in managing their affairs with such a great measure of freedom from the Sublime Porte.

The interaction between the Maronites and the Catholic world encouraged mass emigration among the Lebanese. Through this special relationship with Catholic Europe, especially France, the Lebanese Maronites, later followed by other confessional groups, began to emigrate in large numbers to West Africa and the New World. At the turn of the nineteenth century, the port of Marseilles on the south coast of France had become a major station for Lebanese emigrants seeking their fortunes. They seem to have gone first to the French colonies in the Caribbean and from there to West Africa and Latin America. These waves of emigration, which reached a climax before and immediately after the First World War, were partly responsible for the 'return to Phoenician roots', a political ideology that appears mainly to have attracted the Lebanese Maronites.

These factors—a tradition of interaction with the West, relative economic relaxation, emigration and a well-organized Church and monastic orders—encouraged the Maronites to see themselves as a 'distinct nation'. From here, the idea of seeking Phoenician roots and bestowing upon Lebanon a touch of divinity began to take shape. According to Harik (1982:110), Tannus al-Shidyaq (1794–1861) was 'the first to introduce the idea of Phoenician origin in his search for a Lebanese national identity'. It is no coincidence, however, that al-Shidyaq was writing about the Phoenician origin of the Lebanese towards the middle of the nineteenth century—the century that witnessed the rise of nationalism in Europe and a deep concern with the origin of Christian civilization. This concern had led many European scholars to re-examine the contents of ancient Near Eastern civilizations, including Egypt, Mesopotamia and Phoenicia. The return to Phoenician roots among the Maronites came simply to echo the West's concern with Ashtar, Adonis, Sidon, Tyre, Beirutus, Byblos, Tripoli, Ras Shamra, Arwad, and many other Phoenician gods and sites of this kind.

As a political ideology, the return to Phoenician roots did not receive popular support among the Maronites until the mid-1930s, several years after the foundation of the Republic of Lebanon and the subsequent rise of many opposing political movements calling for (Greater) Syrian or Arab unity. The insistence on a Phoenician origin came as a countermeasure to the insistence on Syrian or Arab origins. At this stage, the Maronites began to transfer their attention from the history of the group's struggle to the unique identity of Lebanon, the divine land. The shift from the one to the other was so spontaneous that it is difficult to distinguish between the 'Lebanization' of the Maronites and the 'Maronitization' of Lebanon. This is reflected in the writings of Daw (1978; 1980) and al-Sawda (1979). According to Daw (1978:13):

> Ethnically the bulk of the Maronites belong to the Lebanese Phoenician tradition. They received the gospel at the hand of St Marun's students who originally came from Syria between the fourth and the sixth centuries AD. The preachers came from Syria, not the people. The people are of Phoenician origin [and have been] living in Lebanon for thousands of years. Many of us confuse the origin of the nation with the origin of the Church. The nation is Lebanese even if the founder of the Church and his students were of Syrian origin.

Moving back and forth between the origin of the nation and the origin of the Church, Lebanon acquired a distinct cultural character, becoming a phenomenological expression that continues uninterrupted in time, and beyond time. It becomes a divine phenomenon that combines the past and the present. Through this process of transformation, the Phoenician Ashtarata, according to Daw (1978:17, 39–50), become 'the Lebanese women who invaded the world and spread the elements of civilization', and 'the Amazonate (the daughters of Ashtarata), who were renowned for chivalry, become a symbol of the women fighters in the Lebanese war of 1975–'.

Lebanon is likewise transformed into the birthplace of religion, humanityand divine messages, even having a message of its own. In describing the way Christ sought refuge in Lebanon, Daw (1980:159) relates:

> Jesus came to Lebanon in order to open the way for his Church and apostles to spread his message amongst the nations of the world exactly as he had done amongst the Jews. His message is universally comprehensive, covering the whole world. To succeed, a comprehensive message like this had to start from Lebanon. The coming of Jesus to Lebanon was meant to reassert the humanitarian message of Lebanon.

Obviously, Lebanon is no longer a geographical or physical given; it has been transformed into a religious image. It is the 'refuge of Christ', the place that 'Christ sought to disseminate his message' in the world. Christ did this in response to Lebanon's call and message, which means that Lebanon is assumed to have a 'call' and a 'message'. On a certain level of analysis, Lebanon seems to be elevated to the rank of prophets and messengers. The same religious images of Lebanon recur in many other places in Daw's writings whereby Lebanon becomes 'the Paradise of Aden in which Adam and Eve, the ancestors of mankind, were born' (1980:287), and Lebanon's Biqa Valley becomes 'the land of the shrines of Adam, Abel, Cain, Noah and Noah's sons' (1980:288–98). Noah becomes a Lebanese and his 'boat is made of the cedars of Lebanon' (1980:322). 'The Cedars Mountain becomes the Mountain of the Lord, the Mountain of divine manifestation' (1980:402–3).

Other Maronite writers convey the same image in different words. In his book, *Maronitism*, Kassab (1980:15–16) says:

> Maronitism coincides with the geographical expanse of the Lebanese culture which is six thousand years old. From it there branched off the three Abrahamic religions: Judaism, Christianity and Islam. Should there be a cause for existence, Lebanon is the cause for the existence of all religions.

Kassab speaks of his book as a 'comedy'; he says that 'the Maronitism' he talks about is a new philosophical approach to life which he learned from the Lebanese philosopher Marun Khoury, a name unknown among the *literati* in Lebanon. According to Kassab, the crux of this philosophy is:

> The belief that the cell/person gives itself up to the [survival] of the whole body/society out of love and loyalty rather than out of a sense of national duty (1980:14).

> It is the fourth theory . . . which is based on love, sacrifice, and unity between person and society, unlike idealism (based on spiritual principles), or materialism (based on natural principles), or the theory of social contract based on rights and duties and subsequently state and law (1980:8–14).

In examining some of these writings—the expressive literature—the intention has not been to learn about the history of the Maronites, but about the Maronites' image of themselves in history, where the sovereignty of a community actually lies. The concept of sovereignty among the Maronites lies in their belief that they are an extension of an old civilization (the Phoenicians) and that Lebanon, their land, is a religious experience rather than simply a geographical expanse. These givens are further enriched by the belief that Lebanon possesses certain qualities which, as Malik (1974:10) puts it, 'define Lebanon in its self'. Of these qualities, Malik (1974:10–11) cites ten:

> The unique mountain, the unique village, the tourist position of Lebanon, its international trade, Lebanese emigration, the Christian-Muslim coexistence, its universal freedom, its openness to the world, the intellectual meaning of Lebanon and Lebanon's role in international affairs.

It is not as important to see these features as actually distinguishing

Lebanon from other neighbouring countries as it is to *believe* that they do. Whoever seeks distinction will somehow find a way to it. Mount Lebanon is no more unique than the Druze Mountain, the Alawi Mountain, the Zaidi Mountains or the Berber Mountains. But what is unique is the *belief* that Mount Lebanon is unique. The same goes for the 'Lebanese village', many of whose features are shared with other rural areas in the Arab world, especially in Palestine, Syria, northern Iraq and the Atlas Mountains of North Africa.

The mental image of Lebanon as a unique creature makes everything in it unique: the Church, the trees, water, snow and skiing. Not to mention dishes such as *kibbi, tabbouli* and *mughrabiyi*. The reverse is also true: those who think that Lebanon is not unique subsequently believe that everything in it is common to Lebanon and its immediate environment.

These ideological givens about Lebanon, the unique identity, are no more than a reflection of the Christian Maronite image of itself as a sovereign community. This sovereignty, in turn, could not possibly have continued were it not for the Maronites' well-organized Church and monastic orders, a topic which is examined in more detail in Chapter 16.

Part Three

The Organization of Sects

12
The Organization of Religion: the Sunni *Ulama*

In writing the preceding chapters on the ideology of religion and sects, two approaches were possible: either to deal with ideology and organization together in relation to each sect, or to deal first with ideology comparatively across sects and then with organization. The second alternative has been chosen in the interests of a comparative approach. The theme is, of course, the same: whereas the Sunni stand for the sovereignty of *shar'* (Islamic jurisdiction) and the state, sects work for the sovereignty of the community. The distinction will become clearer as we examine the organization of religion.

The *Ulama* of Religion in Islam

In his critique of secularization and its protagonists in Lebanon and the Arab-Islamic world, Muhammad Mahdi Shamsuddin (1980:85), vice-president of the Shi'a High Council in Lebanon, writes:

> . . . one of the means of deceit and confusion [the secularists use] is to translate the word 'secularization'—which implies irreligiosity (*la-diniya*) in European languages—as *ilmaniya* from *ilm*, which means science in Arabic. This falsified translation is intended to give the naive person the impression that this doctrine [secularization] is part of science and springs from it, thus manipulating the muddle of linguistic derivation between *ilm* meaning 'science' and *alam* meaning 'world'. We have seen and heard many people, some of whom are educated and even turbaned, who were taken in by this false association between secularization and science and continued to call it *ilmaniya* from 'science', which it is not, instead of calling it *alamaniya* from 'world',

which it is. Perhaps some of the turbaned shaikhs, who we believe are far from being ignorant or negligent, agree to trade religion for worldly commodities, authorities and charms—how deep is the misery of Islam with these people.

After reviewing in impressive detail the Christian environment within which the doctrine of secularization has emerged, Shamsuddin makes the point that this doctrine could not possibly arise in Islamic societies because of the lack of contradiction between 'state' and 'church'. Throughout Islamic history, he argues, there have always been *fuqaha* (pl. of *faqih*, jurist) and *ahl al-hukm wa al-sultan* (men of government and authority), the first clarifying the religious precepts to be implemented by the second; at times they quarrel, but theirs is a dispute of *takamul* (complementarity) rather than *tanaqud* (contradiction). He concludes:

> Never in the reign of Islam did the 'jurists' turn into a separable, distinct *tabaqa* (stratum); and to call them *rijal al-din* (men of religion) is to surrender to a foreign expression that found its way into the Islamic heritage because of European cultural influence. They are known conventionally and conveniently as *ulama al-din* (scientists of religion), which is analogous to saying that engineers are *ulama* in engineering, that chemists are *ulama* in chemistry, and so on. (Shamsuddin, 1980:165).

No one would take issue with Shamsuddin over his contention that the separation between God and Caesar in Christianity provided the ideological prototype for the separation of church and state, or that the *ulama* are alike within their fields of specialization, in the sense of using standardized methodologies to derive or investigate general and universal laws of action; this is irrespective of whether the arena of investigation is religion, chemistry, engineering or any other discipline. The issue is whether *ilm* as 'science' and *alam* as 'world' are operationally as distinct as he wishes them to be, and whether or not the *ulama* constitute a separable, distinct stratum in Islam. Is not science, after all, a method that tries to understand, manipulate and control the 'world', the knowable and researchable? It must be stressed that this meaning of science is only partially implied in the Arabic term *ilm*, which, in addition, connotes knowledge of the invisible and unresearchable, knowledge obtained through private and particularized means rather than through standardized and universalized ones. *Ilm* in Arabic conveys the idea of 'certainty' rather than 'predictability' about the ultimate; an *alim* knows what will befall mankind in the future. The Shi'a believe that religion is *ilm wa amal* (Kashifulghata, n.d:101), that is to say, concerned with knowledge of and belief in *dainuna* (the Day of Judgement) and *mi'ad* (the return to life) as well as worship. In this context, *ilm* means particularized knowledge or certainty about the ultimate rather than science, and *amal* means worship rather than work.

It is in the spirit of this meaning of *ilm* that Khumaini in his book *The Islamic Republic* adduces several *hadiths* in support of his contention that the *ulama* are fit to rule in the absence of the Hidden Imam. Incidentally, this is the reason that the same book is also published under a different title, *Wilayat Faqih* (The Reign of a Jurist). These *hadiths* include: 'the *ulama* are the *waratha* (heirs) to the prophets'; 'the *ulama* of my community are like the prophets of Israel'; and 'the *ulama* have the same rank as Moses and Jesus' (Khumaini, 1979:94–5).

The *ulama* entrusted with this private knowledge have always constituted a separate, distinct category in Islam. The term *tabaqa* (stratum), which Shamsuddin uses, has been deliberately avoided in this chapter because of the double meaning implied in it: it may be used to mean simply a distinct but stratified group or, alternatively, a stratified layer of people whose members keep too much to themselves and have little interaction with society. The term *tabaqa* in Arabic has a derogatory meaning that contradicts the ideological image of society as a unified brotherhood; *inna al-mu'minina ikhwatun* (the believers are brothers), says the Qur'an, 49/10. Indeed, nowhere in the Qur'an is *tabaqa* used to refer to a segment of human society; it is rather used in connection with the layers of the moon, the skies and the earth. It is only in this sense that the *ulama* do not constitute a *tabaqa* in Islam; they not only belong to different social classes, but they penetrate all segments of society as well.

A separable and distinct category, the *ulama* are nevertheless to be found at almost all levels of interaction. They wear distinct and standard costumes, styles of beards and headdresses, which reflect a hierarchy of religious ranks and achievements. They often speak in classical Arabic, punctuating their conversations with Qur'anic verses; their skills in language, religious history and law enable them to play formally definable roles in society. Above all, they consider themselves and are considered by others to be a separate category.

The question remains, however, whether or not the *ulama*, as a socially distinct category, stand in perpetual opposition to the power elite, the emirs, as the clergy in Christianity did in relation to the state. Of course, nobody expects religion in Islam (which is a form of public policy) to adapt to state structures in the same way that religion, as a private system, did in Christianity. The literature on Islam, which focuses mainly on Sunni Islam and always assumes that Islam has no clergy or church, tends to oversimplify the issue.[1] Islam can be said to have no clergy only if we mean by clergy a specialized priesthood empowered (or consecrated) to transfer objects and people sacramentally through ritual from a worldly status to a divine community. Not only is this category absent in Islam, but it would be *shirk* (blasphemy) to have it. Unlike Christianity, which is essentially sacramental and where salvation is sought through the inner acceptance of the Messiah, Sunni Islam is a *shari'a*-oriented religion in which salvation is officially and externally sought through the observation and application of divine law. The word 'officially' is used here because this is not true of other religious communities in Islam: the Sufi movements, Druzes, Ibadis, and so on. If salvation were to be actually sought through the application of divine law, religious specialists would then be jurists, as they are in Sunni Islam. The church then would not be a 'divine congregation' brought together by communion, as in Christianity; rather, it would be a 'community of brotherhood' brought together by submission to God's law.

The belief that 'state' and 'church', or rather, the power elite and the *ulama*, or the emirs and the imams, merge in Islam in a single formulation of action where the first execute the laws or policy decreed by the second, is only theoretically true. While discussing this issue, Shamsuddin (1980:164) often punctuates his sentences by the phrases, 'in principle the merger takes place' and 'in theory it must always be there'. Whether or not the merger actually takes place has always been a subject of controversy, an object of reform, and a cause for political opposition, dissent and rebellion in Islam. Khumaini's Iran is only the most recent illustration. What may happen is that the integration between purity and power could itself turn into a pressing political issue, thus generating a contradiction between the *ulama* and the power elites. Popular uprisings in Islam have repeatedly been against the extent of a regime's deviation from the dictates of God's religion, in other words, the lack of integration between the *ulama* and the power elite. This is precisely what Shamsuddin (1980:165) means by the statement, 'When the governor insists on being Caesar, that may lead to a big protest which may end in rebellion.'

Indeed, many Islamic jurists (such as Ibn Khaldun, for example, who distinguishes between the imam, who derives power from religion, and the emir, who derives it from the use of force and coercion) make it legitimate for Muslims to rebel against the emir but not the imam. In their own way, the Shi'a have ritualized rebellion against the tyrant ruler following the precedent set by Husain at Karbala.

The recurrence of rebellions in Islam centred around the religious orientation of government makes it clear that the contradiction between purity and power, the imams and the emirs, occurs behaviourally or historically at the same time as it is rejected ideologically. It is interesting to note that where state and church are ideologically held to be distinct, as in Christianity, a reconciliation between them in practice was easier to attain than in Islàm, where they are held to belong to a single formulation. This means that the issue of integration or contradiction between the *ulama* and the power elite cannot be dealt with in absolute terms without reference to the dynamics of the situation that contains it.

Needless to say, nobody expects the mode of integration between purity and power in Islam to correspond to the Christian model (the separation between religion and state) simply because religion in Islam is not so much a matter of personal conviction as of public policy. The process of adapting religion to state structures in Islam would have to follow the Islamic prototype, namely, the merger of religion with the state, what is Caesar's belonging to God. Cultures and religions change according to their own traditions. What pattern Islam might take is a question dealt with in the final chapter of this book. We shall now turn to the way in which the *ulama* link to the power elite, and how this linkage varies among the Sunni where religion is adapted to the sovereignty of central authority, and among sects where religion is adapted to the sovereignty of individual communities.[2]

The Sunni *Ulama*

In Sunni Islam there is, strictly speaking, one category of religious specialists, the legalists-judiciary, who officiate on divine law according to one or more of the four standard interpretations: the Hanbali, the Shafi'i, the Hanafi and the Maliki. These interpretations were officially recognized by the state during the reign of al-Mutawakil (846–61), the tenth Abbasid caliph, following a series of legalistic controversies in the empire. Recognizing these schools to the exclusion of others was obviously a political decision that had nothing to do with divine law as such.

The four schools are not alike. Although the exact nature of their differences is outside the scope of the present work, it is important to note that they provided, and will continue to provide, leeway for both states and citizens to follow the dictates of divine law, while still seeking their own political interests. For example, the Ottoman Empire, which included many non-Muslim subjects, adopted the Hanafi interpretation of divine law which is the most permissive of all with regard to the rights of non-Muslims in an Islamic state. According to Hanafi interpretation, a non-Muslim may occupy any post in government short of the caliphate itself. Likewise, Saudi Arabia, which before the discovery of oil had adopted the Hanbali interpretation (the strictest of all with regard to the civil rights of non-Muslims in an Islamic state), seems to be slowly relaxing its rules in favour of non-Muslims as more of them settle there because of the oil industry. By the same token, a Sunni Muslim who has no sons and wishes his daughters to inherit all his property, will opt for the Ja'fari (Shi'a) law which provides for this. Ironically, this is exactly what three Sunni prime ministers in Lebanon (who represented the Sunni in government) did some time before their death in order to allow their daughters to inherit all their property.[3] It must be stressed that by doing so they did not forfeit their membership of the Sunni community, which is yet another example of the incorporative character of religion among the Sunni. (To accommodate a variety of interests, a *faqih* (Islamic jurist) in Islam tends to specialize in one school while receiving training in others.)

Traditionally however, countries, ethnic groups and families are known to follow only one of these interpretations of religious law. While North Africa follows the Maliki interpretation, Egypt, Syria and Lebanon follow the Shafi'i; Saudi Arabia the Hanbali; and Turkey the Hanafi. Within the same city, however, it may happen that different ethnicities and families follow different interpretations. In Bahrain, the Sunni Muslim Hawala, who claim Iranian origin, follow the Shafi'i interpretation, the tribal Sunni follow the Maliki, and the urban Sunni who claim Arabian origin follow the Hanbali. In Tripoli (north Lebanon), high-ranking families such as the Karamis, the Adras and the Kabbaras apply the Shafi'i interpretation, whereas some of the low-ranking tradesmen and craftsmen's families follow the Maliki. It must be stressed that moving from one school to another within Sunni Islam can be done easily and legitimately, although in practice it does not happen as frequently as one might expect. This is because such shifts are often tied in locally with class mobility or shifts from one ethnicity to another. How these various schools of Islamic interpretation fit into the general dynamics of social structure is a fascinating subject that deserves more careful examination on the part of both Islamicists and anthropologists.

Sunni religious officials, who fall into four overlapping categories—*mufti, qadi, faqih* and *ma'dhun* (all can be called shaikh)—are salaried employees paid for from public funds and/or by private institutions. Excepted from this category are some local shaikhs who are paid for by community donations; they are in the lower ranks who perform individual rituals centring on life crises. *Mufti* refers to the highest religious position in the *shari'a* court within the state or district: only cases which are in dispute are referred to him in appeal. *Qadi* is the specialist who serves in the *shari'a* court. *Faqih* is one who is trained in law, and could therefore deliberate on legal matters, but he has no official post, as he is often employed by private, educational or welfare institutions such as schools, colleges and legal councils. The *ma'dhun* (local licensed shaikh) lacks formal religious training but nevertheless executes legal transactions as well as religious customs. These specialists differ widely in the formal training, the tasks they perform, the posts they occupy and the income they earn. In 1981 the range of salaries in Lebanon fell between LL600 (Lebanese liras) for the lower ranks and LL5,000 or more for the higher ones, such as the *mufti* of the republic, which is a cabinet appointment.

The range of salaries reflects the degree of formal training: those who have completed their religious studies at al-Azhar in Cairo, the most prestigious institution for religious training in Sunni Islam, occupy top positions (*qadi, mufti, faqih*), whereas local shaikhs who receive training in local Qur'anic schools and who are simply trained by other local shaikhs, occupy the lower ranks. The data in Table 3 were collected from 128 specialists in Lebanon: they show that whereas top positions are competitive, local ones tend to be hereditary and often contained within the same families. This is not to say that religiosity in Sunni villages and traditional areas of towns and cities necessarily runs in families (as it does among the Alawis and to a lesser extent the Druzes). The element of heredity here is simply a reflection of occupational stability in peasant society. The Alawis, for example, hold that 'a shaikh is the son of a shaikh', which has led to the concentration of religious employment in specific family branches.

Of the 128 specialists, 42 had trained at al-Azhar, and of these, 12 (28%) belong to families that have had no tradition of religious training

Table 3: Distribution of Some Sunni *Ulama* in Lebanon

Ulama of religion	Urban-dominated areas				Rural-dominated areas					
	Beirut		Sidon		North Lebanon		Biqa Valley		Total	
	No.	%	No.	%	No.	%	No.	%	No.	%
Mufti	1	2.7	1	10.0	1	1.6	1	5.0	4	3.1
Qadi	12	32.4	2	20.0	5	8.2	2	10.0	21	16.4
Faqih	6	16.2	2	20.0	8	13.1	3	15.0	19	14.8
Ma'dhun	18	48.6	5	50.0	47	77.0	14	70.0	84	65.6
Total	37	99.9	10	100.0	61	99.9	20	100.0	128	99.9

whatsoever. Compared with the Shi'a, the Alawis and the Druzes, this is a rather high percentage, as we shall see later. In Lebanon, and elsewhere as well, to be trained at al-Azhar is a clear instance of upward social mobility. About 71% of those who received al-Azhar training come from humble social backgrounds: petty traders, urban craftsmen, orphans or peasants. For many of them, becoming a jurist is a definite instance of social advancement.

Sunni specialists differ not only in the extent of their training, but also in the types of task they perform. The lower ranks perform less prestigious functions such as washing and burying the dead, reciting and chanting Qur'anic verses during funerals, calling for daily prayers, signalling the Ramadan fasting schedule, and so on. These tasks, assigned to local low-ranking shaikhs, could in Sunni Islam be performed just as well by the laity. By contrast, the higher ranks, the formally trained jurists, are responsible for the administration of Islamic law and share in the management of religious welfare including *shari'a* schools, colleges, orphanages, vocational training centres and homes for the aged. Along with the power elite, they supervise the *waqf* (endowed property) revenues and expenditures, allocate funds for building and maintaining mosques, and opening or cleaning cemeteries.

All religious specialists in Sunni Islam perform some judicial functions; they are all licensed to contract marriages, for example. However, there is a tendency for the lower-ranking shaikhs to contract marriages for low-income categories and higher-ranking shaikhs to contract marriages for high-income categories. Divorce tends to be controlled by the *shari'a* court, where formally trained *qadis* deliberate on controversial issues, rather than left to the whims of the local shaikh. The fact that divorce falls within the authority of higher religious specialists is a clear indication of the social value of conflict and the place assigned to leadership in dealing with it: the resolution of conflict is an instance of power. We shall return to this point later when dealing with the Shi'a jurists (Chapter 13). Suffice it to say here that court records on divorce in Bahrain and Lebanon show very clearly that divorce, not marriage, seems to highlight most dramatically the dynamics of family relationships.

Links with the outer Islamic world offer a fascinating area of inquiry that reflects on the organization of *al-umma al-islamiya* (the Islamic community). The 42 Azhari jurists mentioned above fall into two 'network constellations' that mirror the power structure of the Sunni community in Lebanon. The *shari'a* courts, on the other hand, parallel the bureaucratic divisions of the country into five districts. At the top lies the Islamic High Council, which is located in the capital Beirut and is headed by the *mufti* of the republic. The High Council includes the *muftis* and *qadis* of the various districts plus a selected number of religious specialists representing a variety of factions in the country. The council meets once a year to consider budget, expenditure, projects and policy. However, this does not mean that it has the authority to deliberate on issues raised at local *shari'a* court level. Far from it: every *shari'a* court in each of the five districts is headed by a *mufti* and has a respectable measure of autonomy. The yearly meeting of the High Council is meant to co-ordinate rather than arbitrate.

Religious structures, large or small, central or peripheral, operate with a fair degree of autonomy; cases are only voluntarily referred to higher learned men for consultation. Segmental autonomy does not mean that there is no unity of action: instead of being built into a graded authority system with lower offices hierarchically linked to higher offices, unity of action is built into a complex system of networks with the less learned religious specialists linked to the more learned ones.

These networks can conveniently be dealt with at three levels: (1) the level of the *ma'dhuns* who operate within a small community, which could be a village, an area within a city, a large family or any other loosely knit structure; (2) the level of the jurist (*mufti, qadi* or *faqih*), who may operate within an officially recognized *shari'a* court, or outside it in a variety of welfare projects; and (3) the level of the Islamic community, in other words, links with the outer Islamic world. It must be stressed, at this juncture, that these networks are drawn on the basis of two fields of interaction: (1) employment and placement, in the sense of who employs whom or who helps find a job for whom; and (2) the process of religious consultation and appeal.

The category of *ma'dhun* accounts for 65.6% (Table 3) of the total number of religious officials in Sunni Islam; this percentage increases in rural areas and decreases in urban areas. Furthermore, the percentage of traditionally employed shaikhs in rural areas far exceeds that of local shaikhs employed by senior officials; the reverse is true in urban areas (Table 4). Almost all of those traditionally employed by the local community have family roots in it, unlike those who are employed by senior officials who may or may not have community roots. About 30% of the local shaikhs who are employed by senior officials are foreign to the communities they serve; they are recruited directly by jurists who serve in the *shari'a* court.

Table 4: Patterns of Employment among Local Sunni Shaikhs in Lebanon

Pattern of employment	Urban-dominated areas				Rural-dominated areas					
	Beirut		Sidon		North Lebanon		Biqa Valley		Total	
	No.	%	No.	%	No.	%	No.	%	No.	%
Directly employed by senior shaikhs	15	83.3	12	25.5	4	80	2	14.2	33	17.01
Traditionally employed by local community	3	16.3	35	74.5	1	20	122	85.7	161	82.99
Total	18	99.6	47	100.0	5	100	124	99.9	194	100.00

Two significant conclusions may be drawn from these data. First, the formally trained jurists are becoming increasingly responsible for the administration of Islamic law, as shown by the high incidence of jurists as compared to other categories in urban areas. Second, as this happens, local shaikhs are increasingly being employed by jurists (the senior officials) rather than by the community. This means that as more professionally trained jurists come to penetrate small communities, the legal definitions of religion will be emphasized at the expense of customarily accepted rituals. Jurists not only avoid taking part in rituals but they are critical of shaikhs whose understanding of religion is restricted to the performance of rituals.[4] It follows then that as religious authority becomes more centralized at the hands of jurists, religion becomes more legalistic; this trend will have an interesting impact upon religious modernization in Islam.

The second set of networks involving formally trained jurists who operate in *shari'a* courts or in private institutions offers an entirely different perspective. The 42 jurists included in this study, who are scattered in four different areas of Lebanon, seem to cluster in two networks, one based in Tripoli (north Lebanon) and the other in Beirut extending into Sidon and Baalbek (Table 5). This division is as much geographical as political, reflecting two different loci of power for Sunni Islam in Lebanon. In both areas, religious welfare (or rather social welfare delivered or endowed for religious purposes) is closely meshed in with the local power structure, with jurists occupying positions subsidiary to the power elites. The jurists tend to be the administrators, supervisors and managers of a welfare system subsidized by the local notables.

Table 5: Religious Training Backgrounds and Employment Patterns in Lebanon

The circle at al-Azhar	Distribution of jurists in Lebanon									
	Tripoli		Beirut		Sidon		Baalbek		Total	
	No.	%	No.	%	No.	%	No.	%	No.	%
MM	3	21.4	8	42.1	3	60.0	2	50.0	16	38.1
AM	7	50.0	4	21.0	1	20.0	1	25.0	13	31.0
KT	1	7.1	2	10.5	1	20.0	0		4	9.5
Miscellaneous	3	21.4	5	26.3	0		1	25.0	9	21.4
Total	19	99.9	14	99.9	5	100.0	4	100.0	42	100.0

All the posts of jurists serving in the *shari'a* courts, including the *muftis*, are political appointments needing the approvement of the government.

In keeping with tradition, the opinions of high religious authorities are solicited, but the final decision lies with the power structure. In the words of one *qadi*, *'na'zum wa yahzumun'* (We intend; they enact). The other jurists, who work in welfare community projects, are employed by the local political elite who initiate, supervise and sustain these projects.

The appointment of *qadis* to the *shari'a* courts has always been the subject of competition between political factions, much like any other high post in government. This type of competition lies outside the scope of the present inquiry, which focuses on the way in which religious authority relates to the power structure, and therefore on the competition between religious authority and the power establishment. Such an inquiry proved difficult to conduct, mainly because the influence wielded by the *ulama* in Sunni Islam tends to be indirect and tacitly executed by the power elites. This is itself a significant ethnographic point, for in Shi'a Islam influence is directly and openly exercised by the *ulama*. In fact, the two contested cases of *qadi* appointments I came to know about in Sunni Islam (and there are undoubtedly many more) involved religious authorities at the centre (Beirut) and power elites at the periphery (in Baalbek and Sidon). The appointments were made by government against the wishes of the local power elite in Baalbek and Sidon, on the recommendation of the Sunni religious authorities in Beirut. The *qadis* recommended by Beirut were better trained and had wide-ranging legal experience. Other appointments were made without obvious conflict between the religious authorities and the power structure, which is an interesting phenomenon without parallel in other Islamic sects.

Although cases of conflict sometimes tend to illustrate the system or norm better than cases of non-conflict, in this particular instance the reverse is true. The involvement of the power elites in the appointment and placement of Islamic jurists does not nullify or disturb the continuity of latent, invisible structures that bind the jurists together in networks sometimes reaching far beyond the political boundaries of a single state. In Lebanon, jurists cluster in employment networks according to the kinds of tutor and seminary they have attended at al-Azhar; indeed, it is no different from the university system in the West and the resulting patterns of employment.

Table 5, which gives a crude summary of religious training backgrounds and employment patterns, reveals two important points. First, religious training can be traced back to a few circles based at al-Azhar (only two circles seem to be prominent in the networks in

Lebanon). And second, unity of training at the top, or 'source', tends to concentrate jurists' employment within the same power syndrome at the bottom. The words 'crude' and 'source' have been used deliberately in order to emphasize the multiplicity of dyadic relationships involved in this process, which is difficult to present in tabular form. What further complicates the analysis is that the circle at al-Azhar, which is known by the name of the most prominent member, includes several pupils who may be equally active in expanding the circle's network outside Egypt. The source at al-Azhar is not an individual; it is a circle, and therefore it has, strictly speaking, no top.[5]

Of the 42 jurists studied in Lebanon, only 4 are in direct contact with the heads of circles at al-Azhar, 11 have contacts with less prominent tutors and the rest (27) have no contact at all. Such contacts comprise, among other things, exchange visits, gifts, correspondence and consultation on legal matters in Islamic law. Only 1 of the first 4 jurists occupies a high administrative post in the *shari'a* courts in Lebanon, the other 3 are employed outside the legal system. In other words, the bureaucratic arrangement of the courts does not necessarily reflect the centrality of interaction in the syndrome of networks that bind jurists together inside or outside the same political entity. It is a fluid system that allows a jurist to hold a central position in a specific network while occupying a peripheral post in the bureaucratic structure of the *shari'a* courts, and vice versa. The networks which arise on the basis of legal consultations (which have the power of appeal in Islamic courts) clearly demonstrate the point. Two cases will be discussed very briefly: the first, the case of the retired *qadi*, shows how legal consultations cut across court hierarchy; the second, the case of a writer, shows how networks cut across individual states.

The Case of the Retired Qadi

This man is around 75 years old, is married to one wife and has two married daughters and a son. One of his daughters is divorced and relies upon him for financial support. The *qadi* takes a special interest in his daughter's middle son who, as he put it, 'has the talent for religious studies'. Originally from south Lebanon, the *qadi* moved to Beirut with his parents in the early 1920s. In Beirut he joined a local Qur'anic school on the recommendation of the local village shaikh who was a distant relative. Ten years later, the head of the Qur'anic school arranged for him to go to al-Azhar to be trained by his tutor there. The *qadi* stayed at al-Azhar for some fourteen years, learning and teaching Islamic law, language and history.

He returned to Beirut in his late thirties, and within a few months was appointed *qadi*. Gradually, he developed the reputation of being learned, discreet, soft-spoken and, most significantly, apolitical. He is said to be apolitical in that, having no family roots in Beirut, he does not take sides in local politics as many other Sunni jurists do. 'Being apolitical served me professionally,' he says, 'but disfavoured me politically.' This is because he was nominated by several jurists to the post of *mufti* of the republic, which at the same time is the head of the *shari'a* court in Beirut, but, lacking political support, he lost to the Beirut candidate. Professionally, however, he became 'a focus of confidence', especially to the well-off in Beirut as well as to other jurists who continually seek his legal advice. Even after his retirement, many of Beirut's 'high society' still go to him for legal transactions: inheritance, property, marriage, divorce and so on, which is rewarding both socially and financially. Likewise, many jurists I spoke to cited his name as the person they would go to for consultation on controversial religious or legal matters.

His records for the four months from June to September 1980 show that he had concluded 22 marriages, deliberated on 2 cases of attempted divorce (but persuaded the parties concerned to 'soften their position'), settled 4 cases of disagreement on inheritance and property, disentangled 1 case of perpetuity inheritance and corresponded on legal matters with acquaintances and classmates located in Abu Dhabi, Java and Egypt. Before interpreting the data on the *qadi*, let us turn to the case of the writer.

The Writer

Aged 38, the writer is married to a German student of orientalism and has no children (as of 1982). Like the *qadi*, he is of village origin (from Mount Lebanon near Zahle); he studied and memorized a large part of the Qur'an at a young age while attending the village school. In the late 1950s he moved to Beirut and joined the Maqasid School in Beirut, a private school sponsored by Sunni Muslims, where he completed his secondary education. Receiving some financial aid from the Maqasid, he went to al-Azhar, where he spent four years studying Islamic law. In those days, under Nasser's regime, al-Azhar changed from a medieval institution to a modern university, which allowed the writer to graduate in four years.

Following graduation, he was appointed secretary to the *mufti* of the republic (in Beirut); in this capacity he met a German orientalist who encouraged him to pursue higher education in Germany. It took him three years to study German and write his PhD dissertation on al-Mawardi's political thought, after which he returned to Lebanon and took up a teaching post at the Lebanese University. In six years of teaching, he became so well known for his writings and religious commentaries that he was appointed editor of a major Arabic quarterly. He also became adviser to the *mufti* of the republic, a member of the Maqasid board of trustees and a prominent member of the High Islamic Council. The friends he had made at al-Azhar and in Germany paid dividends. He came to be known as 'the broker', with access both to 'modernity' as represented by his contacts in Germany, and 'religiosity' as represented by his contacts at al-Azhar.

He cultivates these links in order to enhance and widen the scope of his network at different levels. In the last two years he has helped to place around ten students at al-Azhar, invited six Egyptian jurists to Lebanon (one of whom took a permanent job at the *shari'a* religious college in Beirut, known locally as Azhar Lubnan, 'the Lebanese al-Azhar'), helped find jobs for a Lebanese and an Egyptian jurist at the University of al-Ain in Abu Dhabi, and organized a conference in Beirut on Islamic education to which he invited his former Egyptian and German tutors. Among his colleagues, the jurists, he is known as the *lawlab* (spiralist), meaning the one who, through his networks, renders many varied services at different levels both inside Lebanon and outside it.

These two cases, the retired *qadi* and the writer, make it quite clear that pyramidal hierarchy in the *shari'a* court system does not reflect centrality of interaction on religious (legal) matters. Just as the retired *qadi* deliberates on legal controversies, sometimes referred to him by the court itself, though he is outside it, the writer activates, through religious employment and mediation, a wide network of relationships reaching far beyond the boundaries of the political state. Both the *qadi* and the writer have cultivated links that extend in different directions to different parts of the Islamic world. If the organization of religion looks like this from a peripheral country like Lebanon (peripheral to Islamic religious activity), it would be interesting to see what it looks like in a central country like Egypt, Morocco or Saudi Arabia.

Before discussing the organization of religion in Shi'a Islam, it is worth underlining some major themes that have emerged in our discussion of Sunni Islam:

1. Religious officials—specialists in Sunni Islam—belong essentially to one category, the legalist-judiciary, who are formally employed to officiate in various capacities on divine law, or to participate in religious welfare: in schools, colleges, mosques, and so on.
2. The organization of the *shari'a* courts parallels the bureaucratic structure of the state, irrespective of the size of the community served by the courts.
3. Performing the tasks assigned to them, the religious specialists always co-ordinate with, and often assume a subsidiary function to, the power elite. At this level of action, the social, religious and political merge in a single value orientation.
4. The formally trained jurists, whose higher ranks are maintained by public funds, avoid local customary rituals. By contrast, the local shaikhs, whose lower ranks are often maintained by community donations, regularly participate in such rituals.
5. As greater numbers of formally trained jurists penetrate small communities, the legal, scriptural definition of religion takes precedence over the ritualistic definition.
6. Therefore, as religion becomes more legalized, religious authority becomes more centralized, and vice versa.
7. Centrality or unity of action is not achieved, internally or externally, through pyramid-shaped structures, but through a complex system of networks that cuts across religious institutions, courts and circles, sometimes reaching far beyond the boundaries of a single state.

13
The Imam and the Pharaoh: the Shi'a *Ulama*

Based on their belief that religion in Islam is located both in dogma (the Qur'an and the *hadith*) and in *al-itra al-tahira* (the Holy House, i.e. of Ali),[1] the Shi'a struggle to identify the proper religious models as manifestations of divinity in Ali's descendants. This they relate to the belief that the Qur'anic verse which declares the completion of Islam[2] was revealed immediately after the Prophet Muhammad designated Ali as the *mawla* (succeeding imam). The designation took place on 18 Dhi al-Hujja, 10 AH, in what is known in Shi'a sources as *hadith al-ghadir*, where the Prophet said, 'He whose master I am, Ali is his' (*man ana mawlah fa Ali mawlah*).

The Shi'a interpret the association between the Qur'anic verse and the *hadith* to mean that the completion of religion includes the succession of Ali to the caliphate and his House after him. The Prophet is an infallible messenger, a medium of revelation, and therefore his designation of Ali and his descendants as imams signifies God's will and ordinance. According to the Shi'a, only the imams thus designated by text are capable of grasping the inner, esoteric meanings of the Qur'an that are deemed necessary for the complete and perfect understanding of religion.

The departure from the Sunni here is in the Shi'a belief that Islam is not revealed to man once and for all in the Qur'anic texts; rather, it is a continuous process awaiting the successive rise of imams. Indeed, the controversies that split the Shi'a world are precisely about: first, lines of descent of imams; second, methods of designation; and third, the termination of succession (Figure 2). These controversies are not simply theological exercises; they reflect differences over ways of worship, legal interpretations and the ultimate structure of the divine community or brotherhood. To the various Shi'a sects, the imam is not simply a leader in prayer, as he is among the Sunni; rather, he is the summit of religiosity, the way to salvation and an imitable model in religious actions and behaviour. His *sira* (life-style) dictates the precepts for religious action.

The belief that the Holy House of Ali is as illustrative of religion as it is of dogma led to the emergence of at least three different categories of religious specialists in Shi'a Islam: the *mullas* or *khatibs*, the *mujtahids*, and the *sayyids*. The *mullas* specialize in history and ritual, the *mujtahids* in law and the *sayyids* are simply a genealogical category, non-specialized descendants of imams. Although it is possible to combine these three religious merits in a single personality, as prominent Shi'a leaders often do, the categories themselves are nevertheless separable structures.

The intensity of ritualistic life among the Shi'a is one of the most striking features of their religious practice. The Shi'a are to the Sunni much as the Catholics are to the Protestants. Apart from the first thirteen days of Muharram, during which the Shi'a annually observe a variety of rituals related to the massacre of Husain, his family and supporters in Karbala at the hands of Yazid's troops, they additionally observe eighteen days of *taharim* (the 'death days' of important religious figures) including the Prophet, the twelve imams, plus the Virgin Mary, Christ and many other biblical figures mentioned in the Qur'an. Excerpts from these rituals, especially from Ashura which commemorates the massacre of Husain, are repeatedly read at several solemn occasions: death, funerals, the fortieth day of mourning after death, and *qira'at* (weekly assemblies) held in rotation, especially by women. These *qira'at* are often led by female *mullas* who are the wives or daughters of male *mullas* (Khuri, 1980).

The *mullas* or *khatibs* (*khatib* is a higher rank of the *mulla* category), who know these rituals by heart, recite the details of the death of a particular imam, focusing on the oppression and the atrocities committed against him by central authority and coercive governments—the pharaohs being symbolic of the power elite. The mutilation of the dead imam's corpse is related to the audience in graphic detail, mixing poetry with prose, to provoke cries of grief and sighs of pain. They believe that the better the *mulla*, the louder and deeper are the cries he provokes among the audience; the audience in turn seek paradise by deeper and deeper cries.

Highly reputed *khatibs*, who receive training at the Shi'a seminaries in Najaf, allow themselves a greater measure of freedom in dealing with these rituals. Instead of sticking to the literal text of the ritual as low-ranking *mullas* do, they address themselves to the current issues of the day. In Bahrain and Lebanon I have heard such *khatibs* speak on women's liberation, civil rights, the right to employment, security for the deprived and oppressed, and other politically loaded issues. The imam, the central figure in the ritual, is always presented to the audience as a rebel: either directly, by leading an outright rebellion against the established, centralized authority, as Husain did at Karbala; or indirectly, by championing the cause of the oppressed, the deprived and the under-privileged, as al-Sadiq did in Baghdad during the reign of al-Ma'mun.

Because of the importance of ritual in Shi'a religious life, imams, *khatibs* and *mullas*, who handle such rituals, are able to attain high positions in the hierarchy and exert considerable politico-religious influence. Indeed, this is exactly what Musa al-Sadr did in Lebanon during the last twenty years of his career. However, before examining this point in more detail, we shall turn to the other two categories, the *mujtahids* and the *sayyids*.

The *mujtahids*, who are trained in the *shari'a*, are the closest organizationally, if not functionally and operationally, to religious officials in Sunni Islam. They are called *mujtahids* (interpreters) according to the Shi'a belief that man is incapable of comprehending the esoteric meaning of the texts; he only interprets or 'deduces' judgements on the basis of, first, the exoteric as spelled out in the Qur'an and, second, the esoteric as modelled in the imam's life-style. The *mujtahids* keep detailed records of the actions, works and behaviour of individual imams, much as the Sunni jurists do with regard to the Prophet and the first four caliphs. These actions, works and behaviour form the basis on which legalities in human society are drawn. Like the jurists, the *mujtahids* deal with legal matters and consequently work hand in hand with centralized authority, often assuming a position secondary to the power elites. In Lebanon and Bahrain they are formally employed by government to officiate on legal matters pertaining mostly to marriage, divorce, inheritance, family conflicts and property. Organizationally, the *mujtahids* are divided into the same four categories as the Sunni jurists (*mufti, qadi, faqih* and *ma'dhun*), which are cross-cut or bridged at different points by networks connecting to different Shi'a seminaries in Najaf or in Iran. However, they differ from the Sunni in two ways: in the level of intimacy that binds the *mujtahids* to the Shi'a community and, correspondingly, in the continuity of religious specialization in traditional houses.

The court records I reviewed in Lebanon and Bahrain (some 5,000 cases of marriage and a little under 1,000 cases of divorce) show that while

Sunni *qadis* approach problems of marriage and divorce contractually, the Shi'a add an element of morality, bringing to the fore the weight of the immediate community. In marriage contracts, for example, a Sunni *qadi* may act as guardian or proxy to the bride in the absence of her father, brother or uncle; the Shi'a *qadi*, on the other hand, insists on the presence of witnesses representing the family and/or the community. Divorce in Sunni courts is granted simply and easily according to the terms of the marriage contract, if the husband pronounces it desirable, with or without the agreement of the wife; in Shi'a courts, the *qadis*, speaking for the community, retain the right to interfere even if the two partners are in agreement. This is why some of the divorce cases I reviewed in the Shi'a courts have taken several years to finalize; the tendency in Sunni courts is to finalize divorce contractually and as quickly as possible. In Sunni courts the morality of the case as it reflects the general attitude of the religious community is generally brushed aside.

More important still are the cases of family conflicts, notably between husband and wife, and father and daughter, that are brought before the Shi'a courts and seem never to find their way to the Sunni courts. In the Shi'a records, there were several charges of sexual abuse: wives accusing husbands of anal intercourse, having intercourse during menstruation, committing adultery or having incestuous relationships with daughters and sisters; and daughters accusing fathers of abusing paternal authority by forcing them to marry against their own wishes, or inflicting upon them severe corporal punishment. Likewise, acts of *la'n* (cursing) and *hijab wa kitab* (witchcraft) are frequently brought before a Shi'a judge but rarely, if ever, before a Sunni judge. In Sunni communities such conflicts are dealt with informally at the family and community levels rather than being referred formally to the court. Herein lies the difference between the two communities: what is achieved 'informally' and 'intimately' at court level in Shi'a communities is achieved as such at family level in Sunni communities. Is this not an instance of ethnicity adapting to non-state situations?

Intimacy and personalized relationships between the *mujtahids* and the community are further reinforced by the continuity of religious specialization in the same family or house. Of the 36 high-ranking *mujtahids* I studied in Bahrain and Lebanon and who had training in Najaf, only 2 (5.5% as opposed to 28% among the Sunni) belonged to families that had no tradition of religious specialization; all the rest claimed religious origins or traditions of one kind or another. The tendency among the lower ranks, the local shaikhs, is always to claim such origins and traditions.[3]

In Shi'a communities, the claim to religious origins is a recurrent phenomenon mainly because specialization itself is a diffuse rather than a specific domain of action. In addition to the *mullas, khatibs* and *mujtahids*, there exists throughout the Shi'a communities a large number of *sayyids* claiming descent (often crudely) from the Holy House of Ali. Irrespective of their socio-economic status, they are shown social deference and are paid *zakat* (tribute), especially during the thirteen days of Ashura commemorations that take place in the first part of Muharram. The *sayyids* are a genealogical category often referring to entire family stocks. In Lebanon, for example, the Musawis of Baalbek, the Husainis of Byblos, the Hurrs of Jubai and the Sharaf al-Dins of Tyre all claim *sayyid* origin. Unlike the *ashraf* in Sunni communities who claim descent from the Quraish and enjoy high socio-economic standing—obviously a class situation—the *sayyids* in Shi'a communities range from the rich to the poor, the learned to the illiterate, and include soldiers, shopkeepers, proprietors, civil servants, teachers, farmers, officers and shaikhs.

In contrast to Sunni officials, the Shi'a earn social notability and popularity in proportion to their achievement of pre-eminence in ritual and jurisdiction. Among the Shi'a, notability, popularity and claims to religious knowledge and origin are intertwined phenomena precisely because they are community-based and community-recognized achievements rather than state-controlled or designated insignia. Consider, for example, the names by which religious categories are known and the method by which titles are conferred. The Sunni recognize terms that reflect gradations of formal office (*mufti, qadi* and *ma'dhun*) or imply formal religious training (such as *faqih*). The Shi'a, by contrast, in addition to these, recognize terms that reflect gradations of social status and/or religious knowledge (*sayyid*, imam, *ayatollah, ruhallah, mujtahid akbar, hujjat al-islam*). These titles, which are conferred upon the specialist by his colleagues or followers, indicate not only formal office but also the scale of social influence and power. Because religious achievement is at the same time social achievement, religious officials tend to rise to power in Shi'a, but not in Sunni, communities. This is demonstrated by the rise to power of the religious bloc in the Bahrain parliament (1973–75), all of whose members were Shi'a; by the recurrent rise of religious specialists to high leadership positions in Lebanon; and, most obvious of all, by the *ayatollahs* of Iran.

In their relation to the power-authority structure, the Shi'a *ulama* can be roughly divided into two overlapping categories: the *mujtahids* who deal with the administration of religious law, and the imams, *khatibs, mullas* and others who deal with ritual. The first category, the jurists, tend to accommodate their ways and methods to existing power realities, working more or less harmoniously with regimes and established authority. Nevertheless the Shi'a jurists, while performing their duty, find themselves caught between two conflicting roles: that of government appointee subject to public supervision, and that of 'leader' representing (in the eyes of the community) the ultimate source of legitimacy, the imamate. This ambivalence in the role of the *mujtahid*, which is deeply rooted in *taqiya*, has been primarily responsible for the continued strained relations between Shi'a religious categories and the established authorities. This ambivalence occurs even where the authorities adhere to the Shi'a faith, as in Iran, for example. Work on Bahrain (Khuri, 1980) has demonstrated how the Shi'a, who were the first to support the 'administration reforms', turned against them when the reforms suddenly subjected the authority of the jurists to a centralized court system. Relations between jurists and regimes become especially strained when the former begin to accumulate power and wealth. Following the early Islamic practice of donating one-fifth of the war loot to the Prophet and his House (as in the Qur'an 6/41), the Shi'a donate one-fifth of their earnings, *haq al-imama* (the right of the imam), to religious authorities—each to the one he 'imitates' religiously. This means that as a religious figure grows in popularity, he simultaneously grows in wealth. Because of community pressure and expectations, many religious specialists reinvest some of these titles in religious teachings and welfare, which is also an investment in power and prestige. Whereas the Sunni *ulama* take part in the management of welfare donated by the power elite, the Shi'a *ulama* carry on these projects as if they themselves were the power elites.

The career histories I collected on eight renowned Shi'a religious specialists, six in Bahrain and two in Lebanon, show quite consistently that as they gradually accumulate power and wealth, they correspondingly shift from the practice of law to participation in ritual. This means that instead of simply being jurists deliberating privately on matters pertaining to worship, marriage, divorce, debts, inheritance, property, women's physiology and the legitimacy of children, they become *khatibs* and, if more successful, imams, dealing publicly with ritual and the mobilization of the community for the fulfilment of Shi'a objectives. This is illustrated by an interview I conducted in the spring of 1982 with one of these renowned men, al-Ghumri, in Lebanon.

Social Profile of al-Ghumri

Al-Ghumri started his religious career at 14, working as a clerk for his master-shaikh in Tyre (Lebanon). His job involved the registration of marriages and dowry-filing and copying commentaries on religious texts, in addition to providing the shaikh with general assistance. Partially supported by his master, he went at 19 to Najaf to continue his religious studies in jurisprudence, traditions, history and grammar. Although he excelled in jurisdiction and Arabic grammar (the two are somehow interconnected), his 'soul', as he put it, was in history and traditions. In his late twenties, one year after his return from Najaf where he had met many colleagues from different parts of the Shi'a world, he took up a job in the *shari'a* court in Beirut. He stayed in this job until 1973, when he was invited by a very influential Shi'a religious man to join the recently established Shi'a High Council as officer and then as council member. It must be remembered that the Shi'a High Council became an independent body in 1969 when it split from the Sunni-dominated Islamic Council; this was part of a general attempt to establish a separate Shi'a political wing in Lebanon.

In a very short period of time, the Shi'a High Council, thanks to the efforts of Imam Musa al-Sadr, came to distinguish itself as the main platform for Shi'a lobbying, a central arena for social welfare and services, and an instrument of collective consciousness on behalf of the Shi'a as a deprived minority. As the council grew in size, power and economic capacity, al-Ghumri came to assume in it the role of 'trouble-shooter', responsible for pacifying and softening Shi'a opposition to the council. This opposition came from two political forces among the Shi'a who opposed the council for entirely different reasons. On the one hand, the established feudal houses saw in it a threat to their power and influence. On the other, the 'ideologized' elite, committed to nationalistic and/or socialistic dogmas, saw in it no more than a belated manifestation of traditionalism and backwardness. In dealing with the multi-factional politics of the Shi'a in war-infested Lebanon, al-Ghumri found himself dominated by two concerns: how to establish Shi'a consensus; and how to promote the Shi'a cause in Lebanon which must include, according to him, intensified contacts with Syria and Iran. We are concerned here with the part of his career which relates to the shift from the practice of law to participation in ritual.

Q: How do you compare your job as *qadi* in the *shari'a* court with your job as 'trouble-shooter' in the Shi'a High Council?

A: I am not a trouble-shooter; I am simply a 'trusted' messenger. As *qadi* one deals with private matters, and in this way you come to know the concerns of people as individuals. It is nice doing this, for you learn a lot about the personal problems of the community. However, it presents no challenge; it is routine, scarcely exciting and frequently boring.

As a 'servant' of the [Shi'a High] Council, I deal with big problems; problems that concern the whole community, the whole Shi'a world. We know what will befall us in the future, and we must be prepared for it.

Q: But as *qadi* you also deal with the problems of the community as they come to you one by one?

A: No, no . . . marriage is your problem, divorce is his problem, praying before ablution is a problem for X, swallowing one's saliva during the fast of Ramadan is a problem for Y . . . these are the matters you deal with as *qadi*. As a servant of the council, you deal with schools, hospitals, colleges, group conflicts and Ashura rituals.

Q: How do you deal with Ashura?

A: Many brothers in different parts of the country write to us asking for financial help to organize processions during Ashura. Ashura does not relate to the affairs of an individual, it is a matter for the whole community, Shi'a and non-Shi'a; it is a cosmic, universal catastrophe for mankind.

Q: How much time or otherwise do you allocate for Ashura?

A: A lot. We do not only deal with financial support, but with religious issues as well. In 1981, for example, the issue of women participating in the public rituals of Ashura came into the open. Many colleagues opposed it on the grounds that this has no precedent. I said, yes, it has a precedent: Husain's sister, daughter and other immediate relatives took part in the battle of Karbala. If so, why don't our women do likewise? Those who oppose Ashura don't want to see the Shi'a united. Ashura is our collective consciousness.

Q: I learned that certain Shi'a leaders oppose some aspects of Ashura rituals?

A: It is Ashura that makes up the Shi'a identity. One works for Ashura not only by participating in the processions or the passion play, but also by silent observation at home, by donations to the poor, by clinging more tenaciously to the demands of the community, by defending his brothers morally and politically. Great is the secret of Ashura: it keeps us going.

Q: How do you participate in Ashura?

A: Early in my career, as *qadi*, I used to address the brethren in the *husainiya* [a Shi'a assembly] of al-Borj during the last three days of Ashura. Today, I spend more than four months working on Ashura commemorations; it is a continuous job for me. I go to Najaf and sometimes to Iran to recruit speakers, approach the rich to subsidize local commemorations, and encourage Shi'a villages and towns to organize for Ashura rituals. Through our efforts at the council more than twenty foreign speakers from Iraq and Iran have visited Lebanon this year, and more villages and communities have observed the ritual publicly.

Q: How long do foreign speakers stay in Lebanon?

A: Some stay for ten days, some for a month, some for a year and a few for even longer. Those who stay for a long time lecture in different *husainiyas* on Shi'a history and traditions all year round. They are supported partly by the local communities they visit, partly by us, and partly by other Shi'a welfare institutions.

Q: How do you recruit foreign speakers: directly through your own efforts, or through 'contact men' placed in Najaf or elsewhere?

A: In our correspondence with fellow shaikhs, *khatibs* or imams in Iraq or Iran, we learn about novices or established shaikhs who qualify for the job. Additionally, many of us make frequent visits to Shi'a seminaries, where we spend a few weeks, establish new contacts, strengthen old friendships and learn about the problems of our communities.

Obviously, to al-Ghumri as to many other Shi'a shaikhs, the shift from the practice of law to indulgence in ritual signifies a higher level of religious action and a deeper concern with Shi'a affairs. It is true that Ashura rituals focus on the themes of 'sacrifice' and 'rebelliousness' of a historic battle that took place in 680. Nevertheless, it has come to acquire a generalized, versatile, non-standardized, unstereotyped form of expression that accommodates a wide variety of emerging problems, personal agonies and collective sufferings that befall the Shi'a at any time in history. Ashura is not a salvation ritual as mass in Christianity; it is a ritual of 'rebellion' and 'protest' against the 'usurpers' of power, where the *huquq* (rights)—not necessarily the truths—of the 'weak' and the 'oppressed' are symbolically and collectively sought. In fact, it is the primary task of the 'speaker', whether *mulla, khatib* or imam, to relate the 'meanings' of Ashura to the current socio-economic and political conditions of the Shi'a community or communities, the stress always being placed upon collective grievances of the Shi'a. In brief, through Ashura, the Shi'a consolidate their collective consciousness as an 'opposition' party.

Opposition in Shi'ism is ritualistically built into the organization of religion as executed by top specialists. In Sunni Islam, religion has, from time to time, been used to marshal opposition against what is thought to be a corrupt regime, but when used in this way, it never assumes a ritualistic precedent and is always championed by non-specialists: Sufi leaders, fundamentalists, Muslim brotherhoods, and so on. Whereas in Shi'a Islam 'opposition' is a religious constant expressed repeatedly and continuously in ritual, in Sunni Islam it is a variable, subject to changing political moods. In the first instance, religious opposition is an integral part of ideology, a general world-view of a group adapted to a non-state situation; in the second, it is an expedient instrument of power adapted to state structures.

14

Purity versus Power: the Ibadis, the Zaidis and the Yazidis

What the Shi'a achieve through the observation of rituals, other sects do through what might be called 'religious presence', which includes the diffusion of religious practice and specialization. The status of the *ulama* in Islamic sects can be placed on a continuum ranging from formal office to sacrament, as shown in Figure 6.

Figure 6: Religious Organization between Formal Office and Sacrament

Sunni	Ibadis	Zaidis	Shi'a	Alawis	Druzes

0 ⟵――――――――――――――――――――――――――――⟶ 1

Formal office ... Sacrament

This form of differentiation between sects has an immediate bearing on the hierarchic structure of the *ulama* and the way they relate to society. Among the Sunni, religious gradation follows a somewhat bureaucratic structure, from *ma'dhun* to state *mufti*, whereby the *ulama* who occupy higher rank exercise more power and authority. Among the Druzes, at the other extreme, gradation is measured in terms of the shaikh's relative solitude: the higher his rank, the more solitude the shaikh seeks and the more withdrawn from society he becomes. A shaikh who achieves a top position is said to have reached a stage of sacramental being, the private knowledge of God, which is his secret. This is what Sami Makarem meant by the phrase, 'may God make his secret holy', in his speech commemorating Sayyid Abdullah al-Tannukhi, one of the Druze *maqams* in Mount Lebanon.[1] The stage of sacramental being is a personal experience, a private matter, that cannot be communicated to others. Among the Druzes and the Alawis, as a man moves higher on the religious scale, he gives up the tasks of dealing with people's day-to-day problems.

The adaptation of religion to state structures amongst the Sunni is clearly visible here. The Sunni seem to be the only Islamic community who have thus far developed a religious system congruent with state structure and centralized authority. True, there is among the Sunni a kind of polarity in the practice of religion—ritualism versus scripturalism—but this polarity has never impeded the merger of religion with state structure in a single formulation where the *ulama* occupy a role secondary to that of the power elites. Unlike the Sunni, Islamic sects have not yet developed such a formulation; theirs is one of dual organization where neither the kingdom of God is adapted to Caesar's, nor Caesar's to God's. Hence the continuous struggle between purity and power, government based on religion and government based on force and coercion. Among the Druzes, the Alawis and the Yazidis the struggle is not so obvious, simply because of the ideological separation between the two kingdoms: the question here is not one of a merger that should have taken place, but hasn't; it is one of separation that shouldn't have happened.

Duality in Contradiction: the Zaidis and the Ibadis

Among the Zaidis and the Ibadis, the duality of religious organization takes the form of a lasting struggle between *shar'* and *taghut* (tribal dictates); the first represented by the imam, the second by the emir or the feuding tribal chiefs. In consequence, Zaidi and Ibadi history is full of records of hostilities between the two loci of power. In North Yemen, each feuding tribe adopts to itself a particular strain of *sayyids*[2] who are responsible for the general administration of Islamic justice, teach in Qur'anic schools, work in local and central government offices, collect *zakat* tax, officiate on personal law and help resolve conflicts between feuding tribes. Once a *sayyid* distinguishes himself socially, he joins the ranks of the *ashraf* (religious nobility), and if he makes it to the top he becomes an imam. The *qadi* is a person who normally officiates on religious matters without having *sayyid* origins; his origins are tribal.

Resolution of conflict between feuding tribes, the task of arbitration, is the single most important task ever performed by *sayyids, ashraf* or imams. It is organically linked to the duality of religious organization among the Zaidis. The task of arbitration is not executed by an established court procedure; rather, it is sought after by the imam himself. As self-appointed arbitrator, the imam obtains support in an effort to establish a *mujamma* (tribal coalition), which he will then use to restore the 'word of God' and peace between tribes. While doing so, he inevitably tries to establish his authority and spread his influence into new realms, new tribal frontiers that have already been recruited under the banner of another imam. According to Stookey (1981:354–7), in Yemen, since 1981, there have been no less than seventy imams competing for the imamship, some of whom trace descent to Hadi, some to Abdullah (Hadi's brother), and some to Husain, the martyr of Karbala.

The process of establishing tribal coalitions is not a simple matter; it carries with it the ingredients of contradiction. Whereas the imam is guided by religious motives, the tribes are after loot and gain. As soon as the imam succeeds in establishing the 'word of God', he finds himself fighting against the very tribes who had earlier paid him homage. He works to consolidate the Islamic *shari'a*; they work for *taghut*. Struggling against the tribes who earlier supported him, the imam finds himself building new but similar coalitions. Hence arises the circularity of conflict, the inbuilt contradiction between purity and power, the imams and the emirs.[3]

The same pattern of contradiction between purity and power recurs among the Ibadis, where, although the forms may be different, the processes are the same. The roles the *sayyids* or imams perform in Zaidi society are analogous to those performed by the *mutawa'a* (religious disciplinarians) or *azzaba* in Ibadi society.[4]

In her work on the Ibadis living in the Mzab Oasis (Algeria), Farrag (1969:20–40) observes that the *azzaba* council is composed of around twelve members, only three of whom (the jurist, the imam and the mosque chanter) have had some religious training; the rest are mostly merchants and tradesmen noted for their dedication to religious values. As a body, they exercise a wide range of functions: collecting *zakat* tax, managing *waqf* land, washing the dead before burial, holding marriage ceremonies, arbitrating on divorce and resolving tribal conflicts. In addition, they have the authority to excommunicate, expel, or impose isolation upon those who fail to conform to religious custom. *Tabriya* (imposed isolation) is lifted only when the culprit repents publicly in front of the worshippers following Friday prayers.

The *azzaba* circle among men is paralleled by another among women; the two operate independently. The women's *azzaba* are smaller, composed of about five members, mostly middle-aged, unmarried, divorced or widowed. Except for the right to banish or expel wrongdoers from the community, women's *azzaba* exercise practically the same powers as men's. In Arab culture, the code of honour requires that women 'sinners' are not expelled from the group; they are punished instead.

But the most significant role played by the *mutawa'a* or *azzaba* is in arbitration, the resolution of conflict between tribal factions. This is very much in line with the role the early Muslims played in Arabia at the dawn of Islam. In his work on the Ibadis of Oman, Wilkinson (1972:67, 201) alludes to this role by saying that the Ibadis 'have become since the first century hijra more interested in holy wars than in religious thought', and that 'their imams are closer to war heroes than to the *ulama*'. He adds that 'the ways by which imams are appointed or abdicate correspond to the same patterns followed in the appointment of tribal chiefs. If the imam commits a crime he has to repent, and if he refuses, he will be requested to abdicate', a process commonly known as *waqf*.

The process of appointment or abdication of an imam does not follow a standard procedure, however; it varies with circumstances. Until the nineteenth century, the pattern of seeking the imamship was in line with the Zaidi way (see Chapter 8). With the advent of the nineteenth century the struggle over the imamate began to take a new form, namely the separation between the imamate and the sultanate, which initiated a series of bloody wars until the withdrawal of the imam from Oman in 1970.

During these long conflicts between the imam and the sultan, the former always emerged from the ranks of the *mutawa'a* and other religious authorities, whereas the sultan had to rely on standing armies and on the support of merchants and men of economic power. The contradiction between purity and power is clear: Oman is being governed by a sultan but the imam is not entirely eliminated. The imam may emerge at any time, the manifest stage, calling for the establishment of the 'word of God' and the execution of Islamic justice. The sultanic rule has not yet eliminated the duality of authority which bears upon people both religiously and politically. Mu'ammar (1964:119) insists: 'As long as the *umma* is in custody of the *ulama*, the *umma* is in good shape; once the *ulama* turn to the support of the ruler, right or wrong, the *umma* is in crisis.' Clearly, Mu'ammar sees the duality of purity and power falling into a lasting contradiction, neither one adapting to the other. He does not call upon the *ulama* to seize power, as Ayatollah Khumaini did in

Iran, but urges them to continue threatening sultanic authority with religion.

Why are the Sunni able to adapt religion to state structures and central authority while the Ibadis and Zaidis, who have a great deal in common with Sunni traditions, have failed to do so? This is a question that can be answered only by looking into the structure and fabric of the societies in which they exist.

As mentioned earlier in Chapter 4, the Sunni tend to live in relatively large and fertile countries such as Egypt, Syria and Morocco which have had a long tradition of stable economies and high-density populations, and subsequently came to experience bureaucracies, state systems and centralized authorities. The state in these societies was an instrument of control long before the advent of Islam, which meant that Islam had to adapt itself to a given, a *de facto* situation. By contrast, the Ibadi and Zaidi societies happen to be small and fragmented, with arid and desert-like terrains, which could not sustain a dense population of any size. A society thus structured is unlikely to build a continuing and stable state structure; hence the personalization of power in the image of the imam.

One might take issue with this point on the grounds that many of the small, tribally based, fragmented societies in arid lands and with low-density populations, such as those in the Gulf, Saudi Arabia and Libya, have turned to Sunni Islam without having a tradition of centralized authority. While this is true, it is also true that the prevalence of Sunni Islam in complex societies does not imply that it could not reach the peripheries. Sunni Islam, like any other religion, adapts itself to social givens; its orientation in complex peasant societies is not the same as in pastoral, tribal societies. The rise of contemporary religious movements —the Wahhabis in Saudi Arabia, the Sanusis in Libya and the Mahdis in Sudan—is a clear illustration of this point. Although these movements were conceived in cities (the Wahhabis in Damascus, the Sanusis in Mecca and the Mahdis in Omdurman, a suburb of Khartoum) they all established themselves as systems at the peripheries, amongst tribally organized Muslims. The Wahhabis established themselves among the tribes of Nejd (central Arabia), the Sanusis among the tribes of Barqa of Libya, and the Mahdis among the Baggara tribes of Sudan. Contemporary religious movements in Sunni Islam had little chance of survival in complex, state-controlled societies. Indeed, when Saudi Arabia, Sudan and Libya began, from the second half of this century, to see the emergence of strong state structures, these movements turned into political parties rather than stable sectarian communities.

Parallel Duality: the Yazidis

Among the Yazidis, duality of religious organization takes a very special form; theirs is one of correspondence rather than contradiction. This is a case where social hierarchy corresponds perfectly to and merges with religious hierarchy.

The Yazidis observe innumerable holidays and maintain the community through a comprehensive network of religious fellowships. They open the year with a holiday called Sari Sal (1 April), which marks the day on which the angel Peacock deserted the heavens to establish the kingdom of angels on earth. They celebrate the New Year by performing a wide variety of acts: hanging bunches of red wild flowers on the doors of their houses; offering animal sacrifices and communally eating the sacrificial meat; colouring and boiling eggs; gambling with eggs; distributing gifts of food to the poor and passers-by; and sometimes visiting the dead to invoke God's mercy and blessings (al-Hasani, 1967:122–3).

Sari Sal opens the year with a series of holidays mostly observed in April, the holy month. During this month, everyone abstains from concluding marriage contracts, refrains from digging holes, pits or house foundations in the ground, and avoids entering into long-term commercial contracts. Instead, they engage in a series of festivities, especially on Fridays of every week, at which they offer sacrifices and gifts, pay tithes and *zakat*, and visit shrines and graves. They organize long processions to visit the holy tomb of Adi bin Musafir and parade through the villages carrying statuettes of the angel Peacock.

The various festivities observed in April are followed by another series of holidays, of which the most significant are: Mirba'aniyat al-Saif (the First Quarter of Summer), al-Qurban (the Holy Bread) and al-Jama'iya (the Spiritual Crowd). The first, which is known as the Shaikh Adi bin Musafir holiday, lasts for about five days beginning in the middle of July. In preparation for this day, a brand of religious specialists known as the *kawajik* fast for about forty days. It is noted that they observe the fast strictly during the first and the last three days, during which they visit Shaikh Adi's shrine, staying there to perform a series of complex rituals. The second feast, al-Qurban, corresponds to the Adha feast among the Muslims, the day when God ordered Abraham to sacrifice his only son Isma'il, but at the last moment provided the sacrificial lamb instead. The third feast, al-Jama'iya, which lasts for seven days beginning on 23 September, is the time of forgiveness when all man's sins are wiped out. On the fifth day of this holy week, the Yazidis perform all kinds of joyful acts: singing, dancing, playing drums, offering sacrifices and holding communal meals.

Among the Yazidis, each of these rituals is performed by a specific class or group, an instance of role complementarity. While one group fasts, the other breaks fast; one offers sacrifices on a particular holiday, another one on another day; one retreats to the shrine of Adi bin Musafir to offer prayers, the others parade through the villages carrying statuettes of the angel Peacock. This complementarity in the performance of religious roles binds the various segments of society into a single drama. The Yazidis are further linked, like the Alawis, by dyadic fellowships between master-shaikhs and novices that encompass the whole community (al-Dimluji, 1949:44). The master-shaikhs monitor the religious performance of the novices and see to it that all the latter's duties and obligations are fulfilled. In turn, the novices pay their masters *zakat* and other honoraria on particular holidays.

Yazidi society is highly stratified from top to bottom; every stratum, which is a genealogically defined category, is assigned a specialized religious function. This suggests that the whole Yazidi community, much like Sufi organizations, belongs to a single order of worship.

At the top of the hierarchy stands a tribal, religious figure, called *mir shikhan*, who is the final authority on spiritual and worldly matters. Al-Hasani (1967:5) describes him as 'the possessor of the forbidden and the permissible', which is a clear reference to the final authority he enjoys. The Yazidis believe that *mir shikhan*, a position occupied in the 1970s by Said Bey bin Ali bin Husain Bey, is the representative of Adi bin Musafir on earth, and that his genealogy goes back to Shaikh Abu Bakr al-Arbali (al-Dimluji, 1949:37–9). This is important, for the *basmariya* category, which controls practically all the high religious posts, traces descent to the same genealogical origin as *mir shikhan*. The Yazidis hold that *mir shikhan* is a direct descendant of al-Mansur, the son of Abu Bakr, whereas the *basmariya* are descended from Abu Bakr's brother Malak. Like many other tribo-religious strata in Yazidi society, the *basmariya*, which means the children of the emir, practise an exclusive form of endogamy.

Immediately below the *basmariya* is a category called the *mashayikh*, who are believed to be the direct descendants of Shaikh Adi II as reincarnated in the personality of the famous Sufi shaikh, Hasan al-Basri. Included in this category of *mashayikh* are six endogamous clans, headed by *baba-shaikh*, who together are entrusted with religious training. Having a sort of monopoly of religious knowledge, they lead in the performance of collective rituals and specialize in the upkeep of Shaikh Adi's shrine. The *birat* category is almost equivalent to the *mashayikh* in status, but is thought to be descended not from Shaikh Adi's strain, but from the strains of his companions. In Yazidi land today there are around fourteen different kinship clusters who are collectively classified as *birat*, meaning elderly shaikhs. They are entrusted with the performance of individualized rituals such as washing and burying the dead, witnessing oaths, taking vows on behalf of other believers and acting as proxies in visiting shrines.

Commoners come at the bottom of the religious scale; they are referred to as *muridun* (novices), a typically Sufi term. Every novice is attached to a shaikh or *bir* who sees to it that the novice's religious duties and obligations are fulfilled. From amongst the commoners very specialized religious categories may arise known as the *fuqara*, the *kawajik* and the *qawwalin*. The *fuqara* are those who pledge themselves to the service of *mir shikhan*; they receive and disseminate his orders in the community. They are distinguished by a black headdress and a red belt and lead a very austere life. Should a *faqir* disobey the orders of the *mir*, he loses his headdress and belt.

The *kawajik* are attached to the *mashayikh* stratum but appointed by *mir shikhan* himself. They help the *mashayikh* perform their roles, especially in times of crisis or drought, when they devote themselves to prayer, continuously requesting divine mercy. They are also believed to be able to reach the dead and inform their close relatives of what has befallen them in the hereafter. The *qawwalin*, on the other hand, are the specialists in hymn-chanting; they often provide the chorus during important festivities. It is a hereditary position passed down from father to son (Jule, 1934:90–1).

The duality of religious organization among the Yazidis is expressed in a unique, Sufi-like merger between tribal strains and religious specialists. The groups entrusted with the performance of specialized religious roles are themselves exclusive genealogical categories sustained from one generation to another through the strict practice of in-marriage.

15
God and Caesar: the Alawis and the Druzes

The distinction between the kingdoms of God and of Caesar among the Druzes and the Alawis does not lie in the Christian belief that 'the Sabbath was made for man, not man for the Sabbath' (The Bible, Mark 2: 27), but in the belief that divine knowledge is graded, private and sacramental, and that therefore only the select few are privileged to acquire it. Religious stratification not only includes the hierarchic arrangement of religions, but also divine knowledge itself. As a person's knowledge of religion deepens, his rank gets higher, and the higher the rank the more he withdraws from worldly affairs. A shaikh withdraws from society not merely to seek solitude, but to set an ideal example of religious tradition. At this stage, he represents the consensus of the religious community, which tries to transcend internal conflicts and factionalism.

This form of stratification, the gradation of religious knowledge, is evidenced by the division of the believers into two main categories: (1) those who have been formally exposed to religious dogma according to a standard procedure: known among the Alawis as the *mukallafun* (custodians) and among the Druzes as the *uqqal* (knowables); and (2) the others who have not been formally exposed to dogma, who are classified as the *juhhal* (ignorant). Whoever among the Druzes reaches middle age and is of good repute can opt to join the first category. Among the Alawis, it is believed that whoever reaches adulthood (the late teens) can be recruited into the 'custodian' category through a comprehensive religious fellowship. Unlike the Druzes, who allow women to join the congregation and become full members of the 'knowable' category, the Alawis exclude women from religious fellowships altogether.

However, the duality of religious organization is not derived from the division of society into the knowables and the ignorant, but from the separation between the religious example and the worldly standard: the first operates within the field of religion and the second within the field of power and coercion, and the control of resources and interests. The first is an instance of religious gradation, the second of sultanic stratification; the two neither meet nor correspond, but stand in contradiction to each other.

The Alawi Shaikhs of Religion

Among the Alawis, 'religious presence' is attained through the observance of holidays and the practice of religious fellowship. Sources on the Alawis invariably cite the many holidays which the community observes on a calendar basis, some of which are Islamic, some Christian and some uniquely Alawi. These include al-Ghadir (18 Dhi al-Hujja), which commemorates the Prophet's designation of Ali as his successor; the Adha (10 Dhi al-Hujja) feast and Ramadan which they celebrate along with other Muslims; al-Firash, commemorating the first day of the migration from Mecca to Medina when Ali spent the night in the Prophet's bed; al-Mubahala (21 Dhi al-Hujja) which marks the occasion when the Prophet, as a blessing, spread his robe over the People of the House including Ali; Ashura (10 Muharram) commemorating Husain's martyrdom at Karbala; and al-Ghadir II, when the Prophet informed Hasan and Husain, Ali's sons, of their divine status.[1]

The same sources also indicate the Alawis' participation in many Christian and Persian holidays, including Christmas, Epiphany (6 January), Easter which they call al-Quzali, St Barbara's Day (16 October), al-Zuhuriya (5 April), as well as the Persian New Year, Nayruz.

These holidays, however frequent, are never celebrated publicly in an open, collective way; they are observed privately, mostly in the houses of notables or of renowned religious shaikhs. Indeed, it is only in the 1970s and 1980s that the Alawis have begun to build mosques for open, collective worship. In their worship, they used to follow a voluntary system much like the Sufi circles or Druze congregations—a system contained essentially in religious fellowship. Once a person reaches adulthood, between the ages of 14 and 18, he attaches himself to a shaikh or *sayyid* who supposedly instructs him in religious dogma and practice. Women are excepted from the rule. Religious fellowship, which is concluded according to a standardized ritual of initiation (a feast-like ceremony in which sacrificial meat and wine are consumed and incense burned) establishes a permanent bond between master-shaikh and novice. The master-shaikhs guide and nurture the novices spiritually, continuously monitoring their religious progress. I was told by an Alawi shaikh that this form of fellowship is a lasting, marriage-like arrangement and cannot be broken without the approval of the master-shaikh.

The recurrence of numerous holidays operates to reinforce the religious bond between master-shaikh and novice. Many of the honoraria and *zakat* due to the master-shaikh are paid by the novice during these holidays. The master-shaikh, in turn, could himself be a novice linked to a shaikh of a higher rank, which suggests that the Alawis, at any particular time, are engaged in hierarchically arranged dyadic religious fellowships that wrap the whole community up together.

Religious example among the Alawis is represented by two categories of specialists: the *shuyukh al-din* (shaikhs of religion) and the *shuyukh al-shar'* (shaikhs of the forbidden and the permissible), dealing with dogma and law respectively. The shaikhs of religion specialize in sacramental knowledge, that part of religion which has been concealed from the Muslim masses, which, by itself, perfects religion. They are entrusted with the responsibilities of fellowship and religious instruction according to the Alawi holy text, *The Book of Synthesis*, the major part of which deals with the esoteric interpretation of Qur'anic texts. Dussaud (1900:161–79) relates that the Alawi shaikhs whom he interviewed used to say that *The Book of Synthesis* is 'the foundation stone in religion'.

The shaikhs of religion are not all classed in one rank, nor are they formally classified on a pyramidal, bureaucratic scale with lower offices subordinately linked to higher ones. The Alawis make a distinction between the local *ulama*, whom they call imams or village shaikhs, and the white-turbaned shaikhs, who are very few in number and occupy top positions in the religious hierarchy (al-Tawil, 1966:275). A few shaikhs who live in the Latakiya district today, such as Shaikhs Mahmud Salih, Habib Salih, Kamil Salih, Abdul-Latif Ibrahim and others, are thought to belong to this top category. In the contemporary religious history of the Alawis, many shaikhs have likewise reached the top positions.[2]

Much as their counterparts among the Druzes, the top category of shaikhs of religion lead a very austere, monastic life; they are 'closer to Hindu monks than to the Islamic *ulama*', according to al-Alawi (1972:177). Their practice of austerity and monasticism is evident in the kind of poetry and prose they have written about themselves, or which is written about them by others (al-Alawi, 1972:207–15). Withdrawal from society has a highly symbolic meaning: one withdraws and seeks solitude in order to act as an example of consensus and religious brotherhood, aloof from factional conflict. This is where the passing of prescribed religious roles from father to son (especially among the top shaikhs) becomes expedient: it assures the community of the continuity of symbols that establish consensus in a faction-ridden society. The Alawis contend that a shaikh is 'the son of a shaikh', which means that religious knowledge is inherited.

The element of hereditary roles in religious specialization could likewise be attributed to the emphasis on the principle of esoteric interpretation and the knowledge of the concealed part of religion. If religion is assumed to be a personal experience rather than a public achievement, it is better for it to be acquired privately through father–son association, not publicly in schools.

Unlike the top shaikhs of religion, who stand for consensus and the unity of the religious community and live in solitude pondering upon the destiny of man, the local village shaikhs, in the lower echelons, are directly involved in upholding religious ethics and fellowship among believers. One of my interviewees put it this way: 'They uphold prayer wherever and whenever they congregate.' Some of them roam the Alawi land calling for obedience of and adherence to religious dictates, thus establishing cross-cutting links between the various segments of Alawi society through a series of dyadic religious fellowships. They are distinguished from other shaikhs by wearing unturbaned white headdresses (the turban being a symbol of personal sovereignty). Some of the local shaikhs wear no headdress at all, which signifies the lowest status on the religious scale. According to al-Tawil (1966:477), the shaikhs of religion are 'as numerous as commoners'; while this may be an exaggeration, it indicates the high ratios of shaikhs in Alawi society.

The other category, the shaikhs of the forbidden and the permissible, pronounce on the law and are essentially recruited in public courts that come under the authority of the state. They lie outside the Alawi structure of religion. The courts in which they serve were established by the state in the early 1920s following the Sunni pattern and did not emerge spontaneously from immediate community needs. Should these courts be closed down, the course of religion would not be altered, either negatively or positively.

Religious structure among the Alawis is paralleled by civil standards rooted in power and coercion. The Alawis are politically divided into several competing factions, some based in tribal or clannish coalitions, and some based in religious denominations or sub-sects such as the *Shamsiyun* (Sun People), the *Qamariyun* (Moon People),[3] the *Kalaziyun* (named after the founder of the sub-sect, Muhammad al-Kalazi), and the *Murshidun* (named after Sulaiman al-Murshid, who appeared in the 1930s and early 1940s). It must be stressed that the dyadic fellowships, mentioned earlier, are contained within these sub-sectarian divisions, especially at the lower levels of religious organization.

Tribal divisions among the Alawis are numerous. The most significant of them include the Khaiyatin, Bani Ali, Mahaliba, Haddadin, Matawira, Darawisa, Mahariza and Kalbiya. From each of these strains, there split off a number of smaller segments spread over different parts of the Alawi land. The Haddadin clans trace descent to the Master Muhammad al-Haddad, the son of Mahmud al-Sinjari who was the nephew of Prince Hasan al-Makzun al-Sinjari, a renowned figure in Alawi religious history. It is related that the Matawira tribe, from which the Numailatiya clan had sprung up, came to the Latakiya area along with Prince Hasan al-Makzun around 1223. Salih al-Ali, who led the Alawi rebellion against the French colonial authorities in 1919 and 1921, had the same tribal origins. These genealogical data are very significant in forming political alliances among the Alawis today, as Batatu (1981:335) has demonstrated in his article on 'The Social Roots of Syria's Ruling Military'.

However, the division of Alawi society into two broad strains, one based on the command of religion and the other on power and coercion, does not mean that the two stand in isolation from one another. Indeed, there has been a considerable amount of grafting or oscillation between them, especially at the top leadership level. Whoever emerges as an uncontestable leader, defending Alawi rights, consolidating their power and unity, and maintaining cohesion and solidarity, is given a religious meaning and becomes a historic symbol. This is indeed what has happened to some of their eminent leaders such as Prince Hasan al-Makzun (thirteenth century), Shaikh Hatim al-Tubani (fourteenth century), and contemporary figures such as Shaikh Ali Salih and Sulaiman al-Murshid. President Hafez al-Asad of Syria today may be on the verge of this historically elevated position. These celebrities were able to combine the meanings of both symbols: religion (purity) and power. They are at once imams and emirs. In other words, at times among the Alawis there emerge leaders of some consequence who exemplify unity between the kingdom of God and the kingdom of Caesar—a process that continues to reinforce the image of the Alawis as an independent, sovereign sect.

The Druze *Ajawid*

The Druze pattern corresponds in many ways to that of the Alawis, although there are some variations in content. There exist among the Druzes two formulations, one based on religion and the other on power, coercion and the control of resources. The religious example is characterized by a hierarchic scale based on the depth of religious knowledge and the extent to which this knowledge is recognized by others. A knowledge of religion alone is not enough; it must be coupled with good conduct and reputation in society. The Druzes of Lebanon are reputed to place tremendous emphasis on socio-religious ethics in daily interaction, especially on speech and the avoidance of swearwords. For example, *kadhib* (lying) is referred to as 'the slip of memory'. Those of them who are exposed to religious dogma exercise a very strict and comprehensive ethical code; the higher the religious rank, the stricter the code. They try to avoid drinking, smoking, sarcastic behaviour, speaking in a high-pitched voice, using obscene language and dressing in a suggestive manner. They believe that 'as women are exposed to religion, the veil thickens'.

The generalization or diffusion of religious practice among the Druzes has created a quasi-religious form, the village *majlis* (congregation), which, except for the *azzaba* circle among the Ibadis, is unmatched elsewhere among other sects. These circles and congregations are unique in that they include people who, while they may know very little about religious dogma, still present themselves as embodying religious tradition. In a word, they establish 'holiness' while knowing little about theology.

The Druze *majlis*, which exists in every village and town, is responsible for the general conduct of the community, acting as the main instrument of control. It meets once a week on Thursday evenings, partly for prayer and partly to review the various happenings that have befallen the community at large. The *majlis* is headed by an elderly man called *sayis*, a pious man of good reputation, who, while knowing little about dogma, represents religious tradition. The *sayis* opens the meeting with a brief invocation and then instructs the members of the congregation each to 'search for his self'. Those who feel they are not quite ready spiritually to take part in the discussion leave the room, in the hope of being admitted at a later date. It often happens that the one who withdraws from the meeting is the very person who wants to seek permanent membership in it—a privilege seldom granted automatically. If undesirables are present—people who have committed any of the 'big three sins', as the Druzes call them: murder, adultery or sacrilege—they will be instructed by the *sayis* to leave the congregation. Attending the congregation among the Druzes has, roughly speaking, the same value as communion in Christianity.

Those who have committed the 'big three sins' are not blessed when they die, and the stigma passes down from one generation to the next. A Druze who commits one of these sins withdraws or is expelled from the category of shaikhs, collectively called *ajawid*. This procedure is referred to as *bu'da* (forced isolation) and is analogous to the practice of *tabriya* among the Ibadis. The *ajawid* refuse to invoke God's mercy upon the committers of such sins.

The Druzes refer to those who regularly take part in religious discussion as the 'receivers of religion' or 'the knowables'; others are called 'the ignorant', those who are not allowed or have not yet chosen to attend the open discussion on religious treatises. This does not mean that the 'knowables' know more about religion than the 'ignorant'; it is a matter of whether or not the persons concerned take part in the weekly congregations. Indeed, many an 'ignorant' knows more about religion than a 'knowable'.

These details of religious practice among the Druzes underline the fact that religious presence need not be accomplished through the observation of formal ritual alone, but also through the observance of a very generalized socio-religious ethical code. The Druzes are noted for their lack of formal ritual, but are very strict on the private religious codes.

At the top of the pyramid stand a few elect shaikhs who lead an austere, monastic life; theirs is a spiritual existence continuously seeking the *tawhid* knowledge of the Divine. In Lebanon, they live in al-Baiyada retreat near Hasbaiya town in the western Biqa. The very top among them are distinguished by wearing a crown-shaped turban made of wool or cotton, not silk which is abhorrent to them. Only a handful of shaikhs are thought to reach the stage of *tawhid* knowledge: my interviewee could only name three in Lebanon (Shaikh Abu Hasan Arif from Baruk village, the late Shaikh Bu Hasib al-Sayegh from Aley and Shaikh Muhammad Faraj from Ubay) and one from Palestine (the famous Shaikh Amin al-Tarif). Some say that al-Tarif, who is the head of the Druze community in Israel, does not enjoy the same religious reputation as the others. Unlike the others, who live in solitude, al-Tarif is quite an active political figure.

These shaikhs symbolize the height of religious achievement. They are much spoken about in public: their personalities, style of life, ways of worship and dedication to religious knowledge command respect. They rarely mix with people, preferring to live in solitude where they perform an intensive schedule of what the Druzes call 'bodily exercises': fasting, abstinence from sex and many other of life's pleasures. One of them is said to have agreed to marry his wife on condition that she bear him no children, which is taken to be the height of devotion to religious studies. This position, the crown-like turban, is bestowed upon the person by his own colleagues and followers at a special meeting called for this purpose. The meeting, referred to as *tatwij* (the crowning ritual), is attended only by shaikhs whose level of religious knowledge is no lower than that of the person concerned. If other shaikhs of lower rank happen to be present, their role would be confined to the performance of the ritual rather than taking part in the election.

Second in the hierarchy come the *ajawid*, who wear a cylindrically shaped white turban. They often wear black robes with green, red, yellow, blue or white stripes. These striped colours stand for the 'five boundaries' of wisdom: the mind, the self, the word, the predecessor (or right wing) and the successor (or left wing). Each of these *hudud* (boundaries) is then represented by one of the five disciples (the interpreters) of the Druze religion. Thus the mind (signified by the colour green) is represented by Hamza bin Ali; the self (red) by Isma'il al-Tamimi; the word (yellow) by Muhammad bin Wahhab al-Quraishi; the predecessor or 'right wing' (blue) by Abu al-Khair Salama al-Samiri; and finally, the successor or 'left wing' (white) by Baha al-Din al-Muqtana. This is why the Druz flag today is made up of these five colours.

The cylindrical white turban indicates that the shaikh who wears it has been exposed to *The Messages of Wisdom* and is capable of explaining or interpreting it to qualified believers. The most traditional, or rather strictest, of them all is a category known as *shuyukh al-khatir* or the blue shaikhs; they are called 'blue' simply because they wear blue baggy trousers. Being strict about religious tradition, they refuse, for example, to read or explain the texts to novices dressed in modern, Western clothes.

It is estimated that in Lebanon today, there are no less than 1,500 shaikhs who wear cylindrical white turbans (including the blue shaikhs), i.e. a ratio of 1 shaikh to every 100 persons. They permeate the Druze land, establishing the authority of religion and carefully disseminating the knowledge of *tawhid*. In the Druze setting, such a ratio can be very confusing, simply because religious specialization is not confined to formally recognized *ajawid*, but is diffused throughout the community, including the initiated (those who have been exposed to dogma) as well. The male initiates distinguish themselves by shaving their hair and wearing a *kufiya* headcloth; women initiates wear modest clothes of dark colours and long skirts, with the arms and legs covered, as well as thick white veils covering the head. Women, however advanced they might be in religious studies, do not progress beyond the status of 'knowables'.

The use of different modes of dress, especially head-covers, to distinguish between levels of religious specialization may vary from one region to another. In Syria, for example, the top *ajawid* wear a rounded white turban without a *kufiya*; the second in hierarchy wear a turban underneath the *kufiya*; the third a turban over the *kufiya*: and the fourth, which is the stage of initiates, wear only a *kufiya* without a turban.[4]

The fact that religious specialization is diffuse does not mean that the *ajawid* do not perform specialized roles. They privately monitor and continuously evaluate the 'worth' of every believer—an evaluation which they publicly expose only on death, as part of a person's funeral ceremony. The social and religious value of a Druze is measured in terms of the number of shaikhs who attend his funeral to invoke God's blessing on his soul. The larger the number of shaikhs and the greater the number of blessings they invoke, the higher the value of the person: they bear witness to his conduct and obedience to religion. To be blessed upon death three or more times by a large number of shaikhs is evidence of relatively high religious and social standing. Likewise, to be blessed only once by fewer shaikhs is an index of low standing, if not a punishment inherited from father to son. The Druzes are a small community, and personal information passes on from one village to another very quickly; what their shaikhs do becomes public knowledge in a few days.

The *ajawid* practise endogamy at its highest level. The Druzes maintain that a *jawwid* (sing. of *ajawid*) who fails to marry a woman of the same standing loses his position and title, which explains why religious specialization tends to be confined to particular families. Besides, the fact that religious knowledge is not disseminated publicly according to an open and standardized system places the sons of shaikhs in a more advantageous position than others. They receive private tuition in religious knowledge at home.

The *ajawid* are not only distinguished by the practice of endogamy and access to private knowledge, but also by worship and the kind of congregations they hold. There exist among the Druzes two types of congregation, one referred to as *khilwa* and the other as *majlis*. The *khilwa* is the domain of the *ajawid* category, where they meet to discuss the general affairs befalling the whole Druze community as well as reading the actual texts of *The Messages of Wisdom* (Abu-Salih, H. n.d:21–5). Direct access to *The Messages of Wisdom* is considered to be a very advanced stage in seeking the *tawhid* knowledge of Divinity. By contrast, the *majlis* is the domain of novices and initiates to whom the preliminary tenets of religion are exposed or in the process of being exposed. This is the stage of *wa'z* (instruction) whereby the congregation is exposed to the contents of a book called *Safin* (the Full One) containing the heritage of many Sufi writers such as al-Hallaj, al-Bistami, al-Junaid, Ibrahim bin Adham, Rabi'a al-Adawiya, Ma'ruf al-Karkhi, Hasan al-Basri, and others. The Druzes believe that these Sufi practitioners are blessed with divine mercy: although they lived before the last exposition of Divinity —the *tawhid* knowledge—they might have been exposed to it some time before its proclamation. As the Druze scholar Sami Makarem put it to me, 'They were aware of *tawhid* knowledge at the subconscious level.'

The stage of 'instruction' is followed by that of *sharh* (interpretation) in which texts from *The Messages of Wisdom* are explained to the initiates (not to the novices). Some shaikhs, such as Jamal al-Din Abdullah al-Tannukhi, known locally as Sayyid Abdullah or Shaikh Abu Hilal, are highly praised for their capacity to 'explain' the meanings of the texts. Those who have committed the sins of murder or adultery stop at the interpretive stage and do not proceed any further to the 'reading stage', which is the speciality of the *ajawid* class alone.

The *khilwa* and the *majlis* are stratified areas of worship in more than one sense. Not only is the *khilwa* a higher order in seeking *tawhid* knowledge, where the actual texts of *The Messages of Wisdom* are read and debated, but in this congregation the *ajawid* discuss the general affairs of the community, especially at times of crisis, such as civil war. They do this in order to enforce a united stand among the Druzes. Unlike the local *majlis*, which may reflect political factionalism, the *khilwa* signifies consensus. The *khilwa* is always located outside the village, far from the everyday activities of men. The *khilwa ajawid* act above internal conflict;

they resist the potential rise of internal strife, as evidenced in the several internal conflicts in Lebanon (in 1958, and in the 1975–89 war) which the Druzes were drawn into as a single, united body despite the various attempts to split them into contrary factions. The Druzes are the only sect in Lebanon today who have managed to avoid internal strife, thanks to the *ajawid* class.

The *ajawid* occupy no formal, public office; their function is voluntarily bestowed upon them by the community and by other *ajawid*. They receive no salaries, indemnities or honoraria for the tasks they perform, lest these be defiled by the 'forbidden'. They subsist on their own earnings, especially in agriculture. However, there is another category of shaikhs among the Druzes who oversee the legal aspects of the administration of justice in the religious court headed by Mashyakhat al-Aql, the highest legal authority. Mashyakhat al-Aql and the courts linked to it are formally salaried offices recognized by the state exactly like other offices in the bureaucracy. They are entrusted with the management of the personal affairs of the Druzes, especially with regard to such matters as marriage, divorce, inheritance and the legitimacy of children.

What is true of the state is not true of the sovereign community. Whereas the state considers Mashyakhat al-Aql to represent the highest religious authority among the Druzes, the latter see it as simply the link between them and the state. They preserve the top of the hierarchy for the devout shaikhs who uphold the consensus of the community. Indeed, Mashyakhat al-Aql and the courts attached to it are political appointments rather than self-achieved statuses, and because of this they tend to fluctuate with power and influence. In Lebanon until recently, there were two people occupying the office of Shaikh al-Aql (head of the Druze court system), one representing the Junblati and one the Irslani factions. When the community unites politically, one person emerges for the office; when it splinters, more than one person appears. In Syria, where consensus is lacking, there have been three shaikhs occupying the same office and carrying the same title. This is where ideology is closely linked to organization: just as the Druzes give priority to the search for *tawhid* knowledge over law (Islam), they place the *ajawid* who deal with this knowledge on a higher level than those who deal with law.

The religious law administered by the Druzes has generally been taken from the Sunni Hanafi law as developed by the jurist Ahmad bin Awwam in the early part of the eleventh century (Taqiyuddin, 1979:14). Since then, many amendments have been introduced to this legal doctrine; the last was reviewed by the Lebanese parliament in both 1960 and 1967 (Taqiyuddin, 1979:390–1). The same point can be made about the Druzes of Syria, where the legal doctrines according to which they are judged were formally issued in 1946, 1959 and 1961. Before these dates, the Shaikh al-Aql, aided by four other jurists who collectively symbolize the five boundaries of knowledge, used to administer the legal affairs of the community.

The two religious hierarchies, the *ajawid* (at the top of which lie the crown-shaped turbaned shaikhs) and the jurists (headed by the Shaikh al-Aql), intersect at many different points. They meet in at least three different fields of action: the management of the local *majlis*, the recruitment of jurists to Druze courts and the recruitment of members to the Religious High Council. The *sayis* who chairs the local *majlis* is initially appointed by the Shaikh al-Aql, but the appointment must then be approved by the *ajawid* living in the area. In his decision, the *sayis* is assisted by the *ajawid*, whom he regularly consults, especially over whether to accept or reject novices.

The same style of co-ordination is repeated in the appointment of heads of the local courts, as well as in the recruitment of members of the High Council. There are four Druze courts in Lebanon (Beirut, Aley, the Shuf and the Metn) each of which is headed by a Druze shaikh well versed in Islamic law, and sometimes assisted by judges trained in legal codes. The judges and the heads of the courts are all appointed by the Shaikh al-Aql as approved by the top *ajawid*. So are members of the High Council, which includes the Shaikh al-Aql, several *ajawid*, various Druze ministers and parliamentary members, and those who have distinguished themselves in commerce and industry. The council supervises the endowment of land, welfare societies, schools and all other charities that come under the control of the Druze community as a whole (with the exception of al-Baiyada endowment land, which is managed by its own shaikhs).

The world of Caesar, the other side of the duality of the Druzes, is represented by the men of power and influence, the feudal houses who control people and resources. The Druzes draw a clear distinction between the two polarities by calling the *ajawid* categories *shuyukh al-din* (the shaikhs of religion) and the men of power and coercion *shuyukh al-tariq* (the shaikhs of the highway), owing to the fact that coercive measures are often imposed upon passage rights on roads and highways. Druze policy has long rotated around two main political causes: the Junblatis versus the Irslanis in Lebanon, and the Atrashes versus the

Hamdans in Syria. Other local cleavages, whether built upon family or village conflicts, are in one way or another grafted onto these two broad, competing factions. When the struggle for power is about to break into an open clash, as could have happened in Lebanon in 1958 or during the 1975– war, the *ajawid* intervene and almost always manage to contain the conflict. In all the history of war-infested Lebanon, the Druzes have never fought against each other; they compete in times of peace but not in times of war, which cannot be said of any of the other communities.

As in the case of the Alawis, the kingdom of God and the kingdom of Caesar among the Druzes do not operate in isolation from each other. There are times when the two ends of the duality merge in the personage of the leader, the symbol of resistance, the protector of the sect. Such was the case with the late Kamal Junblat, who was deeply revered by all segments of the Druze community. He was admired for his knowledge of religion, which is well demonstrated in the poems he wrote in his book *Farah* (Happiness), as well as for his political skills and manoeuvres. Junblat's model resembles that of the historic figures who periodically emerged in Druze history, such as the great prince Fakhruddin, Shaikh Muhammad Abu Hilal, known as the Virtuous Shaikh, who lived during the Ma'ni Emirate, or Sayyid Abdullah who lived during the Tannukhi Emirate.[5] These historic celebrities are milestones in the history of a sect and continuously reinforce the identity of the group as a separate, sovereign community.

16
God and Caesar: the Maronites and the Orthodox

It must be stressed that the resemblance between the Alawis and the Druzes on the one hand, and the Christian Maronites and the Orthodox on the other, with regard to the separation between the kingdom of God and Caesar applies only to the formal structure of this duality. The ideological background is by no means the same. Whereas duality among the Alawis and the Druzes is rooted in the episodic manifestation or exposition of divinity, duality among the Maronites and the Orthodox is a comprehensive system covering practically all aspects of religious life. While it is true that all these religious communities recognize the significance of sacramental knowledge, it is no less true that the contents and meanings of the sacrament they recognize are quite different. The Alawis and the Druzes restrict the achievement of sacramental experience to the few elect; the Christians make it the practice of mass worship, attainable by all participants.

Theological issues aside, certain structural aspects of religious authority are the same among all sects. The difference is between, on the one hand, religion adapted to state authority, and on the other, sectarian dogma adapted to the sovereignty of the individual community. The Orthodox, who adapt religion to state structure, are closer to the Sunni way—indeed, they are jokingly referred to as the Sunni of Eastern Christendom—while the Maronites, who uphold religion as an instrument of community sovereignty, present a sectarian phenomenon. Consequently the Orthodox, like the Sunni, have a limited number of religious specialists who occupy secondary positions *vis à vis* the power elites and perform specifically restricted tasks in society. The following comparative discussion on the organization of the priesthood and the monastic orders will help to illustrate the point.

Monasticism is, among the Orthodox, a personal pledge to the service of God and the Messiah, an act of total devotion to worship and of withdrawal from worldly affairs. As Bishop George Khudr put it, 'Monasticism is an expression of the faithful self and not a social system.'[1] The Orthodox monks and nuns live in isolated monasteries subsisting on whatever they raise from the monastery's *waqf* land and on gifts or honoraria voluntarily given to them by the laity. In Lebanon, there are estimated to be around fifty monks and nuns living in four or five monasteries, each subject to the authority of the bishop of the area. An exception is the al-Balamand Monastery which comes directly under the authority of the Patriarch in Damascus.

The bishop in the Antiochian Orthodox Church stands at the top of the pyramid; he is the final authority on religious matters within his diocese. Beirut is a separate, independent bishopric, as are Akkar, Tripoli, Zahle, and Mount Lebanon; Homs, Hama, Aleppo and Houran in Syria; Jerusalem in Palestine; Europe; North America; Canada; and Brazil. These together constitute the Antiochian Ecclesiastical Council headed by the Patriarch, who presides over the council without having the authority to enforce decisions. Decisions are taken by consensus; the Patriarch is a 'first among equals' and can only interfere in the performance of another bishop through the council itself. Even the council does not have the right to expel a bishop from his consecrated office, with the exception of severe cases such as insanity or crime.

The structure of authority in the Antiochian Orthodox Church is composed of a series of local priests operating in villages or districts of towns and cities, sometimes assisted by an aide called *shammas*, who together come under the direct supervision of the bishop, the final authority. If one of the priests distinguishes himself in religious matters and happens to be still unmarried, he might be promoted to the honorary rank of *archmandrit* and perhaps bishop. However, bishops are usually recruited by the council from the ranks of adult monks rather than from the priesthood category. As with the Sunni shaikhs, the number of priests is roughly proportional to the number of villages in the bishopric or sections in the city. It may happen, nevertheless, that one priest may serve more than one village, or one village might be served by more than one priest, depending upon village size and the prevailing political factions. Different factions might insist on being served by different priests.

Bishops or priests, *shammases* or *archmandrits*, all specialists among the Orthodox, are sustained by the limited earnings of the *waqf*, but mostly by the honoraria paid them for the performance of individual rituals such as marriage, baptism and funerals, or collective ceremonies such as the weekly mass on Sunday, or the various seasonal festivities, Christmas or Easter. Their almost total dependence upon the laity for survival accounts for the secondary position they occupy in society in relation to the power elites, the people of resolution and contract.

All these variables—the limited number of religious specialists, the specialized rather than the general nature of the tasks they perform in society, and their subsidiary position in relation to the power elites—emerge basically as a result of religious adaptation to centralized state authority. Although Byzantium fell around the middle of the fifteenth century, the formal structure of its religion has persisted to the present day. At every mass, the Orthodox still appeal to God to 'help the "kings" [symbols of central authority] beat the barbarians' and call for 'obedience to the ruler and the laws of the land'.

This rather loose Church organization among the Orthodox is counterbalanced by the very tight organization of the Maronites. Unlike the Orthodox, the Maronite monastic orders are not simply engaged in acts of devotion and worship; they form an integrated and pervasive socio-religious structure. The Maronites have two native orders: the Lubnaniya (sometimes called the Baladiya or the Halabiya) and the Mar-Sha'iya (or the Antouniya), which cut across various segments of the Maronite community. Since 1987 these orders have been combined in one federation headed by Father al-Hashim with a membership ranging between 3,000 and 4,500 (Dahir, 1981:156).

In addition, there are a large number of branches representing many universal Catholic orders operating in Lebanon: Jesuits, Carmelites, Italians, Franciscans, Capuchins, St Teresa and the Rosarians. There is hardly an order in the Catholic world which is not represented in Lebanon today in one form or another. Each of these orders performs a particular activity: the Jesuits specialize in college education, the Carmelites and Franciscans in primary and secondary education, St Teresa and the Rosarians in the management of hospitals and homes for the aged.

The involvement of the Maronite monastic orders in a variety of social services began around the eighteenth century, following the community's intensive contacts with the Vatican.[2] Before the eighteenth century, there had been only one monastic order and the number of monasteries was very limited, each operating almost completely independently of the others (Harik, 1972:65–7). The intensive contacts with the Vatican have led to many changes in the structure of the Church, the monastic orders and in the ways these link to society at large, changes that came to be known in the history of the Maronites as the 'reformative movement' (Harik, 1972:77). The reforms focused on three related issues: the training of priests and monks, the separation between the Church and the feudal order, and the separation between the Church and the monastic orders.

Before the reforms, the Church was subject to the influence of feudal lords, evident in the fact that most of the bishops were recruited from well-established feudal houses. The monasteries came under the authority of the bishop, much as has always been the case among the Orthodox. After the reforms, which took more than a century to achieve, the Church earned its independence and began to appoint bishops and supervise their activities. Likewise, the monastic orders split from the body of the Church and began to manage their affairs independently.[3] Maronite monasticism grew so strong economically that by the middle of the nineteenth century they were believed to have owned about one quarter of Mount Lebanon and established between eighty and ninety new monasteries (Harik, 1972:88; Dahir, 1981:141).

It is a self-reinforcing system: as the monastic orders grew stronger economically, they recruited more members, which in turn made them even stronger economically. Many of the poor, who initially joined simply out of poverty, provided free labour which subsequently enhanced the orders' capital and resources. The peasant rebellion in Lebanon at the turn of the eighteenth century must be understood from this perspective: the monastic orders supporting the peasantry, their kith and kin, against the feudal lords. The increasing influence of monasticism had weakened the feudal order both economically and politically.

While Maronite monasticism involves itself in a complex system of social services, sometimes staunchly competing with the state especially in the realm of formal education, the Church, headed by the Patriarch, monitors the ritualistic life of the community. The Maronite priesthood performs the same ritualistic roles as the Orthodox do, but unlike the Orthodox, they are not totally dependent upon the laity for sustenance. In addition to the honoraria they receive for the performance of individual and collective rituals and ceremonies, the Maronite priesthood, from the Patriarch down to the village priests, are paid monthly salaries by the Church. The Church's reliance on its own independent economic resources has given it a greater measure of freedom of operation *vis à vis* the power elites, and has led to what appears to be a tightly graded authority structure.

The influence of the Vatican in this respect is quite clear. Although the Maronite Church has some measure of freedom in operating its internal affairs, ultimate authority rests with the Pope. Some Maronite Patriarchs, such as al-Ma'ushi for example, while being heads of the Church in Lebanon, are simultaneously appointed Cardinals in the Vatican's hierarchy, one of about eighty Cardinals who elect the Pope. It is this tight and graded authority structure—the pyramidal form of organization that begins with the Pope and ends with the village priest—which gives the impression that the Maronite Church enjoys a kind of internal cohesion unmatched elsewhere in Christian churches.

These differences between the Church and the monastic orders have left their imprint. Whereas the number of priests is limited by virtue of the Church's own organization (one or two priests to a village), the number of monks and nuns who could pledge themselves to the service of God and the community is potentially unlimited. In his field-work in the 1980s in Ma'ad, a Lebanese Maronite village north of Beirut with a population of 294, Joseph Faris mentions that there were 15 religious specialists (of whom 1 was a priest and 14 were monks and nuns), i.e. a ratio of 1:20. This corresponds perfectly to the data I collected on 6 Maronite villages in north Lebanon, where the ratio was from 1:12 to 1:27, still a high ratio compared to the Orthodox, the religion of the state.

The far higher frequency of specialists recruited in monastic orders can be attributed to the voluntary nature of monasticism. Unlike the Church, which enjoys a bureaucratic structure where appointments are made to serve a set of specific but limited needs, the monastic orders are voluntary organizations which people choose to join out of devotion or vocation. Monasticism among the Maronites, like the *ajawid* among the Druzes or the 'shaikhs of religion' among the Alawis, is an act of religious devotion for the service of God and man. The monks seek solitude in order to establish consensus, aloof from internal conflicts or schisms that may split the community. In times of crisis, it is these consensus organizations that help unite the sect to challenge external threats and establish internal harmony.

The power elite (the emirs) among the Maronites are organized around a multi-factional policy that falls into two opposed coalitions, one calling for sympathy and co-operation with pro-Arab movements or currents, and one standing for an independent, sovereign Lebanon distinct from Arab policies. In the early days of independence, the 1940s and early 1950s, the first coalition was represented by the protagonists of the National Pact, such as the late President Bishara al-Khoury and Henry Far'aoun, who were recruited in the Dastour Party; the second by the National Bloc Party headed by Emile Edde. In the 1960s and 1970s, the two polarities were represented by the successive Shihabi-based regimes, who inherited the attitudes of the Dastour Party, and by the Kata'ib and the Ahrar Parties who stood for the sovereign and distinct polity of Lebanon. When the Kata'ib took hold of the presidency in the 1980s, President Sulaiman Franjiya, a Maronite leader from the North, took issue with them, calling for co-operation with their Arab neighbours, namely Syria. Today (1989), the same polarity is represented by President Iliyas Hrawi calling for co-operation with Syria and General Michel Aoun calling for a free and sovereign Lebanon.

Throughout the turbulent episodes in the history of the Maronites, the monastic orders (and to a lesser extent the Church) have stood for unity and consensus. Just as they are able to mobilize the Catholic Church, of which they are an integral part, they at the same time mobilize tremendous internal support through the impressive services they offer in education and organized charity. Standing aloof from political factionalism, they, like the *ajawid* and the 'shaikhs of religion', reinforce the sovereignty of the entire religious community.

17
Epilogue: Brethren or Citizens?

The foregoing chapters have reviewed several patterns of religious ideology and organization as they adapt either to state structures and centralized authority or, on the contrary, to the sovereignty of the religious community. Many of the concepts and practices among the Sunni have been placed within the first formulation, and those among Islamic sects and the Christian Maronites within the second. As previously mentioned, the Maronites were added to the latter formulation because of the many socio-religious variables they share with Islamic sects, namely, peripheral location, territorial concentration of population in sectarian regions, comprehensive production system, intensity of ritual and duality of religious organization.

There remains one more question: what does it mean, in the course of the evolution of state and religion and the dialectic relationship between them, to have one group adapt to state authority and the others to the sovereign community? By 'evolution' is meant the lasting changes that take place in the structure of states and religions as a result of technological, and subsequently socio-economic, change. In other words, how does religion adapt to state structures *vis à vis* socio-economic change, and how do religious patterns alter in response to socio-economic innovation?

Religious meanings and understandings change not only as they adapt to state structures or to the sovereign community; they also change with the rise of new conditions.[1] In order to deal with these meanings in Islam, it is helpful to distinguish between what might be called 'political nationalism' and 'symbolic nationalism'. Political nationalism rests upon the belief that the nation must be contained in one, independent state;

symbolic nationalism is a form of behavioural convergence, a meeting-point or a 'central mainstream' where people of the same national origin begin to exhibit unified patterns of behaviour in speech, dress, jokes, music, singing, literature, food, shelter and life-style. These behavioural patterns are growing much closer in Arab society today, converging upon a 'national' model of behaviour. The spoken language in Beirut, Kuwait, Damascus, Cairo, and even Tunis and Casablanca, is now much more similar than it has ever been before. The role of the mass media and education has been very effective in closing gaps and narrowing rifts. All Arabs share in the evolution and development of a symbolic Arab nationalism, whether or not they believe in Arab political unity. This is so by virtue of their daily interaction and the transformation of society from peasantry to a mass, urban order.

The process of convergence over a symbolic national model helps to alter all aspects of culture, including religious orientation. Hardly any nationalistic formulation has emerged in the world without religion playing a major role in clarifying its contents. Consider the rise of English nationalism and its association with the Anglican Church, or German nationalism and Lutherism; or the French, Italian, and Spanish nationalisms and the consolidation of the Catholic Church; or Greek nationalism and the Orthodox Church of Byzantium; or, for that matter, American nationalism and the Protestant Churches. Religious symbols are part and parcel of the total symbolic heritage in which the national pattern is embodied.

This applies equally to Arab nationalism and Islam, even if the link between them is still only incipient. One indication is the way in which the originally Islamic concepts of *umma* (nation), *nasr* (victory), *fatih* (conquest), *ukhuwwa* (brotherhood), *siyada* (sovereignty) and *al-risala al-khalida* (the eternal message) have taken on broad, nationalistic meanings. The *umma*, originally meaning the Islamic community at large, is now also used to mean the Arab nation (*al-umma al-arabiya*). *Nasr*, originally meaning a victory for Islam, now also means one for the Arabs. *Fatih*, originally meaning Islamic conquest, is now the name of the Palestine Liberation Organization. *Al-risala al-khalida*, originally meaning divine message, is today a synonym for the Ba'th Party founded by Michel Aflaq, a Greek Orthodox.

In its general orientation, the national symbolic model is comprehensive and universal rather than particularistic. This means that religious concepts are incorporated into the national model only if they are transferred from a private to a public framework, from the concern of brethren in religion to that of citizens in states. Precisely here lies the role of the modern nation-state: just as a nation-state could emerge as the expression of an already formulated national orientation, it could equally be the creator of this orientation. There is a dialectic relationship between state, religion and nationalistic movements; they work mutually to reinforce each other.

The Interplay between State, Religion and Nationalism

The modern state refers to a political, territorial and juristic arrangement. It enjoys a 'juristic personality', in the sense that it sues and can be sued. No religion can be said to be a state, for it sues but cannot be sued. Granted, some religions, like Islam and Judaism, give precedence to legal doctrines, but this is not sufficient to turn religions into states, or states into religions. It simply means that these religions meet with states in one respect, the priority they give to legislation. The mechanism of operation and the system of control are wide apart: states' actions always claim to be generated through public delegation or representation; religion is God's ordinance. In a state structure, the public, however defined, is the ultimate source of legislation; this is what is meant by 'secularization'.

Not only is the state an instrument of force; it is also an instrument of development and a mechanism of redistribution and growth. It is unfortunate that the Arabs have come to be so negatively obsessed with their colonial heritage that they see the state simply as a mechanism of fragmentation, ignoring its developmental role. This negative image of the state has given rise to two prevailing attitudes in the Arab world. First, there is the tendency of governments and rulers not to take the sovereignty of individual states seriously, as evidenced by their continued insistence upon unity and their readiness to merge states haphazardly. In his constant searching for unity, Qaddhafi of Libya is a good example of this attitude.[2] Second, there is the tendency among certain groups, including the intelligentsia, to blame the regime in power for all backward practices, thus safeguarding those social customs, traditions and beliefs which hinder progress.

The negative attitude towards the modern state does not derive only from its being a tool of fragmentation, but also from its essential contradiction with Islamic religious traditions which still dominate the thinking of the Arab masses. The contradiction between 'brethren' and 'citizens' is one of the most obvious examples of this. Brotherhood in religion is a stratified system governed by a set of unstructured reciprocities in marriage, inheritance, mode of interaction, residence, work, images and self-images. All religious communities see themselves as distinct creations, either through perpetual rebellion (the Shi'a), or through being the recipients of the last message (the Sunni), the only people entrusted with the privilege of knowing the 'concealed' texts that perfect religion (the Alawis), the last to have reached the *tawhid* knowledge leading to realization of the unity of God (the Druzes), the 'angelized' society (the Yazidis) or the people of unique civilization (the Maronites). The logic of 'brethren' implies that equality of interaction, both in theory and in practice, is contained within the same religious community. This belief necessarily stands in opposition to the concept of 'citizens', where equality, at least in theory, is thought to be a generalized phenomenon within the state boundaries. State laws apply universally to all citizens; religious laws are by definition particular, applicable only to brethren.

The difference between state and religion is one of theory and herein lies the concept of secularization as an integral part of the modern state. The modern state is secular in two senses: first, the right to legislate lies in the hands of the public through delegation or representation; and second, those rights are based on citizenship rather than on religious brotherhood. To place the right to legislate in the hands of the public does not of course mean that the laws thus decreed are emptied of their religious content. It is a simple formula: the pious public legislates laws of piety.

It is wrong to assume, as many Arab and Muslim writers do, that the secular West is irreligious or that secularization implies 'irreligiosity'.[3] Many of the secular West's civil laws, especially personal and family laws, have been derived from Christianity or given a Christian interpretation. Take, for example, family planning, marriage requirements, divorce, inheritance and even criminal law. These are either directly derived from Christian teachings, or remain in agreement with them. Besides, many a political platform in the West adopts religious issues. Ronald Reagan's position on abortion, on the grounds that it is incongruous with Christian teachings, is one of many issues that earned him a striking majority in the US presidential elections of 1984.

The secularization of the state implies that even decisions concerning religious matters are left to the public and not to the *ulama* class. This shift in the decision-making process weakens the elitist *ulama* authority, but does not eliminate the attachment to religion. On the contrary, it could be argued that the centralization of authority, which is an extension of secularization, has liberated the populace and their ways of worship from religious oppression or coercion, from one group imposing its ways upon the others.

The equation made by some Arabs between secularization and irreligiosity stems basically from a misinterpretation of certain Western practices, especially those relating to sex and sexuality. The West, to many Arabs, is represented by the image of a naked body; it is materialistic and characterized by immoral acts of behaviour. This is only one side of the coin, however; a wide variety of spiritual practices are also found in the West.

The separation of religion from the body of the state does not mean, however, that religion has become split off from society. This is clear from the course of development of religion and statehood in the Christian West, a model that need not be replicated elsewhere, as in the Muslim Arab world, for example. Nor is it to be expected that religious modernization in Islam (where 'man belongs to the sabbath') will follow a Christian model (where 'the sabbath belongs to man'). The issue in Islam is how to merge the kingdom of God with the kingdom of man, not separate them. If so, what pattern or patterns might Islam be expected to follow in the course of its modernization?

Some Future Trends

In the last few years, and particularly since the religious revolution of 1979 in Iran, an unprecedented number of books and articles have been written on modern trends in Islam.[4] These works abound in phrases such as 'Islamic revival', 'Islamic resurgence', 'Islam on the march', 'Islamic awakening', 'Islamic reawakening' and 'the return of Islam'. A detailed evaluation of these writings is beyond the scope of the present work. It is nevertheless worth commenting on two frequently occurring themes, monolithism and fundamentalism, before discussing religious revival and nationalistic movements. By 'monolithism' is meant the treatment of Muslims as if they were an undifferentiated lot—in other words, with no respect for variations of local tradition and cultural orientation, not even the evident fragmentary nature of religious activism. Many of the books referred to above include, under the rubric of Islamic resurgence, reassertion or revivalism, a variety of disconnected organizations stretching from the USSR in the north to Malaysia in the south, and from Morocco in the west to Singapore in the east. These organizations include the Muslim Brothers of Egypt, the Islamic Commando movement in Iran, the Tijaniya movement in Algeria, the National Salvation Party in Turkey, the Basmachi movement in the USSR, the Society of Atonement and Migration in Egypt, the Islamic Liberation Party in Jordan, Muhammad's Youth in Syria and Jund Allah in Lebanon.

Not only do these religious societies or organizations operate independently of each other; they also differ in aims, objectives, structure, and in the historical and social circumstances that led to their formation. Within Egypt alone, Dessouki (Cudsi and Dessouki, 1981) mentions seven autonomous organizations operating independently of each other, some of which have been spontaneously created by the opposition, others by government agencies. In Syria, different branches of Islamic activist organizations tend to emerge spontaneously in different cities without any links to a parent structure. In the city of Hama, Muslim activists assemble under the name of 'Muhammad's Youth'; in Aleppo, they are called the 'Trumpeters', in Damascus the 'Partisans' (Ansar). The same pattern is found in Lebanon, where they operate as the 'Tawhid movement' in Tripoli, the 'Soldiers of God' in Beirut and the 'Islamic Group' in Sidon. This is in addition to the Shi'a fundamentalism which operates in the Biqa and the southern suburbs of Beirut under the banner of the 'Party of God' (Hizbollah). These fundamentalist organizations operate independently of one another, each having its own resources, modes of recruitment, membership requirements, by-laws, policies, platforms and spokesmen. Such an organizationally fragmented situation cannot possibly be considered a united and comprehensive religious revival in Islam.

That a fragmentary structure like this should be seen as a 'monolothic' being reflects, to a large extent, the official, formalistic image Muslims hold of Islam. At the theoretical, formal level, religion in Islam is seen as a single mass, a united community, a community in consensus, even if, empirically, Muslims are fragmented into various groups, states and cultures. They are united by following Islamic law under the governance of the Muslim imam. The religious emphasis on 'consensus', a community in unity, makes it a mental reality whatever it turns out to be in practice. Based on this formula, sects become 'apostates', 'rejectors', 'schismists' rather than an expression of variations in religious traditions. Many of the Druze, Alawi and Ibadi sources lament the lack of official Sunni interest in their religious traditions.

By the same token, *salafiya* (fundamentalism) is understood to include all sorts of behaviours, beliefs, political movements and welfare societies that link to Islamic traditions in one way or another. It is interesting to note that what could be socially classified as 'change' in Islam is perceived by many modern writers on Islam to be a cyclic demonstration of tradition. Consider the conceptual framework in which change in Islam is captured: 'resurgence', 'reassurance', 'return', reawakening', 'pendulum'. Many aspects of behaviour that are sometimes dismissed as measures or indices of fundamentalism are in reality aspects of religious change. Instances of what is called *al-zay al-islami* (Islamic fashion) and of building 'family mosques' illustrate the point.

Large numbers of women and girls in the Arab world have recently begun to appear in public wearing a new two-piece fashion: a scarf that covers the hair, the ears and the neck; and a long gown that covers the body down to the ankles, with long sleeves covering the arms to the wrists. The dress is always in sober colours with as little design as possible. The appeal of the outfit lies entirely in its simplicity and newness, not in its colour, design or decoration. The most obvious feature is the absence of the black veil. Although many elements of the dress can be traced to traditional Islamic precepts, the way they recombine make the overall effect a new phenomenon. Although it has some roots in religious traditions, it has nevertheless come to signify an act of social liberation, as it is often adopted by women engaged in modernized activities: college students, secretaries, civil service employees and policewomen. As a student at the American University of Beirut put it, 'Were it not for Islamic dress, my parents would have never allowed me to go to college.'

The now frequent recourse to building 'family mosques', which is today most evident in the oil-rich countries of the Arab Gulf, is subject to the same interpretation. Outwardly it may be taken to be a gesture of fundamentalist tendencies, but upon closer inspection it may indicate a change in worship—a shift from collective forms of worship to individualized prayer. As these mosques proliferate, the central role of the *jami* (central mosque), which is under the authority of the state, is weakened; so this is a shift from religion as *din* to faith as *iman*.

The proliferation of family mosques, the prevalence of Islamic fashions, the shift from the practice of ritual to law, the preponderance of formally trained jurists, the sharpening of religious debate—all these could be considered aspects of convergence that go hand in hand with religious modernization. The secularization process in Europe has liberated faith from religion. Many aspects of secularization and modernization imply conformity, convergence upon a model of action and behaviour, the contents of which could be religious or otherwise.

Whatever the case, there exists in Islam today a polarity that has not yet been reconciled, a conflict between the Islamic *umma* (i.e. religion) and the modern state, between brethren and citizens. It often takes the form of opposition to state structures, demanding the enforcement of Islamic laws under such mottoes as: 'the Qur'an is our constitution', 'the re-establishment of the caliphate' or 'the [return to the] roots' (*asala*). In their turn, the protagonists of the state respond to these fundamentalist (religious) challenges by emphasizing a new political language: 'national unity', 'public interest', 'the country's sovereignty', 'the maintenance of independence', 'civil and political rights' or 'progress and development'.

The tension between the two polarities is likely to increase with socio-economic change and the emergence of politically enlightened masses. Already, many voices in the Arab world today are requesting standard civil and political rights, arguing that *shawra*, which is an acceptable form of public consultation in Islamic *shari'a*, is actually a numerical rather than a structural concept; that is to say, they are asking for universal suffrage.[5] This is another attempt to give an entirely new meaning to a well-established religious concept, moving from the particular to the universal, an act of merger between religion and nationalism.

The merger between nationalistic tendencies and religious orientations immediately alters our understanding of both nationalism and religion. The two meet at the point of behavioural convergence. The failure of secular nationalist movements or parties (such as the Ba'th, Arab nationalism and Greater Syrian nationalism) to reach the masses is due precisely to their attempt to dissociate religious orientations from national commitments; they remain elitist dogmas. In this connection, the experience of Nasser of Egypt presents a different perspective: his capacity to merge religion with nationalism almost spontaneously made him the unmatchable hero who quickly commanded opinion all across the Arab-Islamic world. Much more disciplined research is needed in this area of study. It is unfortunate that change in Islam is captured by static images of resurgence, revival, assertion, recognition, and so on, rather than by dynamic concepts of change: evolution, development, convergence, fashion, and so on.

One final question remains. If a redefinition of meanings alters both the religious and the national style, then which Islamic model in the Arab world is most likely to adapt to this mode of convergence? The Sunni model would appear to be the most adaptable. This is so by virtue of many interconnected variables. One is numbers: the Sunni constitute more than 80% of the total population of the Arab world. Another is their concentration in cities, the locus of change. A third variable is their control of government and centralized authority, and subsequently the adaptation of religion to power. Fifth is their incorporative rather than separative religious traditions. Last but not least is the precedence they give to legislation in religion, which corresponds perfectly to state procedures—juristic personality.

For the Sunni to play this modernization role, however, two factors would have to be reconsidered. On the one hand, the stratified structure of society and the imposition of inequalities on others would have to be changed. The religious classification of citizens into *dhummis* (apostates) and *rafada* (rejectors) is incongruent with the minimum requirements of civil rights in any modern state. On the other hand, the national model of convergence could only take on a broad or universal orientation if it were within a state structure rather than an *umma* formulation, a role that cannot possibly be performed by the *ulama*, but only by the national heroes, the builders of cities and states.

Notes

Chapter 1

1. The reader is referred to Figure 2 in Chapter 3.
2. See Redfield (1947:293–308).
3. Ibn Khaldun uses the term *wazi* to refer to the process of internalization of law.
4. See, for example, H. Faris (1980), W. Faris (1979), B. Ghilyun (1979), Hourani (1946), Muhyeddin (1980), Planhol (1956) and Qurm (1979).
5. The documents available in London at the Oriental Room and Reading Room of the British Museum and the Public Records Office tend to concentrate on diplomatic and political history and were therefore of limited use in the research for the present book. However, use has been made of some of the statistical and economic data they contain, especially on the Druzes of Lebanon and Syria, the Ibadis of Oman and the Zaidis of Yemen.
6. See Abu-Husain's thesis on Libya (1978), Hanna's on Saudi Arabia (1981) and Juraidini's on the Mahdis of Sudan (1980).

Chapter 2

1. See *ta'ifa* in Abdul-Baqi, *Index for Qur'anic Lexicons* (1945:431–2).
2. In this work the number of the *sura* precedes the number of the verse. For example, 2/130 means *sura* 2, verse 130.
3. To avoid confusion with the word *shar* meaning 'evil', the ain ('), as an exception, will be added at the end of the word *shar'* meaning 'Islamic jurisdiction; God's law' throughout this book.
4. See Uthman (1979:62), who states that the concept of *umma* is based on brotherhood and does not imply a territorial base.
5. This is taken from a comment made by Professor al-Khashshab at a conference on 'The Status of the Social Sciences in the Middle East', Alexandria, summer 1974.
6. Taken from an interview with al-Sharqawi, a well-known writer on Islam, as reported in *al-Majalla* (London), 1982.

7. From a public lecture given by al-Urwi at the American University of Beirut in 1984.

8. The concept of *taqiya* will be discussed in greater detail in Chapter 8 of this book.

9. This may apply to the Alawi-controlled Ba'th regime in Syria today.

Chapter 3

1. See al-Aqqad (1943:27) for more details.

2. See Khuri (1981e:75–87) for further details on the concept of authority among Arabian tribes.

3. See the declaration of Hujat al-Islam Ali Khumini'i, the President of the Islamic Republic of Iran, as published in *al-Nahar* (Beirut), 19 May 1985.

4. The following are shared by all groups irrespective of religion, class or ethnic origin: names derived from tribal traditions such as Adnan, Ghassan, Ma'n, Mundhir; from weather conditions such as Ghaith (heavy rain), Ra'd (thunder), Matar (rain); from celestial conditions and stars such as Suhail, Zahra (Venus), Najm (star), Qamar (moon), Badr (full moon), Badran (two full moons); from colours such as Abyad (white), Aswad (black), Swaidan (blackish), Azraq (blue), Zarruq (blueish); from foods and vegetables such as Dibs (molasses), Kusa (courgette), Mawza (banana); from flowers such as Warda (rose), Yasmin (jasmine); from physical disabilities such as A'war (one-eye), Atrash (deaf), Akhras (mute); and from desirable human qualities such as Karim (generous), Naser (supporter), Wasim (handsome), Jamil (pretty), Kamil (perfect), Kamal (perfection), Sadiq (truthful) and Mubarak (blessed).

5. See Farrag (1969) and Madani (1963) on the Ibadis.

Chapter 4

1. See, for example, Epstein (1978), Gans (1962) and Gordon (1964).

2. See Khuri's (1981b) work on city typology in the Middle East.

3. In Egypt, the urban population constitutes around 44% of the total population, in Morocco 42%, in Algeria 52%, in Iraq 68%, in Saudi Arabia 70%, in Syria 48%, in Tunisia 52%, in Lebanon 78%, in Jordan 60%, in Libya 52%, in Kuwait 90%, in the United Arab Emirates 81%, in Bahrain 81%, in Qatar 87%, in Sudan 21%. See Population Reference Bureau, *World Population Data Sheets for 1984*.

4. See Gellner (1968; 1981:54–62).

5. See also the article about the Yazidis in *Encyclopedia Islamica*, vol. 4 (1934), p.1164.

6. The reader is referred to Table 1 in Chapter 5.

7. See Khuri on Lebanon (1975) and on Bahrain (1980).

8. This is demonstrated by Van Dam's work on Syria (1978; 1979), and Eliya Harik's work on Lebanon (1972).

Chapter 5

1. The local bedouin call it Jabal al-Ali (the high mountain).

2. In Syria, the last census to take note of sects was conducted in 1956 by the Ministry of National Economics under the title *The Census Collection* (1957:18). Other censuses distinguished between Muslims, Christians and Jews, thus lumping the Druzes and the Alawis with Muslims.

In Lebanon, the last national census was taken in 1932. However, the figures quoted in Table 1 are taken from de Vaumas (1955:510–602), who based his calculations on the official figures of 1950, themselves a projection of the 1932 figures. The sectarian percentages for various districts are taken from official estimates issued by the Ministry of Interior in 1954.

The population data on Oman, contained in Category A of Table 1, are taken from the World Bank Report as presented to the Omani Ministry of Labour and Social Affairs in September 1982 (Khuri, 1981c). The World Bank Report strongly disagrees with the official census, which estimates the Omani population to be around 1,500,000. The official census did not take account of sectarian distribution; these figures have therefore been compiled from those in the *Encyclopedia of Islam* (1971:653) and from case-studies, notably Miles, who collected his data in the early part of this century. For the Ibadis living in Algeria, see Farrag (1969:1–10).

The distribution of the Shi'a in Iraq is taken from the official census of 1937 as quoted by Epstein (1978:1050). The same percentage is likewise quoted by Batatu (1978:40) for 1947. However, the national census of 1973 counts Christians and Yazidis and puts the Sunni and the Shi'a in the Muslim category. In Saudi Arabia, the distribution of the Shi'a for 1960 is taken from the *ARAMCO Handbook* (1960:44). Their concentration in the Eastern Province and Qatif is deduced from Vidal's case study (1955:40–3, 106, 216). Most of the census data on Saudi Arabia is very confusing: whereas Philby estimates the number of the Shi'a to be around 100,000, Lipsky (1956:44) quotes the same percentage for 1956, which is difficult to believe. The size of the Shi'a community in Bahrain was mentioned for the first and the last time in a 1941 census. Other percentages were deduced from a comprehensive survey conducted in this country by

Khuri in 1974–75. The data on Kuwait are taken from the national census of 1975.

The Yemeni national census for 1978, which was the first taken in the country, did not count sectarian groups. However, all case-studies on Yemen mention the concentration of the Zaidis in the northern and eastern regions, and estimate their size to be more than half of the total population (Bury, 1915:22, 34–5; Little, 1968:41; O'Ballance, 1971:20).

3. These shrines include Sa'sa near the village of Askar, Maytham in Jufair, Abdul-Aziz in al-Khamis, Emir Zaid in Malikiya and many others of this order.

4. Maqam Shamlikh (sometimes referred to as al-Maqam al-Sharif) is located in Sharun village north of the Shuf in Lebanon; Maqam Ayub around the village of Niha in the Shuf; Maqam al-Amir al-Sayyid in Ubay; Maqam Ain al-Zaman in Suwaida (Syria); Maqam al-Masih in Houran; and Maqam Shu'aib in upper Galilee (Yasin).

5. Other retreats include al-Qatalib in the Shuf area near the village of Ain Qaniya, al-Shawi located in the village of Abey in the same neighbourhood as the Dawudiya School and al-Mounissa retreat near the village of Aramoun.

6. See Serjeant (1985) for more details.

7. See Chevalier (1971), Harik (1968), and de Vaumas (1960) on Lebanon, Weuleress (1940) on the Alawis and Hay (1959) and Kelly (1959) on the interior of Oman.

8. See Khuri (1981).

Chapter 6

1. On the Copts of Egypt, see the National Census for 1976 issued by the Central Statistical Bureau in Cairo. On the Jews of Yemen, see O'Ballance (1971:21); of Libya, see the *Encyclopedia Britannica*, vol. 10 (1972:879); of Tunisia, see *The Area Handbook for the Republic of Tunisia* (1970:115); of Algeria, see *The Statesman's Yearbook* (1979–80:80); of Morocco, see Hoffman (1967:37–8) and Clarke and Fischer (1972:406).

2. After a conversation with L. Rosen at the University of Chicago, 1972.

3. See Khadduri (1955:178, 182–3, 193–4).

4. The Shafi'i law excludes the Zoroastrians from the *dhummi* category and therefore exempts them from the *jizya* tax.

5. For more details, see Fattal (1958), Ibn al-Jawziya (1961), Joseph (1961), Tritton (1928), Zaidan (1963) and Zayat (1949).

6. See al-Qurtubi, vol. II (1967).

7. Information from a conversation with one of the tribal chiefs of the Al-Jmi'a in North Yemen. See also Ali Haidar's manuscript (1973) on revenge in Baalbek (Lebanon).

8. See Khuri (1980:147–8) and Peters (1963).

9. See the Qur'an: 9/60 as interpreted by M. Uthman (1979:268).

10. See Haddad (1971) for details on this subject.

Chapter 7

1. See Gardet (1954:25) for details.

2. This point is taken from a lecture given by Radwan al-Sayyid on 'The Concept of Community in Islam' at the American University of Beirut, spring 1982.

3. For further discussion of these matters, see the works of those Islamic jurists who deal with the structure of Islamic government such as al-Baqlani, al-Baghdadi, al-Mawardi and Ibn Khaldun.

4. On this point, see Geertz (1968) and Hudson (1977).

5. See, for example, Khuri's works on Beirut (1975) and on Bahrain (1980).

6. See: Qabbani (1981: 596–606); Nuhad Itani's articles which appeared in the Lebanese daily *al-Liwa* between 30 Dec. 1980 and 5 Nov. 1981 under the title 'What do the Muslims Want?'; Sa'ib Salam's often quoted statement, 'Let us Gather our Identity, Lebanon is One, not Two'; and Salim al-Huss's proposals to end the Lebanese conflict delivered in a public speech at the Faculty of Sciences, The Lebanese University, 19 Jan. 1980.

7. See Ibrahim (1981) for details.

8. See, for example, Kashifulghata (n.d:87), Maghniya (n.d:22) and al-Zain (1979:29).

Chapter 8

1. For details of the history of the Ibadis in Oman, see the classic work by al-Salimi (n.d) and that by al-Shamikhi (1301 AH). On Yemen, see O'Ballance (1971), Little (1968), Ibn al-Mujawir (1951), Serjeant (1985) and Tritton (1928).

2. For further details on this point, see Zaid bin Ali bin al-Husain (n.d).

3. These excerpts are taken from Shaikh Mahdi Shamsuddin's speech as reported in the Lebanese daily paper *al-Nahar* on 18 Oct. 1988.

Chapter 9

1. For details, see the following Druze writers: H. Abu-Salih (n.d:21), al-Dhubyani (1967) and Najjar (1965:79).

2. For the Druzes see Makarem (1974:58), and for the Alawis see H. Uthman (1980:112).

3. For an illustration, read the works of Dussaud (1900), H. Lammens (1899) and Nieger (1922).

4. 'The Book of Synthesis', which comes in about 19 pages, was first published in 1864 in Beirut by Sulaiman Effendi in a volume titled *al-Bakura al-Salmaniya.* The book was translated into English by Salisbury. Some parts of 'The Messages of Wisdom' are available in the Oriental Room of the British Museum.

5. *Al-Hidaya al-Kubra* (The Great Guidance), written by al-Khusaibi, is one of the most cherished religious books among the Alawis. It discusses these issues in great detail. Unfortunately, I have been unable to locate it anywhere in Lebanon or Syria, or in the well-known libraries of the West.

6. The Alawis add Salman al-Farsi according to a *hadith* related to the Prophet, saying: 'Salman is from us, we the People of the House.'

7. See *al-Nahda*, July 1938.

8. See al-Tawil (1966:201–2) for more details.

9. The Druze sources I have examined include, among others, G. Abu-Salih (1975), H. Abu-Salih (n.d), al-Atrash (1947), al-Dhubyani (1967), Israwi (1967), Makarem (1974), Makarem and A. Abu-Salih (n.d), al-Najjar (1965), Tali (1961), Taqiyuddin (1979), and the *al-Duha* journal published by the Druze High Council in Lebanon. In addition, I have used two other non-Druze sources, al-Zu'bi (1972) and al-Khatib (1980).

10. See Makarem (1974:71–2) and al-Najjar (1965) for details.

11. This is taken from Makarem (1974:64), who in turn refers it to Hamza bin Ali.

12. See Makarem (1974:90–112).

Chapter 10

1. See *Encyclopedia Islamica*, vol. 4 (1934:1165) and Jule (1934) on the Yazidis.

2. See Jule (1934:74–108).

3. See, for example, al-Banna (1964), al-Dimluji (1949), Empson (1928:77) and Taymur (1347 AH).

4. See *Encyclopedia Islamica*, vol. 4 (1934:1165).

Chapter 11

1. 'Invading the world' is a phrase constantly used by the poet Said Akl, a staunch believer in Lebanese nationalism, when talking about the Lebanese-Phoenician civilization.

2. See Abu-Khatir (1977:39–50) for details.

3. The founders include Istifan al-Duwaihi (1629–1704), Tannus al-Shidyaq (1794–1861), Yusuf Marun al-Duwaihi (d. 1780) and Bishop Nicola Murad (d. 1862).

4. See Dahir (1981) and Harik (1982) for details on the era of reformation.

Chapter 12

1. With the exception of the Shi'a, other religious communities such as the Druzes, the Alawis, the Ibadis and the Zaidis are studied from the point of view of their historical performance rather than their religious dogma, ritual or belief.

2. Savory's chapter (1981:129–38) on the distinction between the Sunni and the Shi'a with regard to their adaptation to state structures is of immediate relevance to this discussion.

3. The three prime ministers are: Riyad al-Sulh, Husain al-Uwaini and Salim al-Huss.

4. The same observation is made by Eickelman (1976:237) in his work on Morocco with regard to Maraboutism. See also Geertz (1968:70–1) and Gellner (1981:114–30) for more details on the built-in conflict between the scripturalists and the 'ritualists'.

5. It would be interesting to carry the analysis of these networks all the way through to al-Azhar, the centre of these complex networks.

Chapter 13

1. The Shi'a refer to these two sources as the *waznatain* or the *thiqlain* (the two weights), the Qur'an being the 'heavy weight', and 'the Holy House' the 'light weight' (al-Zain 1979:44).

2. The Qur'an (5/3) says: 'This day have I perfected your religion for your benefit, and have completed my favour unto you, and have chosen for you Islam as your faith.'

3. For an illustration, see the autobiography of Muhammad Jawad Maghniya (1980:130), who headed the Shi'a High Court in Beirut for several years.

Chapter 14

1. Makarem's speech appeared in *al-Nahar*, Beirut (1987).

2. The population of Yemen is about 5 million people, 60% of whom (i.e. 3 million) adhere to the Zaidi doctrine, which works out at one *sayyid* to every sixty individuals.

3. For more details, see Khuri (1984:2) and Serjeant (1985:11–50).

4. The same structure which is called *azzaba* among the Ibadis in Mzab is called *mutawa'a* in Oman.

Chapter 15

1. See al-Alawi (1972) for details.

2. The list includes Shaikh Abdul-Al, locally known as Hajj Ma'alla, who is at the apex of the al-Hajj family, and Shaikh Yusuf May who is the grand ancestor of the al-Hamid family, distinguished in astrological studies. After his death he was succeeded by his son Muhammad al-Yusuf who, like his father, had a deep and extensive knowledge of astrology. It also includes Shaikh Ghanim Yasin, Abdul-Hamid Afandi and Salim al-Ghanim (who was succeeded by his son Muhammad Yasin al-Yunis), as well as Shaikh Mustapha Mirhij, known as *sayyid* (who is the grand ancestor of the Sayyid family of Bi'amra village in Safita) and Shaikh Hasan Ahmad, at the apex of the Muhyeddin family in the village of Jurat al-Jawamis. (See al-Alawi (1972) for details.) People often cite these names when they discuss sectarian history and achievements, group affiliation and personal identity.

3. The Qamariyun today are headed by Shaikh Sulaiman al-Ahmad, who carries the title 'the servant of the People of the House'. He lived in Qirdaha, the same village from which President Asad of Syria comes.

4. After a conversation with Professor Sami Makarem in spring 1981.

5. For more details on the subject, see A. Abu-Salih and Makarem (n.d).

Chapter 16

1. Following a conversation with Bishop George Khudr in 1983.

2. The Maronites have had good connections with the Vatican since 1584 when a Maronite School was established there.

3. For more details on the reforms, see Dahir (1981) and Harik (1972).

Chapter 17

1. For more details, See Gellner (1983).

2. For more details, see Davis (1984).

3. See Shamsuddin (1980:85).

4. Consider only a small sample: *The Politics of Islamic Reassertion* edited by Mohammad Ayoub (1981), *L'Islam et l'Etat* edited by Olivier Carré (1982), *Islam and Power* edited by Cudsi and Dessouki (1981), *Religion and Politics in the Middle East* edited by Michael Curtis (1981), *Recognizing Islam* by Michael Gilsenan (1982), *Militant Islam* by G.H. Jansen (1979), *Covering Islam* by Edward Said (1981). This is not to mention those written in Arabic such as *al-Qur'an wa al-dawla* (The Qur'an and the State) by Muhammad Ahmad Khalafallah (1981), or *Ya muslimi al-alam ittahidu* ('O Muslims of the World, Unite) by Salamah al-Mughir (1982).

5. See the special issue of *al-Mustaqbal al-Arabi* (1985) on *shawra*.

Glossary

Words as used in text	*Full transliteration*	*Meaning*
abd	‘abd	slave
ahl dhumma	’ahl dhumma	the people in trust; the protected weak
ahl al-hukm wa al-sultan	’ahl al-ḥukm wa al-sultān	men of government and authority
ain	‘ain	eye
aish al-Husain	‘aish al-Ḥusain	food prepared at the time of Ashura
ajawid	’ajāwīd	Druze religious shaikhs
akmaltu	’akmaltu	completed
alam	‘ālam	world
alamaniya	‘ālamānīya	pertaining to the world
alim	‘ālim	learned man; a man of religious knowledge
almaniya	‘almānīya	secularization
amal	‘amal	work; labour; worship
amir al-mu’minin	’amīr al-mu’minīn	the prince of the faithful
amma	‘āmma	commoners
anf	’anf	nose
ansar	’anṣār	partisans
anuf	’anūf	notable; dignified
a‘raf	’a‘rāf	pl. of *‘urf*
archmandrit	archmandrīt	Orthodox high religious specialist

arham	'arḥām	kin; pl. of *raḥm* (womb)
asab	‘aṣab	nerve
asabiya	‘aṣabīya	solidarity; internal cohesion
asala	'aṣāla	[return to] roots
asas	'asās	base; foundation
ashraf	'ashrāf	religious nobility
asil	'aṣīl	inbred; thoroughbred
asnaf	'aṣnāf	guilds; craftsmen
aya	'āya	Qur'anic verse
a‘yan	'a‘yān	notables
ayatollah	'ayatollāh	a high-rank Shi‘a shaikh
azzaba	‘azzāba	Ibadi religious circles
ba‘a	bā‘a	to sell
bab	bāb	door; entrance
baba-shaikh	bāba-shaikh	head religious office among the Yazidis
bakhshish	bakhshīsh	tip
basmariya	basmarīya	Yazidi religious category
batin	bāṭin	esoteric meaning; esoteric interpretation
batini	bāṭinī	believers in the esoteric
bida	bida‘	religious innovations
birat	bīrāt	elderly shaikhs among the Yazidis (pl. of *bīr*)
bu‘da	bu‘da	kept in isolation
bughat	bughāt	rebels; tyrants
dainuna	dainūna	Day of Judgement
dala	dāla	to rotate power
dana	dāna	to judge; to sanction
dar al-harb	dār al-ḥarb	the abode of war

dar al-islam	dār al-'islām	the abode of peace
da'wa	da'wa	religious call; religious appeal
dawla	dawla	state; regime; reign
dawr	dawr	evolutionary cycle; stage
difa	difā'	defence
din	dīn	sanctions; religion
diya	dīya	blood money
falaj	falaj	underground canal
faqih	faqīh	Islamic jurist
fasl	faṣl	chapter
fatih	fatiḥ	conquest
fawasil	fawāṣil	Qur'anic punctuation
firqa	firqa	team
fuqara	fuqarā'	the poor; a Yazidi religious category; (pl. of *faqīr*)
hadith	ḥadīth	saying or deed attributed to the Prophet; declaration
hajr	hajr	strain of imams attached to a tribal group among the Zaidis
haq al-imama	ḥaq al-'imāma	right of the imam (one-fifth of the earnings of a Shi'a)
hijab	ḥijāb	witchcraft (warding off evil magically)
hudud	ḥudūd	divine laws; boundaries; [the five Druze] interpreters

hujjat al-islam	ḥujjat al-'islām	a high-rank Shi'a shaikh
hulul	ḥulūl	spiritual occupation
huquq	ḥuqūq	truths; rights
husainiya	ḥusainīya	Shi'a 'funeral house'
ihya	'iḥyā'	cultivation; usufruct
i'jaz	'i'jāz	miraculous
ijma	'ijmā'	consensus
ijtihad	'ijtihād	interpretation
ilm	'ilm	certainty; science; religious knowledge
ilmaniya	'ilmānīya	pertaining to science
imam	'imām	religious leader; that which lines up (blocks or camels)
imam mubin	'imām mubīn	visible path
imamat al-nass	'imāmat al-naṣṣ	the textual imamate
imamiyun	'imāmīyūn	believers in the imamate
iman	'īmān	faith
imtahana	'imtahana	taking on a menial job
isnad	'isnād	ascription
islam	'islām	surrender; obedience
itra tahira	'itra ṭāhira	the Holy House of Ali
jafr	jafr	astrology; astrological techniques
jami	jāmi'	central mosque
jawwid	jawwīd	sing. of *'ajāwīd*
jaza	jazā'	punishment
jihad	jihād	holy war; struggle
jizya	jizya	tax paid by non-Muslims
juhhal	juhhāl	the ignorant

jumla	jumla	sentence
kadhib	kādhib	lying
kamal	kamāl	perfect; complete
kashf	kashf	exposition of divinity
kathafa	kathāfa	corporeality
kawajik	kawājik	Yazidi religious specialists
khalafa	khalafa	to succeed
khass	khass	lettuce
khassa	khāṣṣa	private ones
khatib	khaṭīb	[mosque] speaker
khawa	khāwa	to establish brotherly relations
khawa	khawa	to become weak
khilwa	khilwa	[religious] retreat
khuwwa	khuwwa	forced tax
kitab	kitāb	witchcraft (positive magic)
kowjak	kowjak	collectors of *zakāt* tax
kufiya	kūfīya	men's headcloth
kutman	kutmān	concealment; kept secret
la-diniya	lā-dīnīya	irreligiosity
la'n	la'n	cursing
lawlab	lawlab	spiralist
ma'dhun	ma'dhūn	licensed shaikh
majlis	majlis	counsel; assembly; congregation
malik	malik	king
maqam	maqām	[Druze] shrine; enshrined personage
mar	mār	saint
mas'a	mas'a	achieved position
masakin	masākīn	subdued

mashayikh	mashāyikh	[Yazidi] religious category; pl. of shaikh
mawali	mawālī	the oppressed
mawla	mawla	master
mi'ad	mī'ād	return to life
milla	milla	strain; nation or law
mir shikhan	mīr shīkhān	Yazidi religious figure
mubaya'a	mubāya'a	proclamation; homage
mufti	muftī	head of appeal court
muhakkamat	muḥakkamāt	explicit meanings
muhtasib	muḥtasib	accountable
mujamma	mujamma'	tribal coalition
mujtahid	mujtahid	Shi'a jurist
mujtahid akbar	mujtahid 'akbar	a high-rank Shi'a shaikh
mukallaf	mukallaf	trustee; custodian
mukallafun	mukallafūn	pl. of *mukallaf*
mulk	mulk	possession
mulla	mulla	Shi'a religious official
mulukiyun	mulūkīyūn	kingly loyalists (i.e. the Greek Orthodox or the Greek Catholics)
al-mu'minin	al-mu'minīn	the faithful
muqallad	muqallad	imitable model
muridun	murīdūn	novices
murtadda	murtadda	apostates
musarraf	muşarraf	immune to physical injury
musiqa	mūsīqa	music
al-muslimun	al-muslimūn	the Muslims
al-musta'min	al-musta'min	the made-secure
mutashabihat	mutashābihāt	metaphoric meanings
mutawa'a	muţāwa'a	religious disciplinarians

nakhl	nakhl	palm groves
nasara	naṣāra	Christians
nasr	naṣr	victory
nasra	naṣra	military expedition; support
na'zum	na'zum	we intend
nisba	nisba	in relation to a place
nihla	niḥla	tendency; direction; religion or religious order
nutaqa	nuṭaqā'	speakers; proclaimers
qadi	qāḍī	judge
qawwalin	qawwālīn	chorus
qira'at	qirā'āt	religious assemblies
qiyas	qīyās	analogy
qurba	qurba	kin
rafada	rafaḍa	rejectors
rahm	raḥm	womb
rasul	rasūl	messenger
rijal al-din	rijāl al-dīn	men of religion
al-risala al-khalida	al-risāla al-khālida	the eternal message
ruhallah	rūhallāh	a high-rank Shi'a shaikh
sabiq	sābiq	predecessor
sadr	ṣadr	notables [from chest]
salafiya	salafīya	fundamentalism
al-salaf al-salih	al-salaf al-ṣāliḥ	the virtuous predecessors
sayis	sāyis	leader of congregation among the Druze
sayyid	sayyid	descendant of Ali
shammas	shammās	Orthodox religious specialist

shar'	shar'	Islamic jurisdiction; God's law
sharh	sharḥ	exposition
shari'a	sharī'a	divine law
shawra	shawra	consultation
shi'r	shi'r	poetry
shira	shirā'	spread
shirk	shirk	polytheism
shu'ubiya	shu'ūbīya	schismists
shuyukh al-tariq	shuyūkh al-ṭarīq	shaikhs of the highway
shuyukh al-khatir	shuyūkh al-khāṭir	the blue shaikhs
shuyukh al-din	shuyūkh al-dīn	shaikhs of religion
shuyukh al-shar'	shuyūkh al-shar'	shaikhs of the forbidden and permissible [jurisdiction]
silb	ṣilb	iron ore
sira	sīra	life history; life-style
siyada	siyāda	sovereignty
sunna	sunna	Traditions
sura	sūra	Qur'anic chapter
tabaqa	ṭabaqa	stratum
ta'bi'a	ta'bi'a	mobilization
tabriya	tabriya	becoming innocent; forced isolation
taghut	ṭaghūt	tribal law in Yemen
taharim	taḥārīm	death days of important religious figures
ta'ifa	ṭa'ifa	sect
tajalli	tajallī	divine manifestation
tajassud	tajassud	divine embodiment
takamul	takāmul	complementarity
takshif	takshif	from *kashf*, exposition of divinity
tanaqud	tanāquḍ	contradiction

tanzil	tanzīl	direct revelation
taqiya	taqīya	dissimulation; piety
tarwid	tarwīḍ	spiritual exercise; training
tashri	tashrī‘	legislation
ta'wil	ta'wīl	allegorical interpretation
tatwij	tatwīj	crowning ritual
tawhid	tawḥīd	oneness; united outlook; unity of being; high religious knowledge
tawwus	ṭawwus	peacock
thiqlain	thiqlain	two weights
ukhuwwa	'ukhuwwa	brotherhood
ulama	‘ulamā'	learned men
ulama al-din	‘ulamā' al-dīn	scientists of religion
umma	'umma	community; nation
al-umma al-arabiya	al-'umma al-‘arabīya	the Arab nation
al-umma al-islamiya	al-'umma al-'islāmīya	the Islamic community
ummat al-da‘wa	'ummat al-da‘wa	the appeal community
ummat al-ijaba	'ummat al-'ijāba	the recipient community
uqqal	‘uqqāl	the knowables
urf	‘urf	cultural practices; custom; tradition
wajh	wajh	face
waqf	waqf	endowment property; the process of an imam being appointed or abdicating

waratha	waratha	heirs
wa'z	wa'ẓ	sermon; instruction
wazi	wāzi'	internal deterrent
al-wazi al-sultani	al-wāzi' al-sulṭānī	the sultanic deterrent
waznatain	waznatain	two weights
wili	wilī	[Alawi] shrine; enshrined personage
wujaha	wujahā'	notables (from face)
yahzumun	yaḥzumūn	they enact
yakhruj	yakhruj	to part off
yawm al-din	yawm al-dīn	Day of Judgement
zahir	ẓahir	exoteric interpretation
zakat	zakāt	alms, tax paid by Muslims
zawaj al-kafa'a	zawāj al-kafā'a	status or qualification for marriage
al-zay al-islami	al-zay al-'islāmī	Islamic fashion; fad
zuhur	ẓuhūr	rising; personification of divinity

Bibliography

Works in English and French

Abdul-Rauf, M. (1979) *The Islamic Doctrine of Economics and Contemporary Economic Thought*. Washington D.C: American Enterprise Institute.

Abu-Husain, A. (1978) 'Zawiya and Dawla: the Sanusiyya as a Religious and Political Movement'. Unpublished MA thesis, Dept. of Social and Behavioral Sciences (Anthropology), American University of Beirut.

Abul-Nasr, Jamil (1971) *A History of the Maghrib*. Cambridge: Cambridge University Press.

Antoun, Richard T. (1981) 'Key Variables Affecting Muslim Local-level Religious Leadership in Iran and Jordan'. In Fuad I. Khuri (ed.), *Leadership and Development in Arab Society*. Beirut: American University of Beirut Press.

Ayoub, Mohammed (1981) *The Politics of Islamic Reassertion*. London: Croom Helm.

Badger, G.P. (1971) *The History of the Imams and the Seyyids of Oman*. London: Hakluyt Society.

Baltzell, E. Digby (1964) *The Protestant Establishment: Aristocracy and Caste in America*. New York: Random House.

Batatu, Hanna (1978) *The Old Social Classes and the Revolutionary Movements of Iraq*. Princeton, N.J: Princeton University Press.

——— (1981) 'Some Observations on the Social Roots of Syria's Ruling Military Group and the Causes of its Dominance', *The Middle East Journal*, vol. 35, p. 335.

——— (1982) 'The Muslim Brethren', *MERIP Reports*, no. 110 (Nov.–Dec. 1982), pp. 12–31.

Boas, Franz (1891) *Race, Language and Culture*. New York: Macmillan, pp. 437–45.

Brace, Richard (1964) *Morocco, Algeria, Tunisia*. Englewood Cliffs, N.J: Prentice-Hall.

Bury, George Wyman (1915) *Arabia Infelix: or the Turks in Yemen*. London.

Carré, Olivier (1982) *L'Islam et l'Etat*. Paris: Presses Universitaires de France (in French).

Chapra, U. M. (1970) *The Economic System of Islam*. London: Economic Cultural Centre.

Çhevalier, D. (1971) *La Société du Mont Liban à L'Epoque de la Révolution Industrielle en Europe*. Paris: Librairie Orientaliste Paul Geuthner (in French).

Clarke, J. and Fisher, W. B. (1972) *Populations of the Middle East and North Africa: A Geographical Approach*. London: University of London Press.

Cohen, Abner (ed.) (1974) *Urban Ethnicity*. London: Tavistock.

Cudsi, S. Alexander and Dessouki, Ali E. (eds) (1981) *Islam and Power*. London: Croom Helm.

Curtis, M. (ed.) (1981) *Religion and Politics in the Middle East*. Boulder, Colo: Westview Press.

Davis, J. (1984) 'Principle and Practice in Qadhdhafi's Libya', *al-Abhath* no. xxx, pp. 51–78. Special issue ed. by Fuad I. Khuri. (Beirut: American University of Beirut Press.)

Deffontaines, P. (1948) *Géographie et Religion*. Paris: Gallimard (in French).

Dodd, Peter and Barakat, Halim (1969) *River Without Bridges*. Beirut: Institute for Palestine Studies.

Dumont, Louis (1977) 'Caste, Racism, and Stratification: Reflections of a Social Anthropologist'. In Janet L. Dolgin, David S. Kemnitzer, and David M. Schneider (eds), *Symbolic Anthropology*. New York: Columbia University Press, pp. 72–90.

Dussaud, R. (1900) *Histoire et Réligion des Nosairis*. Paris: Bouillon (in French).

Eickelman, Dale (1976) *Moroccan Islam*. Austin, Tex: University of Texas Press.

Empson, R. H. W. (1928) *The Cult of the Peacock Angel*. London: H.F. and G. Witherly.

Epstein, A. L. (1978) *Ethos and Identity*. London: Tavistock.

Evans-Prichard, E.E. (n.d) *Biographical Notes on Members of the Sanusi Family*. n. pub.

——— (1949) *The Sanusi of Cyrenaica*. Oxford: Clarendon Press.

Fallers, Lloyd A. (1973) *Inequality, Social Stratification Reconsidered*. Chicago, Ill: University of Chicago Press.

Farago, L. (1938) *Arabian Antic*. New York: Sheridan House.

Farrag, Amina (1969) 'Mechanisms of Social Control among the Mzabite

Women of Beni-Isguem'. Unpublished MA thesis, Dept. of Social Anthropology, London School of Economics, University of London.

Fattal, A. (1958) *Le Status Légal des Non-Musulmans en Pays d'Islam*. Beirut: Imprimerie Catholique (in French).

Fischer, W. J. (1956) 'The City in Islam', *The Middle East Journal*, no. 10.

Gans, H. J. (1962) *The Urban Villagers*. Glencoe, Ill: Free Press of Glencoe.

Gardet, Louis (1954) *La Cité Musulmane*. Paris: Librairie Philosophique (in French).

Geertz, Clifford (1968) *Islam Observed*. New Haven, Conn: Yale University Press.

Gellner, Ernest (1968) 'A Pendulum Swing Theory of Islam', *Annales des Sociologie*, pp. 5–14.

———(1981) *Muslim Society*. Cambridge: Cambridge University Press.

———(1983) *Nations and Nationalism*. Oxford: Blackwell.

Gellner, Ernest and Micaud, Charles (eds) (1973) *Arabs and Berbers*. London: Duckworth.

Gibb, H. A. R. (1962) 'Al-Mawardi's Theory of the Caliphate'. In H. A. R. Gibb, *Studies on the Civilization of Islam* (ed. Stanford J. Shaw and William R. Polk). London: Routledge & Kegan Paul, pp. 151–65.

——— (1975) *Modern Trends in Islam*. Beirut: Librairie du Liban.

Gilsenan, M. (1982) *Recognizing Islam*. London: Croom Helm.

Goldberg, Hervey E. (1972) *Cave Dwellers and Citrus Growers: A Jewish Community in Libya and Israel*. Cambridge: Cambridge University Press.

Gordon, Milton (1964) *Assimilation in American Life*. New York: Oxford University Press.

Haddad, Robert (1971) *Syrian Christians in Muslim Societies*. Princeton, N.J: Princeton University Press.

Hanna, Edwin B. (1981) 'The Rise of Wahhabism in Saudi Arabia: A Socio-Ecological Interpretation'. Unpublished MA thesis, Centre for Arab and Middle East Studies, American University of Beirut.

Harik, Iliya F. (1968) *Political Change in a Traditional Society: Lebanon, 1711–1845*. Princeton, NJ.: Princeton University Press.

Hay, Rupert (1959) *The Persian Gulf States*. Washington DC: Middle East Institute.

Hayek, Michel (1964) *Liturgie Maronite*. France: Mame (in French).

Hirschberg, H. Z. (1969) 'The Druzes'. In A. J. Arberry (ed.), *Religion in the Middle East*, vol. 2. Cambridge: Cambridge University Press, pp. 330–48.

Hitti, Philip (1928) *The Origins of the Druze People and Religion*. New York: Columbia University Press.

Hoffman, Bernard G. (1967) *The Structure of Traditional Moroccan Rural Society*. The Hague: Mouton.

Hourani, Albert (1946) *Minorities in the Arab World*. Oxford: Oxford University Press.

Hudson, Michael (1977) *Arab Politics: The Search for Legitimacy*. New Haven, Conn. and London: Yale University Press.

Ibrahim, Saadeddin (1981) 'A Socio-cultural Paradigm of Pan Arab Leadership: The Case of Nasser'. In Fuad I. Khuri (ed.), *Leadership and Development in Arab Society*. Beirut: American University of Beirut Press.

Jansen, G. H. (1979) *Militant Islam*. New York: Harper & Row.

Joseph, John (1961) *The Nestorians and their Muslim Neighbors*. Princeton, N.J: Princeton University Press.

Juraidini, Raed (1980) 'The Origin and Development of the Mahdiya Sect in Sudan'. Unpublished MA thesis, Dept. of Social and Behavioral Sciences (Anthropology), American University of Beirut.

Kelly, J. B. (1959) *Sultanate and Imamate in Oman*. London: Chatham House.

Kerr, Malcolm H. (1966) *Islamic Reform*. Berkeley, Calif: University of California Press.

Khadduri, M. (1955) *War and Peace in the Law of Islam*. Baltimore, Md: Johns Hopkins Press.

Khalidi, Edriss (1975) 'Economic Determinants of Social Change in Levant Peasant Communities'. Unpublished MA thesis, Dept. of Social and Behavioral Sciences (Anthropology), American University of Beirut.

Khuri, Fuad I. (1970) 'Parallel Cousin Marriage Reconsidered', *Man*, vol. 5, no. 4, pp. 597–618.

——— (1975) *From Village to Suburb*. Chicago, Ill: University of Chicago Press.

——— (1980) *Tribe and State in Bahrain*. Chicago, Ill: University of Chicago Press.

——— (1981a) 'History and Social Variance in the Study of New States: the Case of Bahrain'. *al-Abhath*, vol. 28, pp. 69–93.

——— (1981b) 'City Typology, Urbanization and Urban Management in Arab Countries'. In Lata Chatterjee and Peter Nijkamp (eds), *Urban Problems and Economic Development*. The Hague: Sizth & Noordhoff, pp. 83–106.

——— (1981c) 'Sociological Constraints to Rural Development in Oman'. Report submitted to the World Bank, Washington DC.

——— (1981d) 'The Social Dynamics of the 1975–77 War in Lebanon', *Armed Forces and Society*, vol. 7, pp. 383–408.

——— (1981e) 'Social Authority in the Tribal Cultures of Arabia', *al-Fikr al-Arabi*, vol. 22, pp. 75–87.

——— (1984) 'State and Society in Arabia: An Introduction', *al-Abhath*, vol. 30, pp. 1–5. Special issue ed. by Fuad I. Khuri. (Beirut: American University of Beirut Press.)

Lambton, Ann K. S. (1981) *State and Government in Medieval Islam*. Oxford: Oxford University Press.

Lammens, H. (1899) 'Les Nosairis, Notes sur leur Histoire et leur Religion', *Etudes*, no. 16 (Aug. 1899), pp. 461–94 (in French).

Lane, Edward W. (1978) *An Account of the Manners and Customs of the Modern Egyptians* (Written in Egypt under the Years 1833–1835). The Hague: East-West.

Laoust, Henri (1965) *Les Schismes dans l'Islam*. Paris: Payot (in French).

Lapidus, Ira Marvin (1967) *Muslim Cities in the Later Middle Ages*. Cambridge, Mass: Harvard University Press.

Lessa, William A. and Vogt, Evon Z. (1965) *Reader in Comparative Religion*. New York: Harper & Row.

Lewis, B. (1981) 'The Return of Islam'. In M. Curtis (ed.), *The Middle East*. Boulder, Colo: Westview Press.

Lipsky, George (1956) *Saudi Arabia: Its People, Its Society, Its Culture*. New Haven, Conn: H.R.A.F. Press.

Little, T. (1968) *South Arabia: Arena of Conflict*. London: Pall Mall.

Mahdi, M. (1957) *Ibn Khaldun's Philosophy of History*. London: Allen Press.

Makarem, Sami N. (1974) *The Druze Faith*. Delmar, N.Y: Caravan Books.

Nieger, C. (1922) 'Choix de Documents sur le Territoire des Alaouites', *Revue du Monde Musulman*, vol. XLIV (March) pp. 57–68.

O'Ballance, Edgar (1971) *The War in the Yemen*. London: Faber.

Peters, Emrys (n.d) 'A Muslim Passion Play: Key to a Lebanese Village', *Atlantic Monthly*. n.p.

——— (1963) 'Aspects of Rank and Status Among Muslims in a Lebanese Village'. In Julian Pitt-Rivers (ed.), *Mediterranean Countrymen*. Paris: Mouton, pp. 159–202.

de Planhol, Xavier (1956) *The World of Islam*. Ithaca, N.Y: Cornell University Press.

——— (1968) *Les Fondements Géographiques de l'Histoire de l'Islam*. Paris: Flammarion (in French).

Redfield, Robert (1947) 'The Folk Society', *American Journal of Sociology*, vol. 52, pp. 293–308.

——— (1955) *The Little Community: Viewpoints for the Study of a Human Whole*. Chicago, Ill: University of Chicago Press.

Said, E. (1981) *Covering Islam*. London: Routledge & Kegan Paul.

Salisbury, E. (1864) 'The Book of Sulaiman's First Fruit, Disclosing the Mysteries of the Nusairian Religion', *Journal of the American Oriental Society*, vol. VIII, pp. 227–308.

Sapire, E. (1921) *Language: An Introduction to the Study of Speech*. New York: Harcourt Brace.

——— (1951) *Selected Writings of Edward Sapire in Language, Culture and Personality*. Berkeley, Calif: University of California Press.

Sarker, A. (1980) *The Concept of Islamic Socialism*. Dacca: Shahjalal Press.

Savory, Roger M. (1981) 'The Problem of Sovereignty in an Ithna Ashari (Twelvers) Shi'i State'. In Michael Curtis (ed.), *Religion and Politics in the Middle East*. Boulder, Colo: Westview Press.

Serjeant, R. B. (1969) 'The Zaydis'. In A. J. Arberry (ed.), *Religion in the Middle East*. Cambridge: Cambridge University Press, pp. 285–301.

——— (1985) 'The Interplay Between Tribal Affinities and Religious Authority in the Yemen'. *al-Abhath*, vol. XXX, pp. 11–50. Special issue ed. by Fuad I. Khuri. (Beirut: American University of Beirut Press.)

Shils, Edward (1961) 'Center and Periphery'. In *The Logic of Personal Knowledge*, essays presented to Michael Polanyi on his seventieth birthday. London: Routledge & Kegan Paul.

Stookey, Robert W. (1981) 'Religion and Politics in South Arabia'. In Michael Curtis (ed.), *Religion and Politics in the Middle East*. Boulder, Colo: Westview Press.

Tou'mah, R. G. (1977) 'Land Ownership and Political Power in Damascus, 1858—1958'. Unpublished MA thesis, Dept. of Political Science, American University of Beirut.

Trimingham, J. S. (1959) *Islam in West Africa*. Oxford: Clarendon Press.

Tritton, A. S. (1928) *The Rise of the Imams of Sanaa*. Madras.

——— (1930) *The Caliphs and Their Non-Muslim Subjects*. London/Bombay: Oxford University Press.

Van Dam, Nikolaos (1978) 'Sectarian and Regional Factionalism in the Syrian Political Elite', *The Middle East Journal*, vol. 32, pp. 201–10.

——— (1979) *The Struggle for Power in Syria*. London: Croom Helm.

de Vaumas, E. (1955) 'La Repartition Confessionelle au Liban et l'Equilibre de L'Etat Libanais', *Revue de Géographie Alpine*, vol. XLIII, pp. 511–603 (in French).

——— (1960) 'Le Djebel Ansarieh', *Revue de Géographie Alpine*, vol. XLVIII, pp. 267–311 (in French).

Vidal, F. S. (1955) *The Oasis of al-Hasa*. New York: ARAMCO.

Volney, C.F. (1788) *Travels Through Syria and Egypt in the Years 1783, 1784, and 1785*, vol. II. London: G.C.I. and J. Robinson.

Warriner, Doreen (1957) *Land Reform and Development in the Middle East*. London/New York: Royal Institute of International Affairs.

——— (1962) *Land Reform and Development in the Middle East*. London: Oxford University Press.

Weuleresse, J. (1940) *Le Pays des Alaouites*. Tours: Arrault (in French).

Wilkinson, J. C. (1972) 'The Origin of the Omani State'. In D. Hopwood (ed.), *The Arabian Peninsula: Society and Politics*. London: Allen & Unwin.

Wolf, E. (1951) 'The Social Organization of Mecca and the Origin of Islam', *Southwestern Journal of Anthropology*, vol. 7, no. 4.

Works in Arabic

Abdul-Baqi, Muhammad Fouad (1945) *al-mu'jam al-mufahras li alfaz al-qur'an al-karim (Index for Qur'anic Lexicons)*. Cairo: Dar Matabi al-Sha'b.

Abdul-Nasser, Jamal (1954) *falsafat al-thawra* (The Philosophy of the Revolution). Cairo: Dar al-Ma'arif.

Abu-Khatir, Henry (1977) *min wahi tarikh al-mawarina* (From the Inspiration of the History of the Maronites). Beirut: Catholic Press.

Abu-Salih, Abbas and Makarem, Sami (n.d) *tarikh al-muwahhidin al-duruz al-siyasi fi al-mashriq al-arabi* (The Political History of the Druzes in the Arab East). Beirut: Druze Council for Research and Development.

Abu-Salih, Ghalib (1975) *al-duruz fi zil al-ihtilal al-isra'ili* (The Druzes under the Israeli Occupation). Beirut: Dar al-Irfan.

Abu-Salih, Hafiz (n.d) *waqi al-duruz* (The Present Status of the Druzes). Beirut: al-Maktaba al-Asriya.

Aiyash, Sami (n.d) *al-isma'iliyun fi marhalat al-qarmata* (The Ismailis in the Carmathian Stage). Beirut: Dar Ibn Khaldun.

al-Alawi, Ali Aziz Ibrahim (1972) *al-alawiyun fida'iyu al-shi'a al-majhulun* (The Alawis, the Unknown Commandos of the Shi'a). Damascus: n. pub.

al-Aqqad, Abbas Mahmud (1943) *abqariyat al-siddiq* (The Ingenuity of al-Siddiq). Cairo: Dar al-Ma'arif.

Awad, Jurjus (1932) *al-qibt* (The Copts). Cairo: Dar al-Ahliya.

Awni, Mustafa (1964) *saltanat al-zalam fi muscat* (The Sultanate of Darkness in Muscat). n.p., n. pub.

al-Baghdadi, Abu-Mansur Abd al-Qahir bin Tahir (1928) *usul al-din* (The Tenets of Religion). Istanbul: Dar al-Dawla.

——— (1978) *al-farq bain al-firaq* (The Difference between Schisms). Beirut: Dar al-Afaq al-Jadida. (First published in 1037.)

al-Banna, Hashim (1964) *al-yazidiyun* (The Yazidis). Baghdad: Dar al-Umma.

al-Baqlani, Abu-Bakr (1947) *al-tamhid fi al-rad ala al-mulhida wa al-rafida wa al-khawarij wa al-mu'tazila* (The Introduction to the Refutation of the Rejectors, the Kharijis and the Mu'tazila). Mahmud Muhammad al-Khudairi and Muhammad Abd al-Hadi Abul-Rida (eds). Cairo: n. pub.

Barakat, Halim (1984) *al-mujtama al-arabi al-mu'asir* (Contemporary Arab Society). Beirut: Centre for the Study of Arab Unity.

Dahir, Mas'oud (1981) *al-judhur al-tarikhiya lil-mas'ala al-ta'ifiya al-lubnaniya* (Historic Roots for the Sectarian Problem in Lebanon). Beirut: Ma'had al-Inma al-Arabi.

Daw, Butrus (1978) *tarikh al-mawarina: al-wajh al-askari al-maruni* (The History of the Maronites: the Military Dimension). Junieh: Dar al-Bulisiya.

——— (1980) *tarikh al-mawarina: lubnan fi hayat al-masih* (The History of the Maronites: Lebanon in the Life of Christ). Junieh: Dar al-Bulisiya.

al-Dhubyani (1967) *al-taqammus* (Reincarnation). Beirut: Dar Byblos.

Dibs, Yusuf (1905) *al-jami al-muhassal fi tarikh al-mawarina al-mufassal* (The Achieved Collection in the Detailed History of the Maronites). Beirut: n. pub.

al-Dimluji, Sadiq (1949) *al-yazidiya* (The Yazidis). Mosul: Dar al-Ittihad.

Duwaihi, Istafan (1890) *tarikh al-ta'ifa al-maruniya* (The History of the Maronite Sect). Rashid al-Shartuni (ed.). Beirut: n. pub.

Fadlalla, Muhammad Jawad (1973) *al-imam al-rida* (The Imam Rida). Beirut: Dar al-Zahra.

Faris, Hani (1980) *al-niza'at al-ta'ifiya fi tarikh lubnan al-hadith* (Sectarian Conflicts in the Modern History of Lebanon). Beirut: Dar al-Ahliya.

Faris, Joseph (1985) 'al-hala al-amma fi al-mujtama al-rifi al-lubnani'

(Ordinary Rural Life in Lebanon). Unpublished manuscript, St Joseph University, Beirut.

Faris, Walid (1979) *al-ta'adudiya fi lubnan* (Pluralism in Lebanon). Junieh: Dar al-Kaslik.

Ghilyun, Burhan (1979) *al-mas'ala al-ta'ifiya wa mashkalat al-aqalliyat* (The Sectarian Issue and the Problem of Minorities). Beirut: Dar al-Tali'a.

Haidar, Ali (1973) 'al-tha'r fi ba'albak' (Revenge in Baalbek). Unpublished manuscript, Lebanese University, Beirut.

Harik, Eliya (1972) *man yahkum lubnan?* (Who Governs Lebanon?). Beirut: Dar al-Nahar.

——— (1982) *al-tahawul al-siyasi fi tarikh lubnan* (Political Transformation in the History of Lebanon). Beirut: Dar al-Nashr wa al-Tawzi.

al-Hasani, Abdulrazzaq (1967) *al-yazidiyun fi hadirihim wa madihim* (The Yazidis, Past and Present). Sidon: Dar al-Asriya.

Ibn al-Jawziya, Qiyam (1961) *ahkam ahl al-dhumma* (The Regulations of the Protected People). Subhi al-Salih (ed.). Damascus: Damascus University Press.

Ibn Manzur (1956) *lisan al-arab* (The Arab Tongue). Beirut: Dar Sadir.

Ibn al-Mujawir (1951) *tarikh al-mustansir* (The History of al-Mustansir). O. Lofgren (ed.) Leiden.

Israwi, Najib (1967) *al-madhhab al-tawhidi al-durzi* (The Druze Way). Beirut: n. pub.

Jule, Isma'il (1934) *al-yazidiya qadiman wa hadithan* (The Yazidis in Ancient and Modern Times). Beirut: American Press.

Kashifulghata, Muhammad Husain (n.d) *asl al-shi'a wa usuluha* (The Origins and Principles of the Shi'a). Beirut: Dar al-Irfan.

Kassab, George (1980) *al-mawrana* (Maronitism), Beirut.

Khalafalla, Muhammad Ahmad (1981) *al-qur'an wa al-dawla* (The Qur'an and the State). Beirut: al-Mu'assasa al-Arabiya.

Khumaini, Ayatollah (1979) *al-hukuma al-islamiya* (The Islamic Republic). Beirut: Dar al-Tali'a.

Khuri, Fu'ad I. (1981) *al-qabila wa al-dawla fi al-bahrain* (Tribe and State in Bahrain). Beirut: Ma'had al-Inma al-Arabi.

——— (1983) 'mafhum al-sulta lada al-qaba'il al-arabiya' (The Concept of Authority Among Arab Tribes), *al-fikr al-arabi*, no. 22, pp. 75–8.

Madani, T. (1963) *kitab al-jaza'ir* (The Book of Algeria). Algiers: n. pub.

Maghniya, Muhammad Jawad (n.d) *al-ithna ashriya wa ahl al-bait* (The Shi'a

Twelvers and the People of the House [of Ali]). Beirut: Dar al-Kitab.
——— (1980) *tajarib muhammad jawad maqhniya* (The Experiences of Muhammad Jawad Maghniya). Beirut: Dar Jawad.
Malik, Charles (1974) *lubnan fi dhatihi* (Lebanon in Itself). Beirut: Mu'assasat Badran.
——— (1977) *al-muqaddama* (The Introduction). Beirut: Dar al-Nahar.
Ma'ruf, Nayif Mahmud (1977) *al-khawarij fi al-asr al-umawi* (The Kharijis During the Umayyad Era). Beirut: Dar al-Tali'a.
al-Mawardi, Ali bin Muhammad (1966) *al-ahkam al-sultaniya* (The Sultanic Rules). Cairo: Dar al-Sa'ada. (First published in 1909.)
——— (1979) *qawanin al-wizara wa siyasat al-mulk* (The Rules of Government and the Policy of Dominance). Radwan al-Sayyid (ed.). Beirut: Dar al-Tali'a. (First published in 1058.)
Mu'ammar, Ali Yahya (1964) *al-ibadiya fi mawakib al-tarikh* (The Ibadis in the Procession of History). Cairo: Dar al-Kitab al-Arabi.
Muhyeddin, Khalid (1980) *al-mas'ala al-ta'ifiya fi masr*. (The Sectarian Problem in Egypt). Beirut: Dar al-Tali'a.
Najjar, Abdulla (1965) *madhhab al-duruz wa al-tawhid* (The Druze Faith and Tawhid Knowledge). Cairo: Dar al-Ma'arif.
Nasri, Hani Yahya (1982) *asabiyat al-ta'ifiya* (The Asabiya of Sects). Beirut: Dar al-Qalam.
Qabbani, Khalid (1981) *al-la-markaziya wa mas'alat tatbiqiha fi lubnan* (Decentralization and the Problem of its Application in Lebanon). Beirut: Awidat Publications.
Qurm, George (1979) *ta'addud al-adyan wa anzimat al-hukm* (Religious Plurality and Systems of Government). Beirut: Dar al-Nahar.
al-Qurtubi, Muhammad bin Ahmad (1967) *al-jami li ahkam al-qur'an* (The Total Collection of Qur'anic Rules). Cairo: Dar al-Kitab al-Arabi.
Sa'b, Hasan (1979) *islam al-hurriya la islam al-ubudiya* (Islam of Liberty not Slavery). Beirut: Dar al-Ilm li al-Malayin.
——— (1981) *al-islam wa tahaddiyat al-asr* (Islam and the Challenge of Modern Times). Beirut: Dar al-Ilm li al-Malayin.
al-Salimi (n.d) *tuhfat al-a'yan fi sirat ahl oman* (The Outstanding Notables in the History of Oman). n.p., n. pub.
al-Sawda, Yusuf (1979) *tarikh lubnan al-hadari* (The Social History of Lebanon). Beirut: Dar al-Nahar.
al-Sayyid, Radwan (1979) *al-mawardi, abu al-hasan ali bin muhammad* (Al-Mawardi, Abu al-Hasan Ali bin Muhammad). Beirut: Dar al-Tali'a.

al-Shahristani, Abu al-Fatih Muhammad (1967) *al-milal wa al-nihal* (Ethnicities and Affinities). Cairo: Dar al-Halabi.

al-Shamikhi, Abu al-Abbass (1301 AH [1883]) *kitab al-siyar* (The Book of Life Histories). Cairo: n. pub.

Shamsuddin, Muhammad Mahdi (1980) *al-almaniya* (Secularization). Beirut: Islamic Guidance Press.

Sharara, Waddah (1980) *al-ahl wa al-ghanima* (Kin and Loot). Beirut: Dar al-Tali'a.

al-Sharif, Munir (1961) *al-muslimun al-alawiyun* (The Alawi Muslims). Damascus: Dar al-Umumiya.

Tali, Amin Muhammad (1961) *asl al-muwahhidin al-duruz wa usulihim* (The Origins and the Beliefs of the Druzes). Beirut: Dar al-Andalus.

Taqiyuddin, Halim (1979) *qada al-muwahhidin al-Duruz* (The Druze Courts). Beirut: n. pub.

al-Tawil, Muhammad Ghalib (1966) *tarikh al-alawiyin* (The History of the Alawis). Beirut: Dar al-Andalus.

Taymur, Ahmad (1347 AH [1928]) *al-yazidiya wa mansha nihlatihim* (The Yazidis and the Origin of their Faith). Cairo: al-Matba'a al-Salafiya.

Uthman, Hashim (1980) *al-alawiyun bain al-ustura wa al-haqiqa* (The Alawis between Realities and Superstitions). Beirut: Mu'assasat al-A'lami.

Uthman, Muhammad Fathi (1979) *min usul al-fikr al-siyasi al-islami* (From Islamic Political Thought). Beirut: Mu'assasat al-Risala.

Zaid bin Ali bin al-Husain (n.d) *musnad al-imam zaid* (The Sourcebook of Imam Zaid). Beirut: Dar al-Hayat.

Zaidan, Abdulkarim (1963) *ahkam al-dhummiyin wa al-musta'minin fi al-islam* (The Rules of the Protected People and the Made-Secure in Islam). Baghdad: Dar al-Burhan.

——— (1965) *al-fard wa al-dawla fi al-shari'a al-islamiya* (The Individual and the State in Islamic Law). Baghdad: Dar Salman al-A'zami.

al-Zain, Muhammad Husain (1979) *al-shi'a fi al-tarikh* (The Shi'a in History). Beirut: Dar al-Athar.

Zakkar, Suhail (1980) *akhbar al-qaramita fi al-ihsa. al-sham, al-iraq, al-yemen* (The Qaramita in Hasa, Damascus, Iraq and Yemen). Damascus: Dar al-Harsuni.

Zayat, Habib (1949) *simat al-nasara wa al-yahud fi al-islam* (The Characteristics of Christians and Jews in Islam). Cairo: Dar al-Sharq.

al-Zu'bi, Muhammad Ali (1972) *al-duruz: zahirahum wa batinahum* (Visibles and Invisibles Among the Druzes). Beirut: n. pub.

Zuraiq, Constantin (1981) *nahnu wa al-tarikh* (We and History). Beirut: Dar al-Ilm li al-Malayin.

Index of Concepts

Index of Names